American Victimology

American Victimology

Marilyn D. McShane and Traqina Q. Emeka

LFB Scholarly Publishing LLC
El Paso 2011

Library of Congress Cataloging-in-Publication Data

McShane, Marilyn D., 1956-
  American victimology / Marilyn D. McShane and Traqina Q. Emeka.
    p. cm.
  Includes bibliographical references and index.
  ISBN 978-1-59332-417-9 (pbk. : alk. paper)
  1. Victims of crimes--United States. 2. Criminal justice,
Administration of--United States. 3. Victims of crimes--Legal status,
laws, etc.--United States. I. Emeka, Traqina Quarles. II. Title.
  HV6250.3.U5M38 2011
  362.880973--dc22
                                    2010051352

ISBN 978-1-59332-417-9

Printed on acid-free 250-year-life paper.

Manufactured in the United States of America.

Dedication

To my husband Franklin Emeka, my parents, Charles and Jerri Quarles, and my sons.
    T. E.

To my sisters, Sheila and Janet, for all their love and encouragement.
    MMc

Table of Contents

Acknowledgments

The authors gratefully acknowledge the guidance and assistance of many professional friends and colleagues. These include our fellow victimology professors, Janice Ahmad, Camille Gibson, Judith Harris, Bob Jerin, Stacy Moak, Laura Moriarty, and Ed Schauer. A special thanks goes to Shannon Catalano for her explanation of divergence and convergence in victimization data. We would also like to thank Trey Williams for his invaluable assistance in formatting this book and our publisher Leo Balk, who always is patient and supportive.

Preface

Every day, news of victims dominates the media. While the public uses each unique story and scenario to attempt to understand crime and victimization, those in the field must generalize events in ways that allow us to scientifically analyze patterns and trends. It is only through the rational interpretation of evidence that we can build models that will allow us to more effectively predict and prevent future victimization. This text endeavors to provide a framework for discussing the way victim issues impact the criminal justice system. The history, politics and economics of victim-related laws and policies do not exist in a vacuum, rather they are intricately related to the other elements of the criminal justice system and are shaped by the way the public interprets them.

The text is meant to be issue-based and tries as much as possible to avoid weighing the student down with data, the rapidly changing rates, and frequencies of the various types of crimes one might be victimized by. Each chapter attempts to challenge students on the boundaries of roles, definitions and consequences that guide policy-making in criminal justice as well as treatments and interventions. At the conclusion of the chapter, there are recommended books and movies that students might be interested in. These popular culture links to victimology help to personalize and humanize the experiences of those we encounter in the justice system. Not only are their stories important for us to study, but it is also meaningful to understand why some victims and incidents seem more media-worthy than others.

Ours is a diverse and multicultural society so views on victims will reflect that heterogeneity. It is hoped that the moral and ethical dilemmas of dealing with victims will be an important part of the dialogue stimulated by this book.

The authors welcome any feedback concerning the substance and structure of this text. As we continue to teach this course we are cognizant of its dynamic nature and we strive to incorporate the most relevant topics into our material.

CHAPTER 1
The Concept of Victim in Crime Studies

INTRODUCTION

Who Gets to Be a Victim?

A young woman in Texas is charged with second-degree murder in a case where two gangs were fighting in a park. In a startling ruling, the judge accepted a motion from her defense and agreed that the murdered youth who died as a result of a wound she inflicted, would not be referred to as a "victim" in the trial. Many seasoned lawyers were taken aback by the decision. Historically, the dead person got to be the victim. Perhaps the lack of a "victim" in this murder case, or the fact that the deceased was a gang member influenced the final outcome, a hung jury at trial and a subsequent plea agreement to a two-year term of probation for aggravated assault with a deadly weapon (Rogers, 2009). In another case, the founder of an Islamic-oriented television station in Buffalo, New York defended his actions in beheading his wife by claiming that she had abused him for years. The district attorney refuted the idea that the 45-year-old suspect was a victim and simply stated "He chopped her head off. That's all I have to say about Mr. Hassan's apparent defense that he was a battered spouse." (*Associated Press*, January 23, 2010)

Today, we can argue that the concept of victim has been expanded to include all types of civil and criminal wrongs from birth to death that can give a person the status of victim. As social values and attitudes about crime change, as we develop more new crimes and crime areas, the range of victims appears to continue to grow. Some even argue that we have too many victims. Based on an assumption of limited resources and the negative effects of having too large a pool of "victims" on our social conscience, should we restrict our consideration of who is truly a victim and who is perhaps less "deserving" of victim status? Should we prioritize victims by some hierarchy of blameless-ness? Who are the most popular victims and why? Are there any types of victims who should be excluded? Is there too much competition for victim status in our country today?

Concerns about the potential boundaries of victimology leads us to ask several questions about the limits of what can be considered. For example, can a corpse be a victim? An animal? A town square? The answer would depend on your definition of what is a victim. Is there really any such thing as a victimless crime? What determines whether there is a victim—the law? When a Birmingham, Alabama funeral director is charged with felony abuse of a corpse, the implication seems to be that there is a victim of the abuse (Reeves, 2009) the same way there might be with a person charged with harassing wildlife, or desecrating a sacred space.

In order to determine answers to these questions we might want to know more about whether there is suffering, who is harmed, and how we go about assessing that harm. Can victimization be self-assessed? Frequently an individual will say "I am not a victim, I do not want to be considered a victim." Or, in the reverse, someone makes a claim to be a victim. They might say, despite the opinions of others, "I am the victim here." Can someone decide whether or not he or she is the victim? In the case of a person charged with desecrating a corpse, for example, who is the victim? A person who is dead cannot feel pain or experience harm and the law has been fairly consistent in its determination that a person cannot be raped if they are already deceased. Is it instead the family of the deceased who is suffering from the idea that their loved one has been violated? Is it society, who must somehow have faith in those who are entrusted with the care of our departed loved ones? In these cases, does the state represent the victim of the whole and prosecute the case in the name of the greater good of society? Perhaps by the end of this book, you will have a better idea of how we could best address these questions. One way to begin is by looking at the field of victimology in general.

The Legal and Scientific Study of Victims

As Burgess and Roberts (2010) point out, the term victim is not, by itself, a legal or scientific concept. Recognition of the role of the victim in society dates back as far as ancient civilizations. Historically, folklore and literature chronicle the complex relationships between offenders and victims and even those that occur within families such as Cain who slew his brother Able. Often these interactions symbolize the good victim triumphing over the evil offender as in David and Goliath as well as Cinderella and Snow White and their wicked archenemies.

Victims probably had the most input and influence on justice outcomes prior to the emergence of systems of law. Victims and their relatives controlled the extent of retribution and, consequently, the extent of their satisfaction with the punishment meted out to the offender. Ironically, this "most satisfied" version also yielded one of the greatest problems for those societies. Retribution created a disturbing threat of blood feuds which, ultimately, called for a more formal society intervention. Law, or the creation of a third-party interest, began the process of restricting the role of the victim. With the advent of such concepts as "the King's peace," the actual victim was no longer a principle figure in the criminal process and, in a move calculated to reinforce central authority, the state came to represent the aggrieved party in judicial proceedings. True, individual victims appeared to testify at trial or give information to the authorities in a variety of ways, but they were no longer the accusers nor did they have to bear the expense of prosecuting the accused. That role was assumed by the "official" prosecutor.

The state's historically-increasing indifference to the victim is reflected in the changing criminal justice role it assigns to them. One reflection of this indifference is found in the modification of the victim's role from a person who has been harmed in some way to the person who provides emotional credibility to the prosecution. In this fashion, the state ignores the actual harm and instead focuses on the social harm. The symbolic value of punishing the offender, exacting the price for transgressing the legal codes is the basis of retribution and deterrence. Such a process, where the victim is concerned, may lack satisfaction and reduces him or her to a secondary role. Real harm has thus been subordinated to theoretical conceptions of legal harm and the definition of a victim becomes an artificial one. Therefore, the traditional (system-oriented) definition of victim used in victimology is entirely created by law and the legal process.

While the victim is often a prominent feature in cultural identities and moral instruction, the scientific study of victims is a product of twentieth-century positivism, empiricism and the accumulation of data necessary for meaningful analysis. Until we began to collect information about victimization, we could not test theories or develop insights into this critical component of the criminal justice system. While most contemporary criminal justice programs offer a course in victimology it is also found in the fields of sociology and criminology although some theorists have argued that the substantial body of theory and research within the study area warrants its consideration as a separate discipline.

VICTIM TYPOLOGIES

A typology is one of the more primitive forms of theory and thus is frequently used in early forms of scientific analysis. Positivistic inquiry relies on identifying and categorizing subjects into groups according to traits they share with others. A typology is an ordered and systematic classification of phenomena that best describes the characteristics of its members. A typology organizes information about a group according to some theory or rational explanation.

A typology is developed by taking a set of existing subjects, who all fit the definition of a particular phenomenon and further arranging them into subsets. For the purposes of our discussion, we are looking at theorists who said (hypothetically), "after studying all types of victims, I find that they can be sorted and labeled according to the following scheme." The premise is that if all victims can be further subdivided into a range of types, this will help us to improve methods of identifying and servicing victims. It also promises to clarify how we might prevent victimization by recognizing early patterns of behaviors and the need for potential intervention.

What you can discern from the discussion of victim typologies that follows is that the categories of victims seem to evolve over time with changes resulting from new ways of viewing social problems and new events to which individuals are exposed. Categories also seem to reflect the influence of new academic disciplines for example, psychology or forensics.

Hans von Hentig

When Hans von Hentig published his famous study *The Criminal and His Victim* in 1948, *Time* magazine even published a story about it. In the book von Hentig argued that the factors shaping the development of both criminals and victims are varied and complex, including the possibility of physical impairments and disabilities, things that may cause one to be bitter or ostracized and teased by others. In discussing victimization, von Hentig noted, much like earlier cartographers and demographers, that particular times of the day or year may produce a higher likelihood of offenses. He noted that *"...crimes of violence and sex reach their peak in late Spring; most women are murdered between 6 and 8 p.m."* Like our contemporary social-disorganization theories, von Hentig explained that *"Some types of criminals are attracted to slum areas; so are their victims."* And, perhaps being influenced by the writings of Italian physician and early criminologist Cesare Lombroso, he attempted to classify his victims and offenders by their common traits. As the article in *Time* relates:

> Feeblemindedness, common among some types of criminals, is also common among their victims... certain characteristics of law-abiding citizens arouse a counterreaction in the criminal. The inexperienced businessman, for example, invites embezzlement; the nagging wife is flirting with murder; the alcoholic is a natural for robbery. Thus the victim becomes the "tempter." Since society does not yet recognize the close relationship between criminal and victim... the whole machinery of prisons, parole boards and probation is drastically out of date. Until a new theory of crime prevention is adopted, victims will go on being a self-perpetuating group, as dangerous to society as criminals (*Science*, 1948).

In his work, von Hentig discussed a typology that appears primarily sociological and seems to focus on weaknesses or demographics that might make someone more vulnerable or easily preyed upon. He divided victims into:

1. The Young
2. The Old
3. The Mentally Defective/Deranged
4. The Intoxicated
5. The Immigrant
6. Minority Group Members
7. Those with Low Intelligence

Over the years, data have consistently supported the idea that victims, as well as offenders, are disproportionately young. Though those who are older are generally more fearful of crime than their lower rates of victimization seem to justify, that fear may be linked to the seriousness of injuries, when involved in some type of physical altercation, sustained by those who are frail. In the news today, we still see evidence of the logic of von Hentig's classifications. As Barrow (2008, p. 47) explains:

> Von Hentig claims that the vulnerability of the immigrant is less a function of linguistic differences and more a result of the isolation and unfamiliarity with social norms and rules. With respect to minorities, he claims that such individuals do not enjoy the same protections from the law as do the dominant class members, thereby making it easier to victimize them. And finally, a person identified as 'dull' is seen as a perfect victim. They fall, intellectually, outside of the immunity extended to very old and very young by 'honorable thieves' (Sutherland, 1937) and are, generally, not smart enough to know they are being victimized.

Looking at von Hentig's categories, it is obvious that in some events, victims may be represented in multiple categories. A young coed partying on spring break in the islands disappears with some new-found "friends" and is murdered. In the classic Chicago School work (Shaw, 1930), the delinquent, Stanley, and his young friends prey upon old drunks in the alleys, stealing what they can with little risk of physical confrontation, an offense nicknamed "jackrolling" (thus the title of the book, *The Jackroller*).

Von Hentig also created a typology of victims that centers on psychological traits that also may be associated with criminal events. They include:

- The Depressed/Apathetic
- The Acquisitive or Greedy (eagerly enter into schemes or illegal investments)
- The Wanton or Sensual (includes prostitutes or one who uses sex as a weapon)
- The Lonesome and Heartbroken (who today may be victimized through the internet)
- The Tormentor (an abusive person is later killed or rendered unable to inflict harm)
- The Blocked (in a no-win situation, defeated and unable to escape. A good example of this is the battered woman who feels she cannot get away or be helped.)

Overall, von Hentig was instrumental in developing interest in the view of victim as a potential provocateur, someone responsible for their involvement in a crime. At the least, his work called attention to the need for legal and social-psychological analysis of the relationship between victims and offenders. If von Hentig was responsible for the creation of a penal couple (a victim and offender tied in some type of relationship), then our next contributor, Benjamin Mendelsohn would be viewed as advocating the "divorce" of the penal couple (Schafer, 1968) and a more separate view of the culpability or role of each in a criminal event.

Benjamin Mendelsohn

Mendelsohn was an attorney who surveyed his clients to develop a database about crime incidents (Schafer, 1968). Mendelsohn is often called the father of victimology, as he coined the term emphasizing it as the "reverse" of criminology. He developed a typology of six victim types. Unlike von Hentig, Mendelsohn (1956) focused primarily on the idea of blameworthiness in formulating the categories described below.

- Completely innocent victim (victim of traditional crime, no provocation or facilitation)

- Victims with minor guilt or victim due to ignorance (such as venturing into a high crime area or believing what others might consider a transparent scam)
- Victim as guilty as the offender (drug buyers and sellers who pull guns and shoot each other, suicide)
- Victim more guilty than the offender by provoking or abusing (in cases where a neighbor witnesses a burglary and shoots the suspect and public outcry condemns the dead burglar and praises the shooter)
- Most-guilty victim (causes one to use self-defense, home-invasion robber killed by home owner)
- Simulating or imaginary victim (pretends to have or falsely claims victim status)

While these categories seem to be of some "legal" consequence, they do not seem to tell us much about what motivated the behavior or what the underlying causes of a person's victimization might be.

Stephen Schafer

Twenty years after von Hentig wrote his noted work, Stephen Schafer (1968) wrote his classic rebuttal in *The Victim and His Criminal*. The shift in the title reflects a change in focus to perhaps herald the new age of the study of the victim. By putting the victim first, Schafer foreshadows the influence that a more-conservative public perspective on social justice will have on the field of criminal justice. It also reflects the prominent role that the victim will have in shaping criminal law in the next half century.

Schafer's typology included varying levels of victim responsebility:

- Unrelated victims (stranger-activated crimes, with no victim responsibility)
- Provocative victims (victim's behavior is responsible to some degree for the offender's reaction)
- Precipitative victims (make themselves vulnerable particularly by being in certain places at certain high-risk times)

- Biologically weak victims (have no responsibility in the offense such as a youth who is raped in jail)
- Socially-weak victims (like powerless minorities and immigrants who bear no fault)
- Self-victimizing victims (these are fully responsible because of their direct involvements in high-risk activities like vice, prostitution, drugs)
- Political victims (bear no responsibility as they are created by shifts in power)

Typology of Victimization

According to Decker, Shichor and O'Brien (1982), another way to approach the issue of typologies is by classifying the event of victimization itself. An example of this is found in the work of Thorsten Sellin and Marvin Wolfgang (1964) when they assessed the context of an incident by considering the role of the victim. They used *primary victimization* to refer to any direct personal harm such as a person being robbed at an ATM or assaulted by a spouse. *Secondary victimization* was used to designate a non-human victim such as an organization or business, as when a Red Cross worker steals from the organization, a cable company experiences theft from people who rewire connections to obtain free service, or riders enter a subway without purchasing tokens. In this case, consumers suffer, needy citizens may go without support and public services may be restricted by diminished revenues. *Tertiary victimization* refers to a general social harm or a wrong against society as a whole, as when a public official embezzles from the state, vandals destroy a public monument or a terrorist act undermines the feelings of safety within a nation. *Mutual victimization* involves the sharing of the offender/victim experience where there is mutual consent and participation, as in vice activities or conspiracies that backfire on one or more of the participants. This is also the case when someone dies when involved in an illegal drag race, sideswiped by a co-offender. Fifth and finally, Sellin and Wolfgang recognized the potential for an event to be resolved by the determination that *no victimization* had occurred. This is a probable outcome when it cannot be determined that anyone was victimized.

Typologies Within Specific Crimes

More recently, typologies have been developed to help organize the study of certain types of victimization. It may be that legislation, policy, programming, and services need to be more specifically focused within these broader categories of crimes in order to be more effective. For example, Levin and McDevitt (1993) divided hate crime offenders into groups that might help us predict who victims are and to create interventions that might reduce the risk of victimization. They saw three types of motivations behind hate crime: "thrill seeking," which is usually a characteristic of teen perpetrators; "reactive hate crimes," where offenders are somehow threatened by the differences they see between themselves and the victims such as gays and lesbians; and "mission-oriented" offenders, who are more likely to be psychotic on a crusade against individuals who may be singled out for attack such as seniors in a Jewish community center.

Sapp, Holden and Wiggins (1993) also constructed a typology of hate crime on the basis of ideology. To these researchers, hate crimes are rooted in either Christian conservatism which would include the abortion doctor who was slain by a remorseless offender who testified to his belief in his actions as he was sentenced to life in prison for first degree murder; white racial supremacists such as the offenders in Jasper, Texas, who dragged James Byrd to his death behind their pick-up truck; and incidents motivated by an aggressive and exaggerated sense of patriotism or survivalism. By acknowledging that hate crimes can be sponsored by a variety of circumstances, theorists can address the differences more accurately and not attempt to derive a "one-size-fits-all" type of approach. The specificity of research may lead to more practical and effective responses from the criminal justice system.

In the early 1990s, several theorists offered typologies of stalkers, a type of offender who was receiving attention from law enforcement and policymakers as a result of a number of high-profile murders. Gavin de Becker (1994) profiled four types of stalkers. First there was the mentally-ill stalker who pursued a famous person with whom there was no prior relationship. The second was a pursuit of a public figure by someone who is not otherwise identified as mentally ill and with whom the public figure has no prior relationship. The third category is the stalking of a regular citizen with whom the stalker has no prior relationship. The fourth and final category is the stalking of a regular citizen by someone with whom that person has had a prior relationship, such as a former girlfriend or roommate.

In another, somewhat more clinical, typology McAnaney, Curliss and Abeyta-Price (1993) classify four types of stalkers. There are those who display (1) erotomania and deClerambault's syndrome or (2) borderline erotomania; (3) those who are former intimates and (4) sociopathic stalkers. Erotomania is the psychotic delusion someone may have that a famous or distinguished person, particularly someone of high status or influence, is in love with them, even from afar. The term "de Clerambault's syndrome" refers to a similar affliction, except that in this case the subject believes that the object of his or her affection actually initiated the relationship. The syndrome was named after Gaetan de Clerambault, a French psychiatrist of the early 1900s who worked with the insane and wrote one of the first papers on this subject. Today, many refer to these subjects as "obsessed fans" such as Margaret Ray who has been arrested many times for stalking David Letterman, often appearing at his home and claiming to be his wife. John Hinkley is frequently cited as another good example of erotomania. In 1981 Hinkley shot President Reagan and White House Press Secretary James Brady as a gesture to actress Jodie Foster, with whom he believed he was in a relationship and who wanted a sign of his devotion. Because the diagnosis is three times more common in women than in men, the psychiatric literature often refers to it as "Old Maid's Insanity." The difference appears to be,however, that men are more likely to be represented in criminal or forensic samples than women (Kelly, 2005).

STUDYING VICTIMS

As the field of victimology grows its research base becomes broader, what we refer to as the "literature of the field." Many studies are specifically funded by legislation targeting victim needs, such as services for domestic-violence victims and victims of rape. Others are mandated as evaluations of criminal-justice-system policy changes such as the benefits of mandatory arrest or the use of victim-impact statements. Some look at direct effects of victimization while others study less obvious, secondary, or indirect effects such as a child witnessing violence between his or her parents at home.

How victims respond to their experiences with crime varies considerably from person to person. Research has indicated that differences in perceived levels of support from family and friends has an effect on recovery from crimes, as do different levels of involvement in the criminal justice system, particularly the prosecution. Variations in demographics may also influence whether or not victims suffer post-traumatic stress or depression subsequent to an offense or benefit from counseling and therapy. In the past, studies of particular types of victims have relied on such small sample sizes that one could not derive any meaningful generalizations from them. Only recently have larger surveys and databases made it possible to get more accurate estimates of the frequency of various types of victimization and, as a result, we have improved our ability to predict those most likely to be victimized.

For example, in a series of studies of juvenile victimization, Finkelhor and colleagues have identified a phenomenon they refer to as "poly-victims" whereby roughly one-third of all youth victims go on to be subsequently victimized within a relatively short period of time. His survey indicated that 71% of children experienced at least one victimization in the last year, and that crimes against youth are three to four times more frequent than reported to police. Older youth and males are most likely to be poly-victims (Finkelhor, 2007). Finkelhor also suggests that a more specific inquiry into what he calls "developmental victimology," or the study of issues associated with childhood exposure to certain types of risks and crimes, would be helpful in prevention and treatment efforts.

PRIORITIZING VICTIMS

As the following examples will illustrate, most criminal justice textbooks make the same simple assessments about the history of crime victims in the justice system. First, the authors will say that historically victims had been ignored and then refer to the 1980s as a period of expanding awareness of the needs of crime victims and a movement to implement more specific rights for victims in the justice process. According to Reid (2003, p. 380),

Throughout most of our history, victims have been ignored by criminal justice systems. In the past decade, many jurisdictions have tried to remedy this situation, and they have done so in a variety of ways.... The decade of the 1980s was characterized by a strong movement toward the recognition of victims' rights, evidenced by the implementation of changes directed toward the needs and concerns of crime victims in criminal justice systems.

Similarly Bohm (2008, p. 220) explains,

Until recently, victims of crime and their survivors have generally been forgotten or neglected in criminal justice. They had not been important or respected participants in the adjudication process except, perhaps, as witnesses to their own or their loved one's victimization. Beginning in the 1980s, however, because of increased scholarly attention to their plight and a fledgling victims' rights movement, attempts have been made to change the situation.

Elias (1993), on the other hand, argues that the so-called victim's movement that many refer to may not have been for victims at all. He points to the subsequent development of a victim's industry where persons or agencies, business and interests other than those of the victim appear to benefit from the laws, rights, and services. By the year 2000, each American family was spending, on average $4000 related to criminal justice concerns, namely by installing private security devices, replacing stolen property, or repairing harm to victims (Waller & Sansfacon, 2000). Politicians whose careers are built on showcasing their concern for victims, purveyors of security hardware and software, victim's advocates, media, and support services all seem to have a vested interest in the continued social promotion of the victim. As Karmen (2001, p. 7) explains

Commercial enterprises have rediscovered victims as an underserved market for crime prevention goods and services. After suffering through an unpleasant experience, many victims become willing, even eager, consumers searching for services and devices that will protect them from any further harm. Potential victims—essentially everyone else—constitute a far larger market, if they can be convinced that their personal security purchases can reduce their odds of winding up as another statistic.

Ironically, a study (Lee, 2008) of home burglar-alarm systems found that concentrations of burglar alarms in an area protected even those without such systems from victimization. While the security companies that funded the research were no doubt pleased that there were areas of the city studied that had dense concentrations of residential security systems, and that having them did not displace the burglaries to nearby houses, they were probably less enthusiastic about the implication that if your neighbors have burglar alarms, you might not need one.

Famous Victims

With constant media coverage of sensational crime events, some experts argue that the public becomes desensitized to the pain and suffering of others. In economically-difficult times, the citizenry may be less inclined to spend precious taxpayer resources across all categories of victims. Perhaps in a broader assessment of societal views we could argue that contemporary opinions are more cynical and people are more suspicious of what they hear as they struggle to prioritize who the truly "deserving" or "innocent" victims are. And, it may also be hypothesized that the constant barrage of information we receive about various celebrity victims can distract us from the reality of the everyday, unremarkable hardships of the many anonymous victims of crime in our society.

Famous victims represent perhaps the "celebrated cases" or the top-tier of the wedding-cake model that Samuel Walker (2001, citing a concept developed by Friedman & Percival, 1981) references when he separates everyday crimes from those with intense notoriety. One of the problems with these cases, he notes, is that they often give people the wrong im-pression about the likelihood of outcomes in similar but less-publicized cases. For example, Walker refers to the O. J. Simpson trial as one of the most notorious of our lifetimes yet it does not reflect the reality, that most domestic violence trials end in conviction. In fact in a government survey conducted shortly after the infamous verdict, it was found that only two percent of the husbands tried for spousal murder were acquitted (Walker, 2001, p. 30).

We also know that the most famous cases are synonymous with the most resources devoted to solving and processing the crimes. Walker argues that only a small percentage of cases receive significant media attention, public outcry and, thus, law enforcement and other areas of criminal justice system efforts. Though we all recognize that the murders of celebrities like John Lennon or political leaders like President Kennedy or Martin Luther King will result in a significant amount of public and professional attention, what is less understood is why some unknown victims become household names resulting in thousands of newspaper pages, talk-show hours and made-for-television movies such as Polly Klas or Adam Walsh.

Even within the same incident, victims may not be perceived similarly. Characteristics of some victims or the way their experience is dramatized may trigger more emotional responses from the media or its audiences. Shoshana Johnson, the first African-American U. S. female prisoner of war in Iraq, said she felt she was "portrayed differently because of her race, either by media outlets that chose not to cover her experience or those who portrayed her as greedy when she challenged the disability rating she was given for her post-traumatic-stress disorder" (Hefling, 2010*)*. The single mother suffered serious gunshot wounds to her legs and for 22 days was a prisoner of war alongside Jessica Lynch, a 19-year-old, who was captured in the same attack. While Lynch's rescue and medical evacuation captivated the country in a constant barrage of media coverage, far less attention was given to the 30-year-old Johnson, and four male soldiers from the 507th Maintenance Co. from Fort Bliss, Texas, who also survived the ordeal. Rescued by Marines, almost two weeks after Lynch, Johnson described how she has continued to struggle with mental health issues related to her captivity and "how it felt to play second fiddle in the media" to fellow POW Lynch. "It was kind of hurtful.... If I'd been a petite, cutesy thing, it would've been different" (Hefling, 2010).

If over 594,000 people were murdered between 1976 and 2005 (FBI, 2010), why is it that so few are recognized as media events? If over 64,000 of those murders were committed by domestic partners, how is it we only remember a few like Nicole Simpson or Lacy Peterson? Minority advocates argue that the plight of poorer victims of color are overshadowed by upper-class, white victims who die under just the same circumstances as their loved ones, yet without any media, public or criminal justice system interest. In fact, many victims are regarded with cynicism and skepticism in a process we refer to as "blaming the victim."

Blaming the Victim

In "blaming the victim" we often come up with rationalizations or justifications for why someone became a victim. This yields such questions as: What were they doing out so late at night? or Who would want to use an ATM in a crime-ridden part of town? This tendency toward blaming victims is not limited to individuals. The governments of England and Wales have blamed citizens for rising rates of property crime, accusing them of failing to guard their possessions (Bivens, 1991). Often campus security programs encourage women to participate in self-defense lessons, a practice which critics argue is not a legitimate substitute for adequate levels of police staffing.

In defining a victim, Bayley (1991) requires that there be some kind of loss suffered or "significant decrease in well-being unfairly or undeservedly and in such a manner that they are helpless to prevent the loss." The concepts of unfair, undeserved and helpless are, however, quite subjective and open to interpretation. Still, we hear of many cases that seem very clear in establishing a right to victim status, particularly using Bayley's definition. For example, Cari Lightner was a "thirteen-year-old girl killed by a drunk driver while walking in a bicycle lane in a quiet suburban neighborhood to a church carnival." Within that one sentence there are many value-laden terms (drunk-driver, quiet suburban neighborhood, church) as well as images that project innocence (thirteen, bicycle lane and even "girl"). Contrast that with the stripper/exotic dancer who alleged to have been beaten and raped by members of a Duke University lacrosse team during a drunken house party (how many value/guilt connotations can you find in this one?)

The ability or tendency to blame some victims may also stem from the likelihood that we, as a society, get tired of hearing about so many victims and become cynical about how much victims really suffer. Perhaps we are simply asking ourselves if these victims are really worthy of our emotional investment. Sometimes we just feel too exhausted from caring for and about so many people, so we are more apt to view some victims in a negative light. Also, some critics argue, by blaming the victim, perhaps we can excuse ourselves for not having addressed the social conditions that seem to sponsor a great deal of crime, such as poverty, unemployment, social disorganization, and ineffective government services.

The Meaningful Measurement of Victimization

As we will see in the chapters ahead, the study of victims is impacted by the various ways that we define the victimization experience and how we view the inclusion of members, either broadly or narrowly. Feminists, for example, have shunned the term victim altogether and prefer to use the concept of "survivor" as more empowering (Walklate, 1994). The continued use of the word "victim," particularly by the criminal justice system, seems to reinforce stereotypical images of weakness and neediness of the female under patriarchal management that feminists are trying to break down; it also presents the potential for a "second victimization" resulting from treatment by the system itself.

One might argue that a social science approach to the study of victims is destined to be an exercise in symantics. One person's victim is another person's offender with a syndrome, such as battered women's syndrome, post-traumatic stress syndrome, or Stockholm syndrome. For professionals in the criminal justice system, these conceptual battles often play themselves out in the courtroom and we must cope with whatever new syndrome we are dealt. Still, legal scholar Stephen Morse argues that the tendency to create new syndrome excuses for conduct seems to amount to a syndrome in and of itself. He cautions that the law "should not be blinded by psychiatric pixie dust nor lose its legal commonsense" (1995, p. 14).

In his book, *A Nation of Victims*, Charles Sykes describes "the irresistible search for someone or something to blame colliding with the unmovable unwillingness to accept responsibility" (1992, p. 15). He further argues that because of our reliance on the legal enterprise of suing each other so often, a "community of interdependent citizens has been displaced by a society of resentful, competing, and self-interested individuals who have dressed their private annoyances in the garb of victimism" (1992, p. 15).

Whether you think that there are too many or too few victims known to the criminal justice system, we can probably all agree that accurate data on crime and victims is imperative to the study of victimization. Some studies, as we will see, involve the use of official data—crime and victimization statistics that are gathered from various sources nationwide. Other researchers conduct in-depth studies of individual victims or groups of specific victims such as survivors of the Holocaust or children abducted by strangers. In some cases victims themselves write their life stories as a way of conveying the details of the after-effects of their experiences and hoping to sensitize others to the problems that they face. Examples of some of these case studies and life stories can be found at the end of this chapter and they will be referenced throughout the book.

References

Associated Press (2010, January 23). Man accused of beheading wife claims abuse. *Houston Chronicle,* A18.

Barrow, L. (2008). *Criminal victimization of the deaf.* NY: LFB Scholarly.

Bayley, J. E. (1991). The concept of victimhood. In D. Sank & D. J. Caplan (Eds.) *To be a victim: Encounters with crime and injustice* (pp. 53–62). New York: Plenum Press.

Becker, de, G. (1994, June 29). Intervention decisions: The value of flexibility. Paper presented at the 4th Annual Threat Management Conference, Anaheim, CA.

Bivens, M. (1991, March 28). England, Wales crime rates increase; Victims get partial blame. *San Bernardino Sun,* A12.

Bohm, R. (2008). *A concise introduction to criminal justice.* New York: McGraw Hill.

Burgess, A. W., & Roberts, A. R. (2010) Crime and victimology. In A. W. Burgess, C. Regehr, A. R. Roberts (Eds.), *Victimology: Theories and Applications* (pp. 1–30). Boston: Jones and Bartlett.

Decker, D., Shichor, D., & Obrien, R. M. (1982). *Urban structure and victimization.* New York: Lexington Books.

Elias, R. (1993). *Victims still: The political manipulation of crime victims.* Newbury Park, CA: Sage.

Federal Bureau of Investigation (2010). *Supplementary homicide reports, 1976–2005.* Washington, DC: U. S. Department of Justice. Retrieved from http://bjs.ojp.usdoj.gov/content/pub/pdf/htius.pdf

Finkelhor, D. (2007). Developmental victimology. In R. Davis, A. Lurigio, & S. Herman (Eds.). *Victims of crime, 3rd Ed.* (pp. 9–34). Thousand Oaks, CA: Sage.

Friedman, L. M., & Percival, R. V. (1981). *The roots of justice.* Chapel Hill, NC: University of North Carolina Press.

Karmen, A. (2001). Crime victims: An introduction to victimology, 4th Ed. Belmont, CA: Wadsworth.

Kelly, B. (2005). Erotomania: Epidemology and management. *CNS Drugs, 19,* 8, 657–669.

Lee, S. (2008). *The impact of home burglar alarm systems on residential burglaries.* A dissertation submitted to the Graduate School-Newark Rutgers. Newark: The State University of New Jersey.

Levin, J., & McDevitt, J. (1993). *The rising tide of bigotry and bloodshed.* New York: Plenum.

McAnaney, K. G., Curliss, L. A., & Abeyta-Price, C. E. (1993). From imprudence to crime: Anti-stalking laws. *Notre Dame Law Review, 68,* 819–909.

Mendelsohn, B. (1956). The victimology (in French). *Etudes Internationales de Psycho-Sociologie Criminelle, 3,* 25–26.

Morse, S. J. (1995). The "new syndrome excuse syndrome." *Criminal Justice Ethics,* Winter/Spring, 3–115.

Reid, S. (2003). *Crime and criminology, 10th Ed.* Boston: McGraw Hill.

Reeves, J. (2009, February 26). Man allegedly let body rot in hearse. *Associated Press.*

Rogers, B. (2009, September 18). Probation cut short in fatal gang knifing. *Houston Chronicle,* B1.

Sapp, A., Holden, R., & Wiggins, M. (1993). Value and belief systems of right-wing extremists" In R. J. Kelly (Ed.). *Bias crimes: American law enforcement and legal responses.* Berkshire, UK: Office of the International Criminal Justice Administration.

Schafer. S. (1968). *The victim and his criminal: A study in functional responsibility.* New York: Random House.

Science, Go ahead, hit me. (1948, September 20). Retrieved from http://www.time.com/time/magazine/article/0,9171,799202,00.html#ixzz0cLBEggNs.

Sellin, T., & Wolfgang, M. (1964). *The measurement of delinquency.* New York: Wiley.

Shaw, C. (1930). *The jackroller.* Chicago: University of Chicago Press.

Sutherland, E. H. (1937). *The professional thief.* Chicago: University of Chicago Press.

Sykes, C. (1992). *A nation of victims: The decay of the American character.* NY: St. Martin's Press.

Von Hentig, H. (1948). *The criminal and his victim: Studies in the sociobiology of crime.* New Haven, CT: Yale University Press.

Walker, S. (2001). *Sense and nonsense about crime and drugs: A policy guide. 5ᵗʰ Ed.* Belmont, CA: Wadsworth.

Walklate, S. (1994). Can there be a progressive victimology? *International Review of Victimology, 3,* 1–15.

Waller, I., & Sansfacon, D. (2000). *Investing wisely in crime prevention: International experiences* (NCJ 182412). Washington, DC: National Institute of Justice.

Discussion Questions

1. Is the concept of identifying people as victims overused? Are there any characteristics or traits that you think should be used to prioritize some victims over others? Is there any reason to deny someone status as a victim if they believe themselves to be one?
2. Which victim typologies do you think are most accurate? How would you construct a typology of your own either to categorize all types of victims or one particular kind?
3. How are crime victims different from other types of victims such as victims of natural disasters or diseases or wars?

Books (by Victims) you may want to read

Dully, H. (2007). *My lobotomy.* New York: Crown Publishers

Van Derbur, M. (2003). *Miss America by day.* Denver: Oak Hill Ridge Press.

Johnson, S. (2010). *I'm still standing: From captive U.S. soldier to free citizen—my journey home.* Austin, TX: Touchstone.

Movies You May Want To See

Milk (2008)
Innocent Victims (1996)

Web Links

http://www.victimlaw.info/victimlaw/
http://www.ncvc.org/ncvc/Main.aspx
http://bjs.ojp.usdoj.gov/content/pub/pdf/htius.pdf

CHAPTER 2

Victim Data and Research

INTRODUCTION

To answer questions accurately about victimization risk and to develop theories of victimization we must have at our disposal a significant amount of empirical research. Testing hypotheses about various victim/crime relationships is the key to developing meaningful laws, policies, and programs to benefit our society. It is only in the last several decades that we began to amass the data necessary to allow more sophisticated and meaningful analysis of crime victim groups. This means having large samples of subjects from more specific crime victim groups, such as victims of domestic violence and victims of identity theft.

Early studies of battered women, for example, did not include information on sexual assault. Verbal and physical aggression measures appear as standard indicators of domestic conflict without any mention of sexual violence. As data became available on the incidence of sexual victimization in long term relationships, the integration of mechanisms to collect that data became part of the survey protocol. As might be expected, studies of women in battered women's shelters revealed higher rates of sexually abused victims (36% in separate studies by Spektor, 1980 and Giles-Sims(1980) and 37% in a study by Pagelow (1980). In a clinical sample (those who had sought treatment or therapy) of battered women (Walker, 1979) , most felt that they had been raped at one time or another, a finding that is common in this particular group. Recognition of the serious consequences of such destructive behaviors may drive more of these women to seek help and to openly discuss these issues while the general population may have been more likely, especially twenty years ago, to avoid the perceived stigma of admitting sexual abuse in a committed relationship. Still, random sample surveys of the general population like those conducted by Finkelhor and Yllo (10% in 1982) and Russell (12%, 1980) may be the most accurate indicator of the true marital rape rate. What should be noted here is that these earliest estimates come mainly from testimony, reports and essays, less formal sources than peer-reviewed outlets. Until the use of more rigorous random sampling techniques in the research design, studies on this subject were unlikely to be published in academic journals.

In this chapter we will examine the development of the major data sources for studying victimization in this country. It is important to see that the range of theories we can contemplate is tied to the ability to access large data sets that are recognized for their scientifically rigorous standards. The best ways to measure crime and to determine the characteristics of both victims and offenders are difficult concepts for those in the criminal justice system to reach consensus on. Therefore, the presence of multiple formats and collection techniques such as those found in both the Uniform Crime Report and the National Crime Victims Survey should be seen as an asset. Tasks like developing successful strategies for preventing crime, estimating the true costs of crime, assessing the validity of other measures of crime and increasing the reporting of crime call for a variety of different approaches. It is not realistic to assume that only one source of information on crime is right. Continuously improving the data we have available and expanding into topic areas that are of critical social importance make the study of victimology today a dynamic academic field.

OFFICIAL CRIME STATISTICS

The Uniform Crime Report

Historically, American crime data collection was a responsibility of individual states and it was not until 1870 that Congress mandated the U. S. Attorney General to institute a crime reporting system. This was a measure also urged by the International Association of Chiefs of Police although a formal mechanism was not authorized or funded until 1930. From that time, up until the late 1960s, the primary source of information we had about crime was the Uniform Crime Report, official police data submitted to and published by the FBI.

Although the UCR had been federally coordinated since the 1930s, there was not widespread participation from law enforcement agencies did not occur until the late 1950s. Still, theories based on these data tended to emphasize street crime, offenses captured by the index crimes featured in the UCR (also called Part I crimes), and arrests that seemed to overemphasize the representation of poor and minority offenders. Critics argued that a large portion of crime went unreported to police for a variety of reasons and that the dark number or percentage of unreported offenses resembled, for some crimes, a huge mass floating undetected below sea level exposing only the "tip of the iceberg" in crimes known to police.

Text box 2-1 lists a number of reasons for victims not reporting crimes to the police.

Box 2.1. Reasons For Not Reporting A Crime To The Police

1. A victim might not realize that an offense has been committed.
2. There might be no victim in the usual sense of the word (victimless crimes).
3. A victim might fear reprisals.
4. A victim might fear self-incrimination or incrimination of close relative or friends.
5. A victim might fear the personal consequences of the criminal justice proceedings, such as cross-examination, public condemnation, and publicity.
6. A victim might not want to lose working time.
7. The offense might not seem severe.
8. A victim might not believe that the offender will be apprehended and punished.
9. A victim might be unable to identify the offender.
10. A victim might be uninsured or unaware of victim-compensation programs and thus would lack a monetary incentive to report crimes.

Source: Decker, D., Shichor, D., & Obrien, R. (1982, p. 21) *Urban structure and victimization.* Lexington, MA: Lexington Books.

In addition to the possible problem of underreporting, researchers were also concerned with the lack of information about the nature of the crime, specifically the victim- offender relationship. Problems were also suspected in the potential of the reporting officer to interject bias or distortion into the report. In addition, differences in the definitions of various crimes across jurisdictions made it difficult to compare crime rates from place to place or to aggregate their counts into meaningful totals. There were also concerns about the way crime incidents were counted, as in using only the most serious offense in a sequence or spree of offenses conducted at one time. This accounting practice is often referred to as the "hierarchy rule." The determination of which offense takes priority is set out in specific guidelines, as is the process for deciding if a series of crimes is a single incident or multiple offenses. Often, the way criminal acts become distinguished from each other as multiple incidents rather than as part of a unified event is a product of the separation of time and place. Only arson (which was added to the list of index crimes in 1979) and, under certain circumstances, motor vehicle theft and justifiable homicide constitute exemptions from the hierarchy rule. The grouping of attempted crimes into the same category as actual (completed) crimes is another weakness in the earlier versions of the UCR

The methodological concerns about the UCR at this time coincided with a pervasive sentiment of unrest among large segments of the population over civil rights issues, discrimination, and mistrust of government authorities. Watergate, the Viet Nam War, the National Guard shooting of protesting students at Kent State University, inner city riots, and the state police shooting of inmates and hostages at Attica were events that created strained relationships between government and citizens. People wanted independent verification of information they could no longer trust their elected officials to provide.

Given all of these concerns, alternative sources of information were sought which led to the development of a national crime victims' survey. By approaching the crime issue from both a victim and a law enforcement measurement perspective, researchers hoped to balance the picture with more accurate representations of the true crime problem.

National Crime Survey/National Crime Victim Survey

The National Crime Survey (NCS), which is known today as the National Crime Victims Survey (NCVS), was developed in stages over a period of time in a somewhat experimental process. In its initial stage, the survey conducted by National Opinion Research Center (1967) interviewed 10,000 households in the U. S. and asked them to report on experiences with crime over the past 12 months. Initial findings were that police reports underestimated crime overall by as much as 50 percent. Still, it is interesting to know that both collections reflected a similar rank-ordering of crimes, meaning that if burglary were the third most common crime in the UCR it was also the third most frequently reported in the NCVS.

While the results of this early victims' survey clearly indicated a discrepancy between official statistics and victim reports, it also faced its own methodological shortcomings. The accuracy of respondent recall was subject to distortions caused by the phenomenon of telescoping. Telescoping is a form of reporting error that occurs when the person being questioned projects an event either forward into a more recent time period than it actually was or backward into a more distant time period.

By the time the survey was revised and reformed into its second generation (1970–1971) it had instituted records checks to attempt to compare the victim's recall with official reports. In a reverse records check the researcher uses the police file on an incident to locate the victim and see if the victim recalls the same information that is in the report while filling out the survey. In a forward records check the researcher starts with a survey report that the victim has filled out, and if that person indicates that a police report was filed, the researcher tracks it down and compares it to the survey for accuracy.

Another way to improve accuracy and reduce telescoping was to conduct the survey every six months so that respondents only have to recall those events that had transpired in one-half of a year, rather than during the past full year. The six-month interval was determined to be significantly better at reducing recall errors. In addition, by returning to the same households for multiple surveys, which is called a panel design, the researchers can also insure that the respondent is not reporting the same single incident in multiple reporting periods. In this process of bounding, the researcher is able to compare the prior survey against the current one to avoid any error caused by duplicating events.

Verification with the respondent insures that two separate time periods are being assessed. The end of the last survey period becomes the boundary or reference point for the beginning of the next questionnaire. For example, an interviewer would say, "since we last spoke in February...." More successfully, an interviewer will use common benchmarks such as Christmas, school beginnings, or the New Year to help the respondent focus on the time period being examined and to orient themselves toward the proper reference span.

In 1972, the survey was administered in its third design which implemented most of the standard features found in its current use. Using the panel format, 72,000 households are visited every six months for a period of three years. One of the continuing limitations of this target population is that the survey is not administered to businesses or commercial properties. On the other hand, other sources of business/retail crime statistics exist for ascertaining this type of information. Concerns have also been raised about the fact that only one household respondent is selected to provide the information. The use of a single interviewee provides for efficiency and expedience in the process which appears to outweigh any potential benefit of talking to the household member who may have been the one who actually experienced the victimization.

In the fourth and most current version, 49,000 households are surveyed every six months by the U. S. Census Bureau. The use of telephone surveying was incorporated for up to 75 percent of the subjects in any one survey period. Although the early survey years enjoyed response rates of up to 100 percent (Catalano, 2006), reductions over time have not been significant and the survey continues to have some of the highest response rates for research in this field.

CHANGES TO NATIONAL STATISTICS

The National Crime Victim Survey Today

A number of new topics have been entered into the National Crime Victims' Survey that allows research to be done on an expanded array of issues related to the criminal events. Items include whether the offender appeared to be drunk or high, what the victim was doing at the time of the incident, any previous contact with the criminal justice system the victim might have had, crimes that may have been committed by friends and family members of the respondent, and also any defensive or self-protective measures the victim may have taken during the offense. The ability to study victimizations in more detail can build on our ability to design more effective crime prevention strategies. For example, Santana (2007) used information on self-protective behaviors to study four types of victimization (rape, sexual assault, robbery and physical assault). She concluded that:

> ...while no one type of self-protective behavior was effective across all four types of victimization, nonforceful verbal self-protective behaviors were ineffective across all four types of victimization... with the exception of sexual assault, another consistent finding was the effectiveness of forceful physical and nonforceful physical self-protective behaviors. The use of both of these types of self-protective behaviors in rapes, robberies, and physical assaults was associated with a decreased likelihood of a completed, or more severe, outcome occurring (Santana, 2007, p. 156).

The Uniform Crime Report Today

Today the UCR has expanded its information data collection and retrieval systems as new technology has made these improvements possible. Online access for research purposes has meant that studies can more easily and economically generate information in the burgeoning field of crime analysis. In addition, a number of changes illustrate how the data base adapts to meet the needs of an increasingly complex justice system. *The Violent Crime Control and Law Enforcement Act* authorized the tracking of data on stalking, domestic violence, and gang violence (Lynch & Addington, 2007). Other federal legislative initiatives have expanded the range of agencies that would be submitting crime data to the FBI. Since 2000, the UCR has also dropped the use of a crime index and the designation of index offenses which were often used to compare areas and the severity of crime experienced in them. This no doubt reflects the recognition of the diversity of opinions about crime seriousness and the way scores and, consequently, labels assigned to certain geographic areas may be less productive than originally thought. A brief description of some of the current UCR collections is provided below.

NIBRS*: The National Incident-Based Reporting System is an upgrade to the UCR which includes over 50 items of information on 46 different crimes. While all of the traditional Part I offenses are included, the system also reports on crimes such as pornography, bad checks, embezzlement and trespassing. Improvements allow for the tallying of all crimes within a single incident, which was one of the criticisms of the earlier data set. Data are collected on all offenders, victims, and places where crimes occur. The NIBRS also distinguishes between attempted and completed crimes and tracks information on the victim-offender relationship, the use of weapons, and the presence of drugs or alcohol. Because this is a more labor intensive reporting system, departments have been only slowly becoming certified in the collection system so that they can contribute to this important data base. There are those who even predict that NIBRS may someday fully replace the UCR (Bohm & Haley, 2005).

SHR*: Another significant addition to the UCR is the Supplementary Homicide Report (SHR) which was implemented around 1976. This dataset has a wide range of demographic information on victims and offenders, specifics on the homicide itself including the relationship of the parties, the use of weapons and probable motive. The SHR also contains information about the reporting agency and related geographic and census traits. Currently, this data set contains reports for approximately 91 percent of all homicides and, because it is available online, it is one of the primary resources for homicide research. Establishing this data set made it possible to form a Homicide Research Working Group and The Center for Homicide Research has been activated. There is also a journal called *Homicide Studies* where work in this area can be published. None of these would have been possible if large data sets were not available to study. For example, these were the data used by Brewer, Damphousse and Adkinson (1998) when they studied juvenile homicides in Houston. They found that juveniles were more likely to be involved in the interracial killings of strangers during felony robberies with long guns.

LEOKA: The Law Enforcement Officers Killed or Assaulted data base contains information on all officers killed either accidentally or intentionally, as well as those assaulted in the line of duty. Records reflect the type of call or incident the officer was attending as well as the weapon used. The data is broken down by agency of the victim, victim demographics as well as criminal history and traits of the offenders. A report is issued annually and is available on the web (http://www.fbi.gov/ucr/killed/2007/aboutleoka.html). The full data set is accessible to researchers wanting to conduct further study by working with the data services office of the FBI.

Hate Crime Data: The collection of data on hate crimes was mandated by a series of legislative acts designed to monitor a wide variety of incidents through the Hate Crime Data Collection Program. Formally adopted into the UCR in 1996 the program tracked hate crimes defined by bias against race, religion, ethnicity or national origin or sexual orientation. The categories were expanded in 2009 with passage of legislation that added gender identity or disability, this data base is not without some public controversy. The ability and willingness of law enforcement agencies to identify and label offenses as hate crimes is critical to the viability of this program. It will be discussed in greater detail in Chapter 4.

OTHER DATA PROGRAMS

Campus Crime Reporting Data

In a series of legislative acts related to campus crime, security, and the right to know campus crime data, the federal government mandated the reporting of campus crime. Information on the traditional Part I crimes is recorded as well as data on on-campus arrests involving weapons, drugs or alcohol. Because these data must be made available publicly, researchers have been able to conduct studies on a wide range of campus security-related issues. Outlets for this research include a number of school administration journals as well as periodicals in the areas of security management and public safety.

BJS National Prison Rape Statistics Program

As a result of a series of high profile court cases, media accounts as well as public pressure from prisoner support groups, statistics on sexual assaults in prison are now filed annually. Mandated by the 2003 *Prison Rape Elimination Act (PREA)*, the Bureau of Justice Statistics compiles an annual comprehensive report of the frequencies of prison rape. Called The National Inmate Survey (NIS) the program gathers mandated data directly from inmates in a private setting. The NIS uses technology that incorporates audio computer-assisted self interviewing (ACASI) with a touch-screen laptop and an audio feed to insure that the inmate's replies are confidential. It also enables researchers to address potential literacy limitations (Bureau of Justice Statistics at http:// bjs.ojp.usdoj.gov/index.cfm?ty=dcdetail&iid=278). The U. S. Attorney General also provides funding to states for personnel, training, technical assistance, data collection, and equipment to prevent and prosecute prison rape.

The establishment of a uniform national database has allowed for the initiation of a research agenda that will contribute to our theoretical understanding of prison rape. The Office of Justice Programs has funded 9 studies since 2003, covering the following topics (http:// www.ojp.usdoj.gov/nij/topics/corrections/institutional/prison-Rape/ ongoing-research.htm):

- Inmate perceptions of sexual violence and rape in adult prisons.
- Prison rape policies and promising prevention programs.
- Risk assessment instruments needed to identify potential victims and perpetrators.
- The effects of victimization upon prisoner reentry into society.
- Improved security in women's facilities.
- Interventions designed to prevent sexual and physical violence in jails.

Studies indicate however, that inmates are reluctant to report sexual victimization and fear of retaliation. There is also the perception that administrative barriers to remedies may prevent inmates from reporting. For that reason, the Bureau of Justice Statistics is experimenting with an Audio-Computer-Assisted Self Interview (ACASI) instrument that will be used to more privately survey a sample of former prison inmates who are on active supervision in the community. This method is also used to gather the data found in the National Survey of Youth in Custody (NSYC), which contributes to the

National Prison Rape Statistics Program. The ACASI is described as follows:

> ...youth, using a touch-screen, interacted with a computerized questionnaire and followed audio instructions delivered via headphones. The NSYC utilized self-administered procedures to ensure the confidentiality of the reporting youths and to encourage fuller reporting of victimization. The survey also made use of audio technology to provide assistance to youth with varying levels of literacy and language skills (Beck, Harrison, & Guerino, 2010, p. 2).

One of the ways the ACASI may improve our understanding of sexual assault in correctional institutions is that it will not only allow larger samples to be included, but it will offer the instrument in various languages and will automatically exclude faulty or inconsistent reporting patterns. For the NSYC, the program also has a number of other measures to reduce error in data gathering that should improve the validity and reliability of the findings. The system, according to Beck, Harrison and Buerino (2010, p. 6) utilizes

> "hotwords," highlighted in a different color, which youth could access if they were uncertain about their definition; range checks for selected questions to guard against unrealistic values, and logic checks that asked youth to verify their responses. To assist youth having difficulty with the interview, the computer flagged those who spent a long period in particular sections of the interview and prompted the youth to obtain assistance from an interviewer.

The Former Prisoner's Survey is another attempt to measure sexual victimization while offsetting the traditional reporting barriers to victim reporting found in institutions, particularly fear of retaliation. This survey is administered to adults who have already been released from custody and contains information on any sexual assault experiences that occurred during the now-released individual's last incarceration.

Finally, another prisoner database that will be collected in an attempt to offset prisoner reluctance to report sexual violence is called The Clinical Indicators of Sexual Violence in Custody (CISVC). This is a passive surveillance system where medical staff will wait until after the patient has been treated, and then complete an incident form for each inmate exhibiting symptoms or injuries consistent with sexual violence. The CISVC is currently being pretested for feasibility at 25 prison facilities and ten jails. If successful, data collection may be expanded to more facilities and, in combination with other data in this reporting program, will provide a more accurate picture of the nature and prevalence of prison sexual assault.

CRIME RATES

Overall crime rates give us a general sense of safety and risk factors as well as a comparative reference point for an examination of changes in the amount of crime over time. Macro level theories use crime rates to assess the impact of other general social conditions on crime such as unemployment and crime, or immigration and crime. However, rates of crime for specific offenses may be more useful for research purposes as well as for the development of meaningful intervention and prevention strategies.

The crime rate is calculated by dividing the number of a type of crime by the population and multiplying that by a standardized 100,000 for ease of understanding and comparing the figures.

The formula then is:

crime rate = the total no. of crimes divided by the total pop. X 100,000

These numbers may not seem particularly meaningful but policymakers and citizen groups are interested in changes in those rates over time, the reasons for those changes, and how to lower overall rates of crime. One controversy from the use of these figures is an issue of magnitude. How large would a change in crime rates have to be before it is considered significant? Problems also arise when small fluctuations, that may be explained by normal or uncontrollable forces in society, are overemphasized or blamed on political positions or circumstances that are difficult to attribute to actual changes in the crime rate.

Crime rates can also be constructed in terms that help us understand the way crime impacts society. The incidence rate, which is the most common statistic used other than the actual number of events, is the frequency of an occurrence in a fixed period of time against a standard population base, say every 10,000 or 100,000 people. These data reflect how often an event occurs. Or, put another way, for the FBI's Uniform Crime Reports, it is the number of crime events per 100,000 population over a period of a year.

Most people think of this crime rate as specifying the likelihood of their being a victim of crime. That simple interpretation, however, is not true for the simple fact that some groups of the population are associated with a higher or lower likelihood of victimization. Some of them even are victimized more than once in a set period of time. Thus, we need an approach that takes into account the number of victims of crime rather than just counting crime or using a standard population figure.

This approach, the risk of victimization occurring, is referred to as prevalence. Because we are concerned with victims, our prevalence rate incorporates the number of victims rather than the total number of crimes in an area. It is calculated by dividing the total number of victims by the total population. This provides an estimate of proportion or percent of the population who have been victimized. Of course, we frequently don't know the number of actual victims and as a result cannot calculate a prevalence rate directly. Another version of a prevalence rate can also be expressed as a percentage of those who report having been victims of a specific crime out of the total population at risk. Let's call this one an "at-risk" prevalence rate. For instance, let us say that there are 12,000 reported rape victims within a population of 100,000, or 12 per 100 people. Changing this into an individual's "risk level," we could estimate a risk of rape equivalent to 12% for each individual. This is still not satisfactory, because while both males and females are victims of rape, females are more at-risk for rape than males. In our hypothetical example, if females represent about 90% of rape victims and 50% of the population, then the "at-risk" prevalence of females raped over the course of a year would be about 21.6% (males would have a risk rate of 2.4%).

Unfortunately for our attempt to construct a reasonable risk rate, there is more involved. Think of it this way, if we can predict victimization to any degree, then the likelihood of victimization is not the same for all. Not only can victimization be predicted for certain groups of people, but there are two theories, lifestyle and routine activities, that are based on and explain differences in victimization. Each argues that the daily choices made by members of the population affect the likelihood of their victimization. For example, a young person who goes to nightclubs on the weekend has a greater chance of being victimized than an elderly person who is at home at night. Geographical criminologists have also shown that there are areas much more disposed to crime than others. All of this tells us that a simple number or rate based on the incidence of crime or some population figure is misleading. We need an approach that will tell us the risk of victimization, rather than the rate of crime events for a given population. Geographical criminologists use concentration rates, which are based on the average number of incidents per victim in a given area. Even this, though, does not account for the different chances of victimization among various types of people engaged in various lifestyle practices.

As should be obvious by now, one of the major dilemmas confronting researchers in calculating the rate of any specific crime or victimization is precisely what goes into both the numerator and denominator of the constructed fraction. Disagreement occurs on who the actual victims of any offense are, as well as disagreement on who the potential victims might be. Altering either of these could result in greatly overestimating or underestimating the risk of being a victim of any offense. In our rape example above, where should the data on the actual number of rape victims come from and should all claims of rape be included? Should rape be inferred if the small child, Alzheimer's patient, or otherwise mentally- or psychologically-impaired person cannot confirm what actually took place? Who should be included in the list of potential victims? By placing everyone of any age in the potential victim category have we watered down the picture of the true risk of rape?

Which approach below would you argue most accurately represents the risk of rape?

# of Reported Rape Victimizations
Population of US

# of Police – Reported Rapes
Population of US

# of Women 10 to 75 years of age Reporting Rape Victimization
Total # of Women in US ages 10 to 75

What other calculation might you use for demonstrating the rate of rape in the U.S.?

While victims may suggest a certain amount or level of crime when responding to the NCVS, researchers are interested in those crimes that respondents indicate have also been reported to police. Thus, there are three different projected levels of crime:

8. the total amount of crime reported to both the UCR and to the NCVS (seen as the top line on Figure 2-1. below),
9. the amount of crime victims responding to the NCVS who indicate they also reported to the police (the middle line),
10. and then the level of crime reported by police in the UCR (the bottom line).

In Figure 2-1, Catalano highlights these three trends illustrating the concepts of convergence and divergence.

Figure 2-1. Measures of serious violent crime, 1973–2002

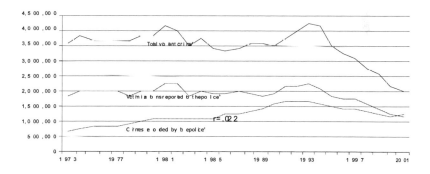

Note: The measures are comprised of the following crimes: homicide, rape, robbery, and aggravated assault.

Source: [a,b]National Crime Victimization Survey, [c]Uniform Crime Reports

Convergence and Divergence

When the NCS was instituted there were many who viewed it as a remedy to the weaknesses and biases of the UCR. The competitiveness of the two models was based in an assumption that there was only one true measure of crime and that by approaching the issue from two conflicting perspectives, a holy grail of crime measures might be reached. The taking of sides on the crime statistics issue was fueled by the early findings that official crime statistics appeared to significantly underestimate the occurrence of crime. This disparity continued for many years until about 1990 when the gap between the two overall crime rates narrowed significantly. By 2000 the two had converged, a phenomenon Catalano (2006) attributes to a number of factors. First, improved methodologies and collection techniques mean that we are able to capture more of the crime that actually occurs. Second, social changes such as more professional policing mean that people may be more comfortable reporting, knowing that they will be taken seriously and that a complaint system exists if they are not. Third, the increased responsiveness that police offer may be due to legal liabilities that translates to additional training and layers of supervision. Finally, demographic changes in the population may have increased not only the concentrations of the types of crimes more likely to be reported to police (such as car theft) but the types of people more likely to report offenses to police (younger or older citizens). This period of convergence, or confluence between the two data sets however, may be short lived.

More recent crime data indicate that we may be returning to more divergent crime rates. Divergence is the concept of difference between the two reporting methods and Lynch and Addington (2007) argue the UCR and NCVS should be viewed as a complimentary system and not a negative attribute. The existence of disparate measures, they explain, gives us unique information and helps us further analyze and respond to crime trend changes. They clarify with this example:

> ...in looking at the recent trends in rape, the UCR shows a steady increase in rape since 2000, whereas the NCVS shows no increase or a decrease. In interpreting this divergence, it is important to know that the UCR includes victims under age 12

whereas the NCVS does not. This would suggest that one reason for the divergence could be changes in the treatment of the sexual assaults of younger children, such that events previously treated as incest or as a child protective matter may now be treated as rape. If further investigation shows this to be the case, then our understanding of what this increase means has been improved by using the two series in concert (Lynch & Addington, 2007, p. 5).

Victim Research

Today, there are many opportunities to conduct meaningful research on victim issues. Some of the areas include the study of fear of crime, research on crime seriousness rankings, and how victimization affects those views, as well as other studies on how victimization experiences impact members of our diverse society. It remains theoretically interesting that those who most fear crime are least likely to be victimized and those least fearful are more likely to be victimized. The relationship between risk and fear is an important area to study because we know from research that people often curtail activities, as well as their community exposures, and reduce their quality of life because of concerns about potential victimization.

The field of victimology like other criminology areas is subject to popular public and media views of issues and causes. For example, the "Mugging Thesis" is a position that anyone who does not have an aggressively tough sentencing orientation is simply a person who has not yet been mugged. This assumes that those who have been victims of crime will be tougher in their punishment views. The purpose of research, then, is to confront these popular beliefs and insure that policy is based on legitimate findings and not anecdotal experiences and personal biases. For example, research has been mixed on whether victims do have more punitive orientations and even some findings indicate they may have less punitive. Still, in deference or respect to victims, many politicians feel that it is politically expedient to be extremely punitive calling for longer sentences, more restrictive release policies and quicker revocation actions.

For the most part, research on the question of whether those who have been victimized by a certain type of crime will view that crime as more serious also has had mixed results. The type of victimization, and the individual's personal experience and perhaps how recent the victimization was seem to influence survey respondents' attitudes about the seriousness of certain types of crimes in some research studies. Other studies have found more uniformity in public perceptions of the seriousness of certain types of crimes regardless of anyone's victimization history.

While research may answer questions about fears of victimization and how prior victimization experiences alter our attitudes and perceptions, it is also useful for answering the question, "What do victims really want from the criminal justice system?" One of the ways we test this question is to ask survey respondents their experiences with crime victimization at the same time as we assess their views on sentencing and punishment. Researchers attempt to correlate the types of victimization events such as the murder of a loved one, or the person's own experience being robbed with changes in attitudes toward criminal justice system outcomes. In an in-depth examination of those who had lost loved ones in capital murder events, the researcher (Vollum, 2008) was able to access and analyze comments from those he called "co-victims" by compiling newspaper accounts, most often in online databases by searching on every execution ever held in the state of Texas. His conclusions in this very unique and insightful study state that:

> The fact is that very few co-victims report that the execution brought them closure (2.5%) and that many report it brings no healing or closure (20.1%). What seems more accurate, based on the statements of co-victims, is that co-victims see the execution as a conclusion to a long process of grief and pain…. Moreover, in nearly half of the cases, co-victims stated dissatisfaction with the death penalty process and/or execution itself, with the leading complaint being the length of time it took to carry out the execution. On the other hand, a substantial proportion of co-victims stated that the execution brought them satisfaction or that it brought them justice. Overall, co-victims seem to be expressing more relief that the whole ordeal is over than any kind of true catharsis or psychic closure—both essential human needs for healthy grieving and healing (Vollum, 2008, p. 233).

Vollum also found that attending the execution seemed to have some mediating, and what he called humanizing, effects on both offenders and co-victims. Offenders were more likely to express regret and contrition when their own families and loved ones were present at the execution as well as the families and loved ones of the victims. In addition, these co-victims were more likely to express sentiments of justice and forgiveness when they themselves were present when the death penalty was administered. This seems to suggest that there is support for the presence of the vested parties at executions and that attempts to exclude them and make the process more administrative would not serve the interests of the system.

INTEGRATING VICTIMS INTO THEORY

As we have seen, academic interest in the victim was a natural extension of both popular public sentiments and improved research methods and capabilities. In the 1970s, human rights issues were in the forefront of political debates as the civil rights movement reshaped constitutional interpretations of equality. Womens' rights, as well as the rights of the elderly, handicapped, and mentally disabled, also evolved during this period of time. The entire population was sensitized by widespread media coverage showcasing the abuses of discrimination against this wide range of potential victims. Today, the coming together of both interest in addressing the needs of victims and more sophisticated methods for studying victimization spawned a broader, multi-faceted array of victim-related theories, as we will see in the next chapter.

References

Beck, A. J., Harrison P., & Guerino, P. (2010). *Sexual victimization in juvenile facilities reported by youth, 2008–2009.* Bureau of Justice Statistics: Special Report. Washington, DC: U. S. Department of Justice.

Bohm, R., & Haley (2005). *Introduction to criminal justice.* 4th Ed. Boston: McGraw Hill.

Brewer, V., Damphousse, K., & Adkinson, C. (1998). The role of juveniles in urban homicide: The case of Houston, 1990–1994, *Homicide Studies, 2,* 321–339.

Catalano, S. (2006). *The measurement of crime: Victim reporting and police recording.* New York: LFB Scholarly Publishing.

Finkelhor, D., & Yllo, K. (1982). Forced sex in marriage: A preliminary research report. *Crime & Delinquency, 28,* 459–478.

Giles-Sims, J. (1980). Stability and change in patterns of wife beating: A systems theory approach. Unpublished Ph.D. Dissertation, University of New Hampshire, Durham, NH.

Lynch, J. P., & Addington, L. A. (Eds.) (2007). *Understanding crime statistics: Revisiting the divergence of the NCVS and UCR.* Cambridge, UK: Cambridge University Press.

Pagelow, M. (1980). Does the law help battered wives? Some research notes. Paper presented at the annual meeting of the Law and Society Association, Madison, Wisconsin.

Russell, D. (1980). The prevalence and impact of marital rape in San Francisco. Paper presented at the annual meeting of the American Sociological Association, New York.

Santana, S. (2007). *Self-protective behavior and violent victimization.* New York: LFB Scholarly Publishing.

Spektor, P. (1980, February29). Testimony delivered to the Law Enforcement Subcommittee of the Minnesota House of Representatives.

Vollum, S. (2008). *Last words and the death penalty: Voices of the condemned and their co-victims.* New York: LFB Scholarly Publishing.

Walker, L. (1979). *The battered woman.* New York: Harper and Row.

Discussion Questions

1. What are some of the barriers you can see to the collection of accurate and reliable statistics on crime victims?
2. Describe some of the current data sets that collect information on victims and how they might be used to solve some of the persistent problems of victims today.
3. Visit some of the websites that either supply the victimization data or reports generated from the various victim data sets. How difficult are they to use or interpret? Why? What could be done to make the information more consumer-friendly?

Books You May Want to Read:

Parsell, T. J. (2006). *Fish: A memoir of a boy in a man's prison.* New York: Carroll & Graff.

Bui, Hoan. (2004). *In the adopted land: Abused immigrant women and the criminal justice system.* Westport, CT: Praeger Publishers.

Movies You May Want to See:

The Burning Bed
Precious

Web-Links

http://www.fbi.gov/ucr/killed/2007/index.html
http://bjs.ojp.usdoj.gov/dataonline/
http://www.ncjrs.gov/spotlight/Hate_Crimes/Summary.html
http://www.ojp.usdoj.gov/programs/victims.htm

CHAPTER 3
Victims in Criminological Theory

INTRODUCTION

As larger data sets have been compiled and made available for sophisticated computer analysis, testing and revising theories of victimization have become easier and more popular. The National Crime Victim's Survey, the National Incident-Based Reporting System, the UCR Supplementary Homicide Report, Campus Crime Reports, Sexual Victimization in Prison Reports and a national database on domestic violence are all examples of the types of information that contribute to theorizing about criminal events and the relationship between victims and offenders. In this chapter we will examine a number of criminological theories that address the issues of victimization and victims. Though there are obviously others that would be useful in explanations of specific types of crime, these represent direct applications of theories you are likely to have studied in your criminal justice coursework. In conducting research, it is important to call upon these theories to predict what factors might influence not only the chances of victimization but also the way society and, in particular, the criminal justice system would respond to different types of victims.

LABELING THEORY

Victims in the Labeling Process

Victimologists will argue that the early study of criminology was offender-based and it wasn't until after the typology work of Hans von Hentig (1948), Benjamin Mendelsohn (1959) and Stephen Schafer (1977) that conceptual frameworks expanded to include a broader spectrum of actors. Labeling theory in the 1950s and 60s was particularly suited for questioning traditional interpretations of events and for challenging the status quo about the designation of someone as an offender or as a victim. The recognition of the victim as a socially constructed label led students to question why some people were more likely to acquire victim status and others were not.

When examining why some people reported victimization to police and other people did not, as well as why some people reported specific types of crimes but not others, criminologists recognized that the stigmatization of certain types of experiences played an important part. Rape and sexual abuse, particularly at the hands of trusted others such as priests, scout leaders and coaches, made it not only embarrassing for young male victims but it often leads them to conclude that they may not be believed or taken seriously. As one of three young friends sexually abused by their priest, Jim O'Brien explains that each of them thought they were the only one it was happening to and none of the three spoke to each other about it. He feared the other boys would tease him, and that he would no longer be popular. He admits "I didn't want to have anyone look at me in a different way" (Associated Press, July 29, 2007). Looking at people in a different way is what labeling theory is all about.

In his classic work, *The Discovery of Child Abuse*, Stephen Pfohl (1977) argues that a behavior or event may pass unnoticed in society until a formal label is introduced and endowed with the power to change how people will now perceive an event through a new value lens. The introduction of a label begins the process of transforming a formerly insignificant event into a social problem that now must be addressed by the agencies vying for power and control of this new issue and its resources.

Sociologists recognize that, as a problem gains priority, experts emerge and attempt to manipulate not only the definition of the problem, but also its solution. In this process, groups and agencies vie for funding, grants, manpower and reputation that can be gained by affiliation with the social problem. Attention is focused on the ability to manipulate people's perceptions of the problem to one's advantage or, as symbolic interactionists would argue, to define the situation.

Labeling theory argues that the development of deviant stigma regarding a certain behavior is predicated on social attitudes about who the victim is, who the offender is, and what current views are about that behavior. It is a complex interaction of the time period and the actors. Gaines and Miller (2008) argue that the public expects law and, consequently, law enforcers to evolve to keep up with the norms and values of its members. As an example, we will use child sexual abuse, as a deviant phenomenon. Not that long ago child sexual abuse was a taboo subject, one that was not discussed by victims or community members who might suspect, but would never publicly accuse anyone of the offense. After celebrities like a former Miss America and Oprah Winfrey acknowledged a history of child sexual abuse, people seemed to unite on the idea that these victims should be taken very seriously.

Likewise, stalking was not considered a serious and potentially deadly phenomenon until relatively recently. To many it seemed like it was not until a well-known young actress starring in a popular television series was gunned down at her doorstep by an obsessed fan that people began to pressure their representatives to develop laws. Still, in a study of social science students at Texas Christian University, Kinkade, Burns and Fuentes (2005) found that respondents were more likely to view a scenario as stalking if the victim were not involved with drugs or did not have a history of physical abuse. Offenders were more likely to be viewed as stalkers if they engaged in gift-giving and did investigative spying on the victim. As labeling indicates, in the case of both child sexual abuse and stalking, it did matter who the victims were and not all potential victims were viewed as credible.

According to labeling theory, the way society reacts to a crime is determined not only by who the victim was, but also by who the offender is and how that particular offense is viewed in the context of contemporary events. As noted earlier, wealthy and famous people as both victims and offenders tend to get more media attention for their experiences—which can work both for them or against them. Discrimination studies have also examined why offenses involving certain groups of victims or offenders may draw more serious charges or punishments than others. Some have argued that the murders of over 500 poor young Hispanic women in the Juarez area over the last decade have led to no charges or arrests primarily because they are a powerless and thus disposable population (*The Toronto Star*, 2006) and also because police, businessmen and area officials have also been implicated in their deaths. Along the same lines, a recent study of federal death penalty cases found that crimes involving white victims had a higher risk of being filed under capital punishment eligible charges than those where the victims were non-white (Chapman, 2009).

Labeling theorists also were quick to critique the process that made so many behaviors into offenses. Edwin Schur argued that delinquents are created when they are tagged and their activities are redefined as crimes. In a sense, juveniles were viewed as victims of the system that perhaps overreacted to what many considered normal adolescent mistakes and locked kids into an unhealthy juvenile justice system. This appeared to be the Supreme Court's view in *In re Gault.* This decision held that exposing a youth to detention for an act that would not have been a crime for an adult, namely making a prank phone call, was unconstitutional. Indeed, the deinstitutionalization movement of the 1970s was a product of the scandals arising in juvenile halls and detention centers after accounts surfaced of youth being sexually and physically abused. Accounts of predatory staff as well as other detainees who victimized weaker juveniles can be found in movies such as *Sleepers,* and books such as *Fish: Memoir of a Boy in a Man's Prison* by T. J. Parsell and *I Cried, You Didn't Listen: A Survivor's Expose of the California Youth Authority* by Dwight E. Abbott.

Edwin Schur (1973) believed that through radical non-intervention, or not doing anything, in response to less serious and first-time offenders, one could avoid the stigmatizing and often self-fulfilling prophecy that comes with widening the net and officially processing youth as juvenile delinquents. Although this view was popular with many practitioners, it lost ground as politicians and media focused on violent juvenile offending and the movement to get tough with criminals that began in the 1980s.

CONFLICT THEORY

As the turbulent 1960s unfolded and led into the 1970s, conflict-oriented theories were a particularly popular reflection of the unrest and criticism of the times. Conflict theorists believed that social problems were rooted in the unequal distribution of societal resources, particularly power and wealth. The division of society into class factions based on income, race, and political influence meant that members of the weaker, lower strata faced more hardship and burden without the benefits of privilege and access to resources. Conflict theorists used examples of the victimization of less powerful groups throughout history to defend their position. One example was early immigration in America.

Immigrants and Victimization

As our fledgling country was striving to become a powerful and respected nation, it was clear that American cities would have to reflect the best parts of our culture and our ingenuity and resolve to address what were common negative consequences of our rapidly industrializing world. It was the hope and promise of the opportunities waiting in this growing economy that fueled the great waves of immigration in the Nineteenth and early Twentieth centuries. Between 1820 and 1931 millions of immigrants were processed through the various depots situated in the area that became known as Ellis Island. Today, over 100 million people, more than 40 percent of this country's population traces its history to this entry point (Coan, 1997). Unfortunately, the process of assimilation was not always the romantic picture that our family history relates either. In fact, then, as it often does now, the presence of immigrants lends itself to hatred, blame, exploitation, and victimization.

As Peter Morton Coan explains, the "immigrant experience" had its very dark side and those who had endured long sea passages were particularly vulnerable to those who would take advantage of their lack of skills, language and resources.

> Still in shock, trauma, or depression from the long boat ride, many immigrants endured verbal, physical, even sexual abuse from opportunistic guards, medical staff, and even fellow immigrants (1997, p. xxvii).
> Inspectors forced immigrants to pay bribes, and young girls to give sexual favors; railroad ticket agents inflated the price of passage and pocketed the difference; clerks at the money exchange wantonly lied about international currency rates. The atmosphere of graft and sin became so overt and untenable that news reached President Theodore Roosevelt,

who in 1901, ordered a major cleanup and replaced the top Washington officials in charge (Coan, 1997, p. xxiv).

The idea that immigrants face possible victimization not only at the hands of predators and individual exploiters but from the state as well was argued in a study of conflict theory by McShane (1985) Examining the criminal history and sentences of prisoners in Texas, she found that inmates with immigration detainers or holds for deportation hearings had shorter sentences and fewer commitments than non-detained inmates. However, they were serving larger portions of their sentences incarcerated under a more punitive classification status based solely on their pending immigration review. In addition, the inmates awaiting immigration processing were significantly more likely to be parole-eligible than their counterparts in the general population but were unable to be released to streets while waiting for federal resolution of their status.

It is not surprising then that von Hentig categorized the immigrant as a specific classification of victim in his typology. Conflict theory finds the resource-restricted immigrant politically and socially power-less enough to raise the likelihood of victimization within this population. It also recognizes that intervening to prevent the physical and mental abuse of prisoners and illegal immigrants would be a lower priority for law enforcement as well as law makers than perhaps cracking down on fraudulent software pirating or cable television theft.

Political and Economic Factors in Victimization

Central to conflict theory is the focus on a capitalist industrial economy. The division of labor, particularly in a more sophisticated technological society will create a surplus of workers, high unemployment and competition for jobs that may mean employees suffer under harsher, more dangerous conditions. The victimization of the worker, according to conflict theory, would be a natural product of the pressure for profit. Often we hear about workers being exposed to hazardous chemicals or situated in environments without required safety equipment. Preventable deaths and injuries suffered on the job as a result of violations of various codes and regulations are the evidence conflict theorists use in this argument. The government's lack of motivation in investigating and prosecuting such crimes is also a product of the influence of lobbyists who represent the interests of wealthy business owners.

Conflict theorists sought a broader definition of victim as well as expanded concepts of crime and criminality. Therefore, a variety of immoral activities and behaviors committed in the name of capitalism or in the interests of extending state powers were considered. The manipulation of hostage victims in Iran in the beginning of the 1980s, on the cusp of a change in American presidencies, has long been an issue for conflict theorists. Similarly, a concerted effort by the FBI to interfere with and neutralize the grass roots work of Dr. Martin Luther King has been discussed in the conflict literature. Victims of genocide perpetrated by groups sponsored by U. S. intelligence operations or supplied with arms from deals made between governments are all examples of non-traditional victimizations studied by criminologists under conflict theory. Similarly, theorists undertook an examination of the state treatment of various types of victims by the criminal justice system, particularly those who suffered in the hands of the state (Schwendinger & Schwendinger, 1970). Today, this would include those who, under the War on Terrorism, have been victims of abuse at U.S. military prisons at Abu Ghraib and Guantanamo Bay.

FEMINIST THEORIES

Much like conflict theory, feminist theory sees that society's traditional male-dominated economic and political structures create barriers and constraints that perpetuate the victimization of women. Women, as one of the powerless groups identified by conflict theory are less likely to receive the benefits of independence and success in the marketplace. Similarly, they are less likely to receive legal protections from the criminal justice system. For feminists, law and business are patriarchal networks that condone the suppression of women, particularly through their role as mothers, and their continued subjugation in the family by means of economic dependency and economic marginalization.

The fact that women continue to earn less than men, are more often caught up in low wage jobs referred to in the literature as the "pink-collar ghetto," and are less likely to receive promotions facing the "glass ceiling" are all research areas for feminist theorists. More recently, analysts have argued that mothers face even greater economic sanctions than their childless sisters, a phenomenon referred to as the "mommy wage gap." As economist Heather Boushey, explains in a report by Kleiman (2005), "For the first child a woman has, the wage differential in comparison to non-mothers is from two to ten percent less. For the second child, the gap is from four to 16 percent less than for women with no children." Figures Kleiman (2005) cited also indicated that the ratio of women's pay to men's decreased between 2002 and 2003, where it stood at about 75.5%. Discrimination, sexual harassment in the workplace, and the creation of a hostile work environment for women are also types of victimization that fit within the framework of feminist theory.

In a feminist victimology, one would look at a combination of the definition and priority given to crimes against women, the resources devoted to the treatment of victims, and the prevention of crimes against women. One particular example would be the study of the development of laws against rape within marriage, or marital rape.

Marital Rape

One of the basic tenets in common law is the principle that there can be no prosecution of a husband as the sole actor in the rape of his wife. This is known as the spousal rape exemption as it indicates that the husband is exempt from being prosecuted for rape. In the mid-nineteenth century the legal precedent was set that, as marriage is a contract, the wife has irrevocably entered into a consent status which would be incompatible with a legal definition of rape which implied "without consent" (Sir Matthew Hale, 1847) . Other legal arguments examine the restrictiveness of rape definitions in that an element might be "unlawful" sexual intercourse, which would be difficult to establish given the "lawful" union of marriage in most jurisdictions. It is further argued that patriarchal courts viewed the privacy of families as sacred and were reluctant to invade marital relations. It wasn't until the late 1970s that courts began to critique the historical tradition as an artifact that was out of touch with modern times.

In *State v. Smith*, the first case to attack the spousal rape exemption, it was held that the antiquated doctrine resulted in a kind of bondage for the wife which "leads to insidious deprivation of sexual privacy to a victimized married woman" (1977, p. 391). The court urged that, as in other areas of contemporary law, the concept of equal protection should be used to give married women the same protection as women in general. Over time, the spousal-rape exemption was gradually eroded. Courts initially provided relief to women who were legally separated and had filed for divorce, recognizing that they had withdrawn that implied consent, and then also provided relief to those who were physically separated. Although some states have simply removed the exemption, others have specified circumstances under which those who are married or cohabiting may face charges of sexual assault.

For feminists, legal barriers to the recognition of certain offenses as serious crimes remains a point of study and of political action. Areas of concern also include the prosecution of women or the creating of women victims of the law when women are singled out for harsher treatment in incidents that involve pregnancy, parenting, and parental liability. Critics argue that aggressive prosecution of pregnant female drug addicts under fetal abuse statutes only seems to drive the women further from view and keeps them from utilizing services that would address not only their health but that of the baby as well. Laws that hold a parent legally and financially accountable for the offenses of their children, such as truancy and gang activity, have a disproportionate impact on women as they are more likely to be single mothers, the primary caregivers, and the custodial parents. The use of the law to further penalize, and thus perhaps victimize, women is a central tenet of both conflict and feminist theories.

SUBCULTURE THEORIES

Subcuture theories were popular in the 1950s and 60s as a way to explain juvenile gang activity, particularly in the work of Albert K. Cohen, Walter B. Miller, and Richard Cloward and Lloyd Ohlin. For subculture theorists, the reasons juveniles join gangs is to alleviate the stresses and strains of poverty, disenfranchisement, and alienation from traditional middle-class pathways to success. Thus, subculture theories predict that acts of theft, vandalism, and public disorder are more likely to be carried out by gang members, with their primary targets located in the middle and upper classes. Victims of subculture crime would also include symbols of authority and state control.

An exception to this would be Richard Cloward and Lloyd Ohlin's (1960) concept of the conflict subculture or gangs that form in the absence of both legitimate and illegitimate opportunities for income and advancement. In these competitive areas, gangs find themselves in conflict with each other and high levels of gang-on-gang crime result. Researchers have substantiated that only two-to-five percent of gang homicides involve nongang victims (Kein & Maxson, 1989, p. 231). The Uniform Crime Report (UCR) indicates that homicides by juvenile gang members increased 500 percent between 1980 and 1994 as gang violence within prisons and juvenile detention facilities also rose dramatically. What Cloward and Ohlin saw was competition and tensions between rival gangs living in close proximity to each other. This was common in densely-populated neighborhoods but could also be found in overcrowded institutions like prisons and jails.

Within the subculture, there are important daily cues and messages about the value of owning, carrying, and using weapons that would explain these data. Gang initiations that involve being dropped off without a weapon to make your way back from inside a rival gang's territory reflect the group's emphasis on toughness, bravery, and street smarts that Walter Miller (1958) described as the focal concerns of the lower-class subculture. As Rodriguez (2010) explains, being "jumped in" (beaten) or "sexed in" (gang raped) for female gang initiations creates not only a subculture of offending but a subculture of victims as well. The 2008 UCR reflects 711 juvenile gang homicides with male victims and 35 female victims supporting the predominantly male subculture premise.

Subculture of Violence

Subculture theory has been used extensively in sociology as a way to explain the formation of groups along the lines of shard traits. These traits encourage cohesiveness and solidarity in, among other things, work groups (police subculture), recreational groups and political groups. Hate groups, neo-nazis, militias, and skinheads have all been linked theoretically to the subculture of violence concept.

The subculture of violence is explained as a set of norms instituted within a group that values and supports defending one's honor and establishing one's superiority through conflict and contest, by dominating or suppressing threats to that group's valued traditions. Violence is regarded as a means to protect the sentiments, beliefs and customs of one's close associates. It is expected and revered, it is taught to one's young and passed down in generational messages about appropriate responses to real or imagined transgressions. Theoretical work on the subculture of violence is rooted in the writing of Marvin Wolfgang and Franco Ferracutti who argued that the subculture of violence will be ingrained in areas where guns, male aggression, fighting, machismo and patriarchal family structures are idealized. Self-defense killings are common within the subculture of violence as are those in retaliation for prior disputes or injuries.

SOCIAL CONTROL THEORY

Social control theorists view the individual as striving to find ways to appear socially conforming for the sake of approval and for any benefits gained from being accepted into peer and family groups. Society provides social constraints to induce conforming behavior that otherwise may be shunned by an offender in order to obtain more immediate and self-gratifying rewards. Thus, although individuals are encouraged by society to adopt normative behaviors and maintain social approval, they are at times naturally subject to their own self-interested, and nonconforming, behavior. As mentioned earlier, a common critique of our modern society is the accusation that too many people are trying to excuse illegal and immoral conduct and avoid accountability by not taking responsibility for their actions.

Self-Control

Low self-control, Hirschi and Gottfredson (1990) argue, is a product of inadequate socialization, particularly when parents fail to exercise proper discipline. Combining what might be a predisposition or propensity to delinquency and criminality with an opportunity to engage in what appears to be an attractive and beneficial event, those with lower impulse control are more likely to offend. High-risk behavior and need for immediate gratification are characteristics of low self-control that predict not only increased criminality but higher risk for victimization.

Surveying Florida residents, Holtfreter, Reisig and Pratt (2008) found that those with low self-control were more likely to be victimized by consumer fraud and schemes that seem "too good to be true." Maria Garase's study of road rage found that low self-control was related to what is perhaps one of the most common forms of victimization in America. Figures indicate that in a seven-year-span (1990–1996) over 10,000 aggressive-driving incidents resulted in over 200 deaths directly attributable to road rage and 12,600 injuries. In 4,400 of those incidents perpetrators used weapons such as firearms, knives, clubs, fists, or feet and, in almost half of the cases where a weapon was used, that instrument was the car itself (Garase, 2006).

Techniques of Neutralization

The process of identifying oneself as a victim, that is, blaming someone else for one's own conduct is a common defense mechanism found in the early psychological writings of Sigmund Freud (although the term was formally introduced by his daughter Anna Freud around 1936). The idea that one reduces one's psychic guilt by repressing one's own blame, or projecting the blame onto someone else, was adapted by Gresham Sykes and David Matza (1957) in their work on delinquents in the late1950s. They found patterns in the excuses juveniles used that were consistent with attempts to neutralize their blameworthiness and to reduce their culpability. One of these techniques is referred to as "denial of responsibility." Using this mechanism, a juvenile looks for someone or something else to blame that will absolve him/herself of any direct responsibility for what has occurred. This reaction is closely tied to the tendency to deny the victim, where one attempts to cast the victim as the aggressor or instigator who set into motion whatever consequences occurred. Children often resort to "He started it!" when confronted by parents with an injured sibling. In rape cases, men have often argued that women were "asking for it" by dressing "provoca-tively" or "leading them on" by being out in certain places late at night.

When Dan White was tried for the murders of San Francisco Mayor George Moscone and Supervisor Harvey Milk in 1978 there was little argument as to whether he committed the offense; many eyewitnesses saw him walk into the office where the shooting occurred. However, his defense relied on the influence of junk food. Notoriously referred to as "the Twinkie defense," this tactic shocked the legal world as well as the average citizen. While it seemed far-fetched that a bad diet of sugar-laden foods could support the burden of diminished capacity necessary to reduce the charges from murder to manslaughter, it was indeed used successfully. When Lyle and Erik Menendez were tried for shooting their parents in their Beverly Hills home, they attempted to portray their parents as tyrannical abusers leading them to believe their use of deadly force against them was necessary (Morse, 1995).

Sykes and Matza's (1957) "denial of the injury" is another technique that attempts to minimize the scope of the damage or deny that any harm occurred at all. Employing this technique, the transgressor simply refuses to accept the idea that anyone was harmed by his or her actions. Often criminal trials and lawsuits seem to prioritize lasting or permanent physical injuries and attempt to downplay psychiatric pain or injuries from which the victim appears to have recovered.

RATIONAL THEORIES

Rational theories argue that behavior is a predictable set of responses geared to maximize one's own benefit and self-interest and to avoid punishment or pain. These arguments are much like early theories of hedonism, behaviorism and even Freudian descriptions of the pleasure-seeking id. Like Classical philosopher Jeremy Bentham, rational theorists see people as calculating and able to read cues in the environment that would indicate whether certain action and activities, such as crime, would likely be successful. Victims would be part of that formula as offenders target those who seem more vulnerable or more rewarding, such as the weak and the wealthy. Choosing a victim is a rational process involving a number of assessments and evaluations about the level of risk and the probability of a worthwhile outcome.

The way a victim appears in specific environmental contexts would be critical to these assessments and crime prevention, under rational models, involves providing protection for the victim in the forms of escape, surveillance by others and the presence of capable guardians who could deter potential criminals.

Routine Activities

Lawrence Cohen and Richard Felson's (1979) work on routine activities studies the patterns of everyday life in our society for trends that might explain changes in crime rates, in the types of crimes committed, and the time and place during which they occur. These researchers argue that since the end of World War II, life has evolved in ways that situate family members away from the home for longer periods of time each day. This means that some victimizations are less likely to take place at home and are more likely to occur in urban areas, work sites, schools and even at fast food establishments on the way to and from residences. While personal victimizations shift to adapt to where people are located, burglaries and thefts may also shift to times when family members are not home, or not near their vehicles. The development of malls, parking garages, and even cyberspace alter the dynamics of interactions between offenders and victims.

Cohen and Felson's (1979) view was that the flow of people through various social settings created criminal opportunities. The chances of any one person becoming a victim at any given time was dependent upon three things: (1) the suitability or attractiveness of that victim as a target, (2) the willingness or motivation of the offender at that time, and (3) the perception that the potential victim will not draw the attention or assistance of any capable guardian. Guardians could be anything from surveillance cameras to pet dogs and neighbors looking out the windows. The patterns of everyday life determine the coming together or convergence of the three crime elements, which may explain variations in crime rates across different areas. For example, very early in the morning, it may be dark and a relatively small person, on crutches, may appear to be a vulnerable target outside of an ATM on a street that has yet to become busy, or where the nearby bank has not yet opened and no security guard is present. As Cohen and Felson assert, the lack of any one of the above three elements is sufficient to prevent the successful completion of a direct-contact predatory crime, and that the convergence in time and space of suitable targets and the absence of capable guardians may even lead to large increases in crime rates without necessarily requiring any increase in the structural conditions that motivate individuals to engage in crime (1979, p. 589).

They believe that even if the number of worthwhile victims and likely offenders stays the same, changes in the way the rest of society interacts and moves about our environment is enough to alter the crime rate through the variations in perceived opportunities.

Rational Choice Theory

As is the case in Routine Activities theory, a rational-choice per-spective is grounded in the notion that a decision process is the impetus in any criminal action. The offender, according to Cornish and Clarke (1986, 1987), engages in a two-step evaluation, characterized by varying degrees of rationality, that leads them to either engage in or withdraw from a particular crime event. The steps are first an involvement decision and then an event decision. As Williams and McShane (2010, p. 182) explain

> Involvement decisions are those in which the choice is made to become involved in an offense, continue with an offense, or withdraw from an offense. These types of decision are instrumental in weighing the costs and benefits.... The other form of decision making, event decisions, is that in which the tactics of carrying out an offense (the demands placed on the offender) are determined. If the tactics are easy, the involvement decision gains potential benefits. If the tactics are difficult, the involvement decision loses potential benefits.

Although rational-choice theorists would argue that the factors being weighed in a crime scenario are specific and difficult to predict, the presence of weak or more vulnerable targets would influence the choice structuring in a favorable way. Thus, an environment with higher concentrations of disabled and handicapped offenders might draw a disproportionate rate of victimization. To offset this, crime prevention measures may be strengthened in these areas and laws have been passed to increase the penalties and enhance the sentences of those who commit crimes against disabled persons.

Lauren Barrow (2008) asserts that the deaf may be viewed as an attractive target because they may not hear the offender approaching or be able to call out to someone for assistance. In addition, that they may be more insulated and isolated socially, and less willing to interact with police because of the inherent difficulties in interacting in a hearing-based justice system.

Lifestyle Theory

One of the dominant themes of victimization statistics is that males, young people, minorities and the poor appear to be at much higher risks for victimization than the rest of the population. Those in multiple categories, such as young black males, increase exponentially the probability of victimization. Lifestyle theory addresses the impact of these demographic qualifiers with some clarification about the relationship between personal traits and increased risk of becoming a victim. As with other contemporary crime theories, researchers need to find models with higher predictive powers as it is obvious that not all poor, black males are at equal risk. Distinguishing between those at risk, even within specific population subsets is an important task for theory.

Lifestyle theory argues that the choices one makes in adapting to the constraints of one's demographic limitations set the stage for what jobs, recreation and lifestyle activities he or she may become involved in. Having made these choices, one then adopts routines that increase contact with certain types of people at certain times and in specific places (exposures). The more one comes in contact with potential offenders, those with high-risk traits, at high-risk times, the more likely it is that one will experience victimization (Hindelang, Gottfredson & Garofalo, 1978). The crux of the theory is similar to something your mother always told you: "If you associate with delinquents or are in an area with a high concentration of delinquents, you are more likely to be preyed upon by those willing to offend." This means that the more your lifestyle exposes you to disproportionate levels of high-risk people, places and times, the more likely it is that you will be victimized.

The choices one makes in their associations and activities may shape a victim-prone lifestyle. For example, Koo, Chitwood and Sanchez (2008) found that 22% of the active drug users they interviewed had been a victim in the past 30 days. Likewise, getting off work at 2:00 am in an area concentrated with bars and clubs, and then seeking out an ATM, is more likely to result in your victimization than using an ATM inside a mall at lunchtime. In yet another case, a young woman who moved from a farm town in Iowa to a low-income area in Los Angeles took in drug addicts she felt she could help remain clean. She hoped to engage the substance abusers she met on the streets in a meaningful religious conversion. She was murdered in her apartment a short time later. Lifestyle theory helps us to understand why someone with fairly low risk demographics, an educated, church-going, middle class, white female from Iowa, might still become a murder statistic.

IMPLICATIONS OF THEORY

According to Sandra Walklate (1994), noted sociologist Donald Cressey once argued that victimology is oriented to examine human suffering. In society today there is much evidence that the process of determining who is a victim is laden with politics, socio-legal traditions, economics, and cultural values. That a judge or jury can deliberate and come up with a monetary award for one person's loss or calculate the replacement value of a parent or spouse is testimony to our mixing of science and humanism.

Applying the theories of criminology to the study of victimology gives us a broader range of ideas about the nature of events as well as their prevention. More-sophisticated contemporary theorizing that examines a number of factors in the context of a victimization seems to give us more options for reducing crime. For example, Elias's (1993) discussion of the violence of poverty creates a more challenging scenario for intervention than a narrow focus on one offender and one victim isolated in time and space. The idea that one can be victimized by an environment will be discussed in more depth when we cover the victimization of places.

References

Ballon, M. (1999, September 22). Captive work force filling labor gaps. *Los Angeles Times*, C1, C12.

Abbott, D. E. (2006). *I cried, you didn't listen: A survivor's expose of the California Youth Authority.* Oakland, CA: AK Press.

Associated Press (2007, July 29) Clergy abuse: Beyond bond of friendship was a dark secret. *Las Cruces Sun News,* 12A.

Barrow, L. M. (2008). *Criminal victimization of the deaf.* New York: LFB Scholarly Publishing.

Carcaterra, L. (1996). *Sleepers.* New York: Ballentine Books.

Chapman, B. (2009). *A re-analysis of the role of race in the federal death penalty system.* Unpublished dissertation, University of Maryland, College Park, MD.

Cloward, R. A., & Ohlin, L. E. (1960). *Delinquency and opportunity: A theory of delinquent gangs.* New York: Free Press.

Coan, P. M. (1997). *Ellis Island interviews.* New York: Barnes & Nobel.

Cohen, L., & Felson, M. (1979). Social change and crime rate trends: A routine activities approach. *American Sociological Review, 44,* 588–607.

Cornish, D. B., & Clarke, R. V. (Eds) (1986). *The reasoning criminal: Rational choice perspectives on offending.* New York: Springer-Verlag.

Cornish, D. B., & Clarke, R. V. (1987). Understanding crime displacement: An application of rational choice theory. *Criminology, 25,* 933–947.

Elias, R. (1993). *Victims still: The political manipulation of crime victims.* Newbury Park, CA: Sage.

Frued, A. (1936). *The ego and the mechanisms of defense.* Trans. By C. M. Baines. New York: International Unversities Press, 1946.

Gaines, L., & Miller, R. (2008). *Criminal justice in action: The core.* Belmont, CA: Wadsworth.

Garase, M. (2006). *Road rage.* New York: LFB Scholarly Publishing.

Hentig, H. von (1948). *The criminal and his victim: Studies in the sociobiology of crime.* New Haven, CT: Yale University Press.

Hindelang, M., Gottfredson, M., & Garofalo, J. (1978). *Victims of personal crime: An empirical foundation for a theory of personal victimization.* Cambridge, MA: Ballinger.

Holtfreter, K., Reisig, M., & Pratt, T. (2008). Low self-control, routine activities and fraud victimization. *Criminology, 46,* 189–220.

In re Gault, 387 U. S. 28 (1967)

Kinkade, P., Burns, R., & Fuentes, A. I. (2005). Criminalizing attractions: Perceptions of stalking and the stalker. *Crime & Delinquency, 51,* 3–25.

Kleiman, C. (2005, August, 29). Mommy's pay worse. *Houston Chronicle,* D5.

Klein, M., & Maxson, C. (1989). Street gang violence. In Wolfgang, M. & Weiner, N. (Eds.) *Violent crime, violent criminals.* Newbury Park, CA: Sage.

Koo, D., Chitwood, D., & Sanchez, J. (2008).Violent victimization and the routine activities/lifestyle of active drug users. *Journal of Drug Issues, 38,* 1105–1138.

McShane, M. (1985). *The use of the detainer in the correctional setting: An examination of conflict theory.* Unpublished dissertation, Sam Houston State University, Huntsville, Texas.

Mendelsohn, B. (1974). The origin of the doctrine of victimology. In Drapkin, I. & Viano, E. (Eds.). *Victimology.* Lexington, MA: Lexington Books.

Miller, W. B. (1958). Lower-class culture as a generating milieu of gang delinquency. *Journal of Social Issues. 14,* 5–19.

O'Neill, A. W. (December 8, 1995). Tells of years of torment: Trial. *L A. Times,* A1.

Parsell, T. J. (2006). *Fish: A memoir of a boy in a man's prison.* New York: Avalon Publishing Group.

Pfohl, S. (1977). The discovery of child abuse. *Social Problems, 24,* 431–33.

Rodriguez, K. (2010). *An explanation of theoretical and cultural aspects of female gangs.* Unpublished Masters Thesis, University of Houston Downtown, Houston, TX.

Schafer, S. (1977). *Victimology: The victim and his criminal.* Reston, VA: Reston Publishing.

Schur, E. (1973). *Radical non-intervention: Rethinking the delinquency problem.* Englewood Cliffs, NJ: Prentice Hall.

Schwendinger, J., & Schwendinger, H. (1970). Defenders of order or guardians of human rights? *Issues in Criminology, 7,* 72–81.

State v. Smith, 148 N. J. Super. 219, 372 A. 2d 386, 1977,391.

Sykes, G. M., & Matza, D. (1957). Techniques of neutralization: A theory of delinquency. *American Sociological Review, 22,* 664–670.

Murdered Women of Juarez, The (2006, February 19). *Toronto Star,* A10.

Williams, F. P., & McShane, M. (2010). *Criminological theory. 5th Ed.* Upper Saddle River, NJ: Prentice Hall.

Discussion Questions

1. What theory or theories do you think best explain(s) why some victims do not report crimes? Is there a theory that might explain why some victims do report?
2. How can theory be used to help us reduce the amount of victimization that takes place today?
3. Think back over the theories discussed in this chapter, how do they vary in how they would view the offender-and-victim relationship?

Books You May Want to Read

Abbott, D. E. (2006). *I cried, you didn't listen: A survivor's expose of the California Youth Authority.* Oakland, CA: AK Press.

Rodriguez, T., Montane, D., & Pulitzer, L. (2008) *The Daughters of Juarez: A True Story of Serial Murder South of the Border.* New York: Atria Books.

Movies You May Want to See

Sleepers
Munich (2005)

Web Links

http://www.bradycenter.org/
http://www.ncvc.org/ncvc/Main.aspx

CHAPTER 4

The Politics of Victimization

INTRODUCTION

In this chapter we explore some examples of how politics comes into play when victims' needs are considered in our complex and very diverse society. As we will see, the enactment of legislation related to crime and victimization is often the way the public demonstrates its commitment to those who have been adversely affected by crime. We will examine how specific social problems, such as certain types of crime and criminals, come to attain a priority position on political agendas. This usually occurs through the experiences of famous or celebrity cases, or through relatively unknown individuals who somehow capture the public's attention and create a national media frenzy. One might argue that there is a "right time" and "right place" for the recognition of certain issues such as stalking or domestic violence and that the creation of laws is just a natural product of our government in action. Others might argue that high-profile cases such as those involving O. J. Simpson or Columbine High School will stir up public and political energy to the point where laws are passed to address the needs of victims, as well as groups and agencies that champion their causes. Either way, a new law generates a complex array of programs and policies that at the time seem essential to the well-being of our society. Certainly the creation of new laws dictates the way our criminal justice system responds. Police, courts and corrections agencies must adjust appropriately every time changes are made to criminal law. It is also our duty to systematically assess the effects of those changes through meaningful research and analysis.

Little Words Mean A Lot

State laws vary tremendously across the country and thus courts are overwhelmed with trying to interpret and evaluate their constitutionality and enforceability. For example, victim compensation may involve criminal or civil remedies depending on statutes in any jurisdiction. In some areas, restitution is considered a "debt" which may allow collectors more power in extracting that payment while such terminology may also qualify the debt for discharge under federal bankruptcy law. This was the opinion of the U. S. Supreme Court in *Pennsylvania v. Rutherford* (1990) when they cited a 1984 decision that "restitution is intended to promote the rehabilitation of the offender, not compensate the victim" (*In re Pellegrino*, 1984). In other discussions, it has been argued that because there is no right to victim restitution, it cannot be considered a "claim" and thus, a debt. This would preclude it from being negated in a bankruptcy judgment.

While many people may equate restitution with some type of repayment to victims, the concept of victim compensation is more accurately applied to that process. It is likely that offenders would be confused by supervised release orders to pay victim compensation and/or restitution and it is as likely that the public would be confused as well.

Victim assistance is also a vague concept that many take on many functions and services. In a critique of the way this popular concept has been abused by prosecutors and other agents of the criminal justice system, McShane and Williams (1992) outline the specific provisions of most victim assistance programs. Many components of such programs appear to focus on improving prosecutorial conviction rates and perhaps enhance their political reputation for "getting tough." Examples of these components are:

> *Victim notification:* notifying victims of the status of court proceedings involving the offender, such as plea negotiations, sentencing and parole decisions;
> *Victim impact statements*: informing the judge of the physical, financial and emotional impact of the crime on the victim, or the victim's survivors, to be used in consideration of the offender's sentence;

Court orientation: providing information on the operation of the criminal justice system and emphasizing the victim's or witness' responsibilities in court to assist in the prosecution of the defendant;

Transportation: transporting the victim or witness to and from court, so that their presence may be used in the trial to help convict the defendant;

Escorting: accompanying victims or witnesses to the courtroom and sitting with them during proceedings against the defendant (McShane & Williams, 1992, p. 264).

While these activities may benefit the political careers of aspiring district attorneys, they only seem to address the needs of a subset of victims who are specifically interested in being involved in the punishment of the guilty.

Many victims have personal reasons for not becoming involved in the criminal-justice processing of their offenders. For example, Caroline Seawell was one of thirteen victims shot by Washington, DC, area snipers over a three-week period in 2002. Although ten others died in the highly publicized attacks, she never even told her younger son, now almost a teenager, about the case. She says she has relocated, moved on, and become a stronger person, but one with no interest in attending the convicted murderer's execution (Potter, 2009). On the other hand, the father of one of the Columbine High School victims, Brian Rohrbough, used the memorial created near the campus to vent his feelings about government lies and cover ups, abortion, and moral decline in general. He argues that his inflammatory inscriptions as a permanent part of the stone panel in the "ring of remembrance" was the way he wanted to remember his son (Banda, 2007).

Legislation: The Process and the Products

The legislative process is a complex system of governance that uses the checks and balances of three different branches of government: the legislative branch made up of the Senate and the House of Representatives, the Executive branch anchored by the Presidency and the Judicial branch that reviews laws and makes rulings on their constitutionality.

A piece of legislation, or a Bill, may have a number of different titles that come together under it and each title may have sections or subtitles that address various areas of concern. Even these subtitles may be divided into chapters that are more specific in the types of activities and services called for. In many cases a piece of legislation will have funding attached to it in order to carry out the required mission, such as providing the training, research, data collection or equipment necessary to be in compliance with the law. These monies are usually distributed in the form of grants that states, counties, agencies, private entities, and other jurisdictions may apply for. Unfortunately, however, the funding is often limited and expires after a set period of time unless new funds are allocated and approved in subsequent years. One of the consequences of bipartisan government is that what was popular and well-funded under one administration is often abandoned in the next. This makes it difficult to determine which law enforcement or treatment efforts really are successful and it is often frustrating for the criminal justice system to be continually redirected to new initiatives and new priorities.

Since the 1980s, it has been common for each Presidential Administration to introduce a crime bill that brings together issues to be prioritized during the forthcoming term. Victims, as a popular political topic, have figured prominently in these crime bills and several victim-related issues have had significant staying power or longevity. However, the type of victims and the range of responses or services, funding and programming receiving attention will change with society's values and attitudes.

LAW AS A RESPONSE TO A PERCEIVED SOCIAL PROBLEM

Experts who study social problems argue that there is a set life-span to an issue; that is, the problem will only be controversial and engaging for a limited period of time. We often call this the "lifespan" of a social problem, which follows a fairly predictable chronology. During that time period, proponents of various positions on the issue will debate the merits of particular approaches to addressing the social problem and compete for resources to be spent on one solution or another. Experts will claim control over the definition, measurement and evaluation of that social problem. Laws will be passed and agencies will be designated to provide certain programs or services. Monies will be allocated for research, training, treatment or enforcement of the strategies most successfully competing in the political arena. Over time, the problem will be eclipsed by some new crisis and the "fifteen minutes of fame," so to speak, will be over for the social problem.

There is much evidence to support the cycle, or "rise and fall," of phenomena such as drunken-driving, cyber-bullying, missing children, and terrorism. In this chapter we will focus on a number of specific laws that have been passed dealing with victims and how certain high profile cases or causes may have generated interest and effort toward these various issues. We will also compare various types of legislation and examine their short- and, possibly, long-term effects.

One important aspect of the politics of legislation that will be noted is the name of the legislation. While Romeo may not have felt that names mattered in that famous Shakespearean play, for the study of victimology, the name is often the most obvious indication of the politicization of the process. For example, California voters passed a referendum in 1990 called the *Crime Victims Justice Reform Initiative.* This complicated piece of law was a collection of bills that had all been previously rejected by lawmakers and offered little if anything to victims. The thrust of the act was a series of shortcuts in the judicial process which seemed oriented toward improving the "get tough" records of judges and prosecutors at a time when the public was high on expectations and short on patience with the courts. Legislators who supported the initiative were attempting to ride the wave of law and order embraced by the voting public. Faced with spending caps on their own election campaigns, political candidates backed this referendum with their excess campaign funds. Thus, they were able to successfully run for office on a single popular issue while avoiding legal limitations on campaign spending. Both the candidates and the initiative benefited from their association with "pro-victim" rhetoric. Meanwhile, the primary message that caught people's attention was that their chances of becoming a victim were greater than ever before and that something needed to be done about it (as suggested by the summary of the proposition on the ballot).

Legislation related to victim needs seems to be generated in two distinct patterns. One is a broader and slower progression of efforts in recognition of human rights and social responsibilities, as discussed in Chapter One, while the other is a quick and sporadic knee-jerk change in response to some high-profile criminal event that appears to need an immediate and showcase response. We will look at examples of both types of legislation and evaluate the impact these laws have had on victims and victim services.

LEGISLATION AND POLITICALLY-POPULAR CAUSES

Hate crime laws are a good example of this first type of implementation process. The emergence of hate crime as a social problem is consistent with forces that generated progress in the overall victims' rights movement. While there were significant events and notable cases, they were combined with energetic grassroots efforts, powerful leadership, and lobbying efforts to make it the right time in history for broad-based support for a range of hate crime laws to be consistently enacted across the country. People at this time were generally amenable to not only enhanced penalties for violent offenders but also official recognition of the social harms caused by bias and hate perpetrated against vulnerable populations. Popular media and literature on hate crime developed its own hate crime vocabulary with terms such as "bashing" for assault, "heterosexism" and "ethnoviolence" for what had previously been termed "racial incidents."

Still, there are many weaknesses in existing hate crime laws that make them difficult to use in the legal system, often resulting in frustrating and painful experiences for victims. Technically, a hate crime is not a separate offense, but an enhancement to an existing crime such as assault, attempted murder, arson, or criminal threats. Theoretically, an affirmative finding of a hate crime allows for longer sentences to be imposed, as well as more stringent restrictions on possible probation or parole and the recording of such a finding in one's criminal history. In the case of a 17-year-old Hispanic student in Texas who was seriously beaten and sodomized with a piece of pipe, one of the perpetrator's affiliation with supremacist groups, their use of racial slurs, and their attempt to carve a swastika on his chest were enough to raise a vehement public outcry to have the attackers charged with a hate crime. However, the fact that the crime took place in a private citizen's backyard resulted in the authorities' inability to use the federal law's enhancement under a hate-crime statute. Critics have also complained that discrepancies in the sentencing structures of the state and federal courts mean that hate crimes are pursued more often as regular crimes in the state judicial system where the penalties are already more severe than federal law permits (George, 2007).

Violence Against Women Act

The Violence Against Women Act is another good example of legislation that was part of a greater social movement of awareness of victims and the need for services and programs. *The Violent Crime Control and Law Enforcement Act of 1994* was a crime bill signed into law by President Bill Clinton. Its Title IV contained the *Violence Against Women Act* (VAWA), which was a comprehensive law aimed at reducing bias against women, offering legal protections for women victims of crime, and clarifying the incorporation of gender as a distinct and protected status. The VAWA produced seven separate subtitles related to gender-based violence.

Subtitle A was called "Safe Streets for Women." This section introduced lengthier sentences for repeat offenders whose crimes were committed against women. Through this initiative, $800 million was dedicated to the program STOP (Services Training Officers Prosecutors) which was to strengthen law enforcement and prosecution strategies to reduce violence against women with special emphasis on safety in public parks and on public transit. Probation and parole officers also received $2 million over two years to work with sex offenders upon release. Another important feature of this section was the barring, under most circumstances, of evidence in criminal court about a victim's other sexual conduct as had been used in the past to erode the testimony of rape victims. Subtitle II, "Safe Homes for Women" focused on domestic violence and, in particular, brought full faith and credit to the restraining orders of one state so that they might be honored and enforced in another state. Subtitle III, "Civil Rights for Women" created the first civil-rights remedies for gender-based violence, although the right of these victims to sue in federal court was later struck down by the Supreme Court (2000). Subtitle IV, "Safe Campuses," specifically allocated funds to research problems facing women on college campuses. Subtitle V, "Equal Justice for Women in the Courts," provided training for judges so that they might be better equipped to solve some of the problems of gender bias in the legal system.

All of the efforts sponsored under the VOWA have helped to launch programs and research specifically designed to use gender equality as a means for reducing the level of victimization of women in society. Similar measures have been undertaken in legislation to protect children from abuse and exploitation.

Child Victims of Pornography and Sexual Abuse

In 1982, California legislators lined up to be associated with the *Roberti-Imbrecht-Rains-Goggin Child Sexual Abuse Prevention Act.* After careful examination of this legislation, one could argue that it had been mislabeled. While discussing this act, an assistant in the California Attorney General's Office told a meeting of the Association of Criminal Justice Researchers-California in Pomona, California, that mislabeling was a misleading, but common, ploy to gain voter's support. In reality, this popular bill was not directed at preventing child sexual abuse nor offered assistance to victims, *per se*; it simply instituted harsher punishments for those caught molesting children, extended the statute of limitations for filing charges, and provided funds for police and prosecutors to be trained in handling cases. A more appropriate and, perhaps just as popular a title, may have been, "The Child Sexual Abuse Prosecution Enhancement Act.*"* Likewise, the *California Child Protection Act of 1984* was similarly misnamed. The act did nothing to directly protect children, rather it allowed the state to confiscate property derived from the profits of child pornography and the cameras, film and lights used in such a criminal enterprise. Another interesting feature of this law was that it eliminated the need to prove intent in the prosecution of child pornography, a change that made it easier for prosecutors to obtain convictions. While it can be argued that putting child pornographers in prison is a way to protect children from future victimization, one can't help but wonder if there are other ways to address the prevention of child pornography than indirectly through prosecutorial enhancements, with a secondary purpose of enhancing prosecutors' political careers.

The impetus to make broad and sweeping claims beyond the direct or practical scope of a piece of legislation is perhaps one way to appear to be serving and addressing the needs of victims. Otherwise, it may be more controversial to say, "We need more resources to go to police and prosecutors" when many taxpayers may believe that these agencies have sufficient resources, and that the funds may just need to be re-prioritized. In a sense, law enforcement agencies are willing participants in this manipulation as they can claim that they cannot possibly address this deserving victim group without additional funds. In hindsight it is often the case that such appropriations were used for personnel overtime, additional hires and equipment that is only tangentially related to the task at hand. Still, it is a rare agency that will reject an opportunity for more funding.

Cybersafety and Cybersecurity

Another area that is popular with politicians is preventing victimization on the internet. Whether it is children being stalked by predators or elderly couples being bilked of their savings, fears about vulnerability and exposure have led many citizens to demand more be done about network protection. Still, legislative initiatives in the realm of cyberspace have been extremely controversial and, thus, limited in their scope and impact. When the Rockefeller-Snowe bill was proposed there was a outpouring of criticism from all areas of the technology industry over provisions that would allow the government to shut down or take over the internet and other computer networks in order to address a crisis or threat. In such a vast business empire, it is understandable that any measures, regardless how noble the intent, will be difficult to reach consensus on. A more indirect and low-level plan to shore up cybersecurity was recently passed by the House in the form of the *Cybersecurity Enhancement Act of 2009*. This measure, with far less invasive features, provides funding to train technology students and allows them to offset their expenses with national service. It funds academic consortium arrangements that would coordinate with agencies like the National Science Foundation and the Department of Commerce to advance security in cyberspace.

LEGISLATION ON SIGNIFICANT VICTIMS AND EVENTS

Anti-Stalking laws are a good example of legislation that researchers and analysts frequently tie to a significant victim, this time via the murder of a popular young actress in 1989. When an obsessed fan showed up at the door of television star Rebecca Schaffer and shot her, the media seemed to rally around the cause, gathering up any related cases that could be used to identify this phenomenon as a fear-inducing social problem. As Kinkade et al. (2005, p. 4) explain,

> To add to the furor, statistical estimates related to stalking began to emerge and suggested that its occurrence was at an epidemic level.... Legislative action directed toward stalking behavior became a 'hot issue' agenda item for state legislators and subsequently resulted in the creation of many new laws that criminalized such activity...to stem a perceived increase in stalkers victimizing the American citizenry....

The idea of crime victims providing a powerful media image and creating a political force to be reckoned with is controversial and often a psychological dilemma. In the more notorious cases, lobbying and legislative efforts often become directed at whatever measures are believed to be relevant to a crime. Table 4–1 illustrates a number of well-known cases and the laws resulting from them. As the chronology indicates, more punitive and restrictive sanctions seem to be evolving over time as older laws and policies appear ineffective in preventing new cases.

For others, however, there is great reluctance to allow politicians to use their personal victimization experiences to further their careers. In California, the use of a highly-publicized case of a murdered child to dramatize issues in a heated political race backfired when relatives challenged the politicization of their little girl. A newspaper article (Bailey & Reza, 1994) summarized the situation this way:

> Atty. Gen. Dan Lungren and other Republican candidates are "dancing a jig" on the grave of Polly Klaas to push their own agenda on crime,the murdered girl's grandfather charged Tuesday at a campaign event for Democratic challenger Tom

Umberg. Joe Klaas lashed out at Lungren, Gov. Pete Wilson and GOP senatorial candidate Mike Huffington and is appearing in an Umberg television commercial that blames Lungren for contributing to 12-year-old Polly's death. Lungren, Wilson, and Huffington—who is co-chairman of Proposition 184, the so-called "three strikes" initiative—have all used Polly's death to push for stricter sentencing laws.... Umberg joined Klaas in charging that the girl's death might have been prevented if Lungren had maintained funding for a statewide computer database designed to give officers quick access to criminal records. Umberg and Klass contend that if the system had been operational, Polly's alleged killer, Richard Allen Davis, could have been apprehended before she died.

Still, as we all know, the "Three Strikes" legislation passed.

As mentioned earlier, politicians also can claim support for a popular victim group based on the title of a proposed law, knowing that most citizens will never read the actual content of the bill. At campaign events they can boast in short sound bites what they have done to reduce or prevent crime simply based on the title of the legislation. Often, the images projected by the memory of a particularly heinous crime or offender are enough to popularize a proposed law regardless of the merits of its content. The Son of Sam Laws are a goodexample of the dramatic impact that legislators can obtain simply by choosing a high-profile name with which to associate policy changes.

Son of Sam Laws

The infamous serial killer, David Berkowitz, is the namesake of the Son of Sam laws that swept through most jurisdictions in the 1990s. However, efforts to control profits generated by the stories of convicted felons actually dates back a little further to another case that, though no less notorious, would not have had the same dramatic effect because they would have been called "Henry Hill laws." In 1985, Nicholas Pileggi

Table 4-1. Examples of popular legislation related to high profile crimes

Law	Victim & State	Crime	Terms of Law	Date	Comment
Megan's Law	Megan Kanka, 7 years old, New Jersey	rape/murder by neighbor sex offender	States must notify public of addresses of known sex offenders, Electronic list to be posted	1996	Amended Jacob Wetterling Act
Jessica's Law	Jessica Lunsford, 9 years old, Florida	Rape/ murder	Various terms depending on state: Bans predators from living near where children gather, longer mandatory sentences & electronic monitors	FLA law passed 2005	Controversial, 42 states have similar laws but no federal law resulted
Amber Alert	Amber Hagerman, 9 years old, Arlington, TX	Kidnapped & murdered	Emergency notification via coordinated effort of law enforcement, media & transportation	1996	Not a law, but government program, service, DOJ tasked w/assisting states w/setup
Jacob's Law	Jacob Wetterling, 11 year old, St. Joseph, MN	Abducted, never found	State sex offender websites required by federal, must post residence though jobs & schools suggested	1994	Set national standards for sex offender registration
J. Clery Act	Jeanne Clery, 19 years old, student in Pennsylvania	rape/ murder in college dorm room by another student	Broader mandatory campus crime reporting & public dissemination w/sanctions for non-compliance	2000	Parents pressured for change; revised previous legislation

Table 4-1 (Cont'd). Examples of popular legislation related to high profile crimes

Law	Victim & State	Crime	Terms of Law	Date	Comment
Chelsea's Law	17-year-old, San Diego, CA	rape/murder by paroled sex offender	Proposes life electronic monitoring for all sex offenders, life w/out parole for force sex crime against child	Not passed	Being proposed around the U.S., controversial sentencing
Matthew Shepard & James Byrd Hate Crimes Prevention Act	Shepard, Wyoming; Byrd, Texas	Shepard: gay college student tortured & murdered Byrd: African-American dragged to death by young men w/ties to Supremacist groups	Adds gender, sexual orientation, gender identity & disability to categories considered bias-motivated, funds for training CJ system personnel & monies to aid in investigation & prosecutions	10/28/09	endorsed by over 300 law enforcement, civil rights, civic & religious groups
Adam Walsh Act	Adam Walsh	Abducted & murdered	Increased penalty for failure to register, adds DNA, photo & fingerprints, allow fed prosecution if fail to register— involves travel between jurisdictions, establishes three tiers of registrants	2006	Amended Jacob Wetterling Act, launched TV career of father, John Walsh
Pam Lyncher Act	Pam Lyncher, Houston founder of Justice for All	Pam Lyncher victim of attempted sex assault, became activist, killed in plane crash	Requires lifetime registration for certain sex offenders, FBI to maintain national sex offender registry	1996	Amended Jacob Wetterling Act

wrote a book called *Wiseguy* based on the life of mobster Henry Hill which later became the basis of Martin Scorsese's Oscar-nominated film, *Goodfellas*. Under existing New York laws, the state had empowered the Victim Compensation Board to seize profits from depictions of crimes and use them as payments to any victims who successfully sued an offender for compensatory damages. It was this law that became the basis of a suit filed by the publisher, Simon and Schuster, who claimed that the law was written in a way that was overly broad and thus in violation of the First Amendment.

In *Simon and Schuster v. Members of the New York State Crime Victims Board,* the U. S. Supreme court analyzed two important questions in order to determine whether to uphold the law. The first question was whether the state had a compelling interest in the process New York had adopted that would outweigh the possible infringement of First Amendment rights. The Court determined that it did not. While it might be a function of justice to keep offenders from profiting from their crimes, it was not part of that obligation to then transfer garnished earnings into victim-based accounts. This is important because later versions of these laws that have been found to be constitutional simply prohibited those convicted from being paid or compensated through the sale of accounts of the crime. Secondly, the court wanted to be sure that laws specifically focused on controlling the exploitation of the crime, its details, and its effects on the victim—not on other subject matter that might involve the offender but not that particular offense (Vaughn, 1996). This means that the writing of prisoner narratives, their life stories, and their experiences in the justice system were protected so long as the basis of the work was not the perpetrating of the crime for which victims had suffered.

Clarification of what profits are and what parts of the criminal's history are permissible in the writing of a book, play or movie has continued since these laws were adopted. Jean Harris, the elite private school headmistress who shot and killed her former lover (famous Scarsdale diet author Herman Tarnower), also ran into a publishing prohibition for her work *Stranger in Two Worlds* and *They Always Call Us Ladies*.

There are several important facts to remember about these high profile cases. First, David Berkowitz (Son of Sam) never tried to profit from his crimes. He never sought money or opportunities to produce media versions of his story. Harris had planned to donate all of the proceeds from her publication to a non-profit charity that sponsored visits for the children of inmates. The rush to pass legislation barring offenders from profiting from the sale of their "stories" was generated by perceptions that publishers, media outlets, film writers, and popular culture agents would generate interest in products that were believed to be offensive to victims, their survivors, and society in general (and that the offender was going to profit from the crime). Today the concerns of victim advocacy groups, legislators, and policymakers have expanded beyond the concept of a book or personal accounts of a crime to the internet marketing of items associated with serial killers and other high-profile criminals. The term "murderabilia" connotes the promotion of any items or artifacts tied to the crime itself, or the offender charged with the crime.

Murderabilia, a concept that appears unsavory and morally reprehensible to many victims' advocates and citizens, seems to have been distinguished to some degree from memorabilia which has been used to raise money to make awards to victims and survivors. After winning $8.5 million in compensatory damages and half of $25 million in punitive damages against O. J. Simpson in wrongful death litigation, Fred Goldman, father of the deceased victim Ron Goldman, sought to recover the football legend's memorabilia as part of that judgment. The collectable items included Simpson's Hall of Fame certificate, autographed footballs, a gold watch, and the suit he wore during his criminal trial that ended in an acquittal (Marquez, 2007). Had he been convicted, would this material be murderabilia? Is the civil verdict enough to change the category from memorabilia to murderabilia? Obviously, the issues are not as simple as some would have us believe.

Since the earliest court cases, laws have had to be revised to best meet First Amendment standards. Some states have attempted to force offenders who are entering into contracts for some type of potentially-profitable product to first have that contract reviewed and approved by the state's attorney general. In what might be their most constitutionally viable form, these laws would allow offenders to write and to engage in free expression in areas that do not specifically address the particular victimization for which the offenders are currently serving time. There is much we can learn about childhood abuse, and abandonment, as well as juvenile and mental health system shortcomings, in these biographical works. However, attempting to control access to murderabilia may be more difficult. Language that relies on a somewhat vague assessment of the value of items that increases because of the notoriety of the offender may be legally problematic (Hurley, 2009).

Still other forms of legislation appear to have elements of both evolving social movements and celebrated cases, which become the faces and the forces behind their passage. Another crucial element of the issues resulting in many of the widespread legal changes is the organized lobbying efforts of victims' families and support groups. Campus Crime legislation illustrates these concepts well. As we will see, it took a number of pieces of legislation, revised and implemented using various strategies over a period of years, to come up with the comprehensive campus-crime-reporting system that we have today.

The Clery Act and Campus Crime

Early research on campus crime seemed to indicate that only about 60 percent of victims reported offenses to campus police. Victims as well as authorities seemed to be confused about jurisdiction and many students indicated that they did not report crimes because they did not have confidence in campus police or believed that the officers would not be able to do anything. Those who were younger and more economically disadvantaged were also less likely to report. Still, studies reflected that women were more worried about crime on campus regardless of the time of day or the location (parking lots, gyms, auditoriums, library, etc.). Ironically, the crimes most likely to be experienced, larceny/theft, harassment, vandalism, and threats, were not even those that would be tracked by the early reporting systems (Fisher, 1995).

During the 1980s there was considerable pressure on the government to employ more accountability measures, particularly in the reporting of crime, spending, and any information that might affect the health, safety and well-being of all citizens. Inefficient and underperforming government agencies were phased out or reorganized. New management and budgeting processes were experimented with and more computerized data-systems set up to track and report social statistics.

The *Student Right-To-Know and Campus Security Act* of 1990 reflected all of these trends. Parents were concerned about graduation rates, not only for student-athletes but across higher education. Making choices about where to send their children and invest their college savings meant being well-informed as higher percentages of high-school graduates sought degrees. More assertive and protective baby-boomer parents wanted trustworthy information about campus crime rates, something both they and legislators had reason to be suspicious about. Attempting to enhance recruitment efforts, universities were often less than honest about the risk of victimization on campus and in the surrounding areas. These concerns were the focus of the campaign waged by Jean Clery's parents.

After 19-year-old Jeanne Clery was raped and murdered in her Lehigh University dorm room, her parents pressed for changes in Pennsylvania law that would require reporting campus crime. They, like many other parents, were unaware that their daughter's school had recorded 38 violent campus crimes in the three years prior to Jeanne's murder. On this issue, the efforts of parents, victims and security organizations, as well as policymakers, all combined to develop a meaningful reporting system for campus crime. As a result of the various federal and state laws passed, schools receiving government funds and federal financial aid were required to annually and publicly report their traditional index-crime statistics in a Uniform Crime Report format, much like cities and towns across America. In addition, schools were required to track the number of arrests on campus for alcohol and drug violations, as well as any weapons offenses.

The passage of the *Campus Security Act of 1990* began a long and slow process of developing a culture of accountability in colleges and universities which they had no history of, and little support for, accomplishing. The Act was unfunded and colleges often stumbled along unclear about how to designate reporting authorities and train, staff, and manage a sophisticated reporting system. It was also unclear just how the information had to be disseminated and how validity and reliability could be enforced. The 2000 *Jeanne Clery Disclosure of Campus Security Policy and Campus Crime Statistics Act* added crimes committed in areas bordering campuses, as well as the reporting of hate crimes and manslaughter. To provide some incentive for compliance, punishments have been put in place for not meeting reporting mandates. The political activity of Connie and Howard Clery later became channeled into the founding of "Security on Campus Inc." Their website pledges to insure that Jeanne's death would continue to have a purpose. Today, one of the organization's interests is supporting the use of unified campus alert systems. These private-vendor-supplied, emergency web-based notification systems are used on most campuses in one form or another. However, effective implementation of such mechanisms in an actual emergency has yet to be fully realized, as has been noted in several high-profile events, including a shooting episode at Virginia Tech.

Transparency in the Interest of Victims

Popular political trends (like transparency in government, accountability, and more public access to information on how government agencies operate) that have arisen in this past decade have influenced a number of victims' issues. In 2010, a law went into effect in Texas requiring Child Protective Services, a state agency, to publically release information and reports on any child who dies from abuse. In a newspaper article, Langford (2010), reports on some of the law's requirements:

> ...within five days of a child abuse death, the agency will have to provide the child's gender, age, date of death, and whether the child was in a foster home or living with a a parent or guardian or someone else at the time of death.... CPS will now have 10 days to produce a report to the public after the agency completes its own investigation into how the child died.

Other indications of the move toward more openness in reporting have been the Senate Judiciary Committee hearings on the possibility of closing Guantanamo Bay (used for incarcerating persons suspected of crimes against the United States), political refugees, and persons held indefinitely under the *Patriot Act.* Ironically, it was not until the media exposed prisoner abuses by U. S. military forces in Afghanistan and in Iraq that the public became aware that these same procedures had long been practiced at Guantanamo. Various forms of torture were used, such as water boarding, short-shackling detainees to the floor in awkward positions, using duct tape over their mouths, and threatening to kill them and their families. Also, tactics that degraded prisoners and violated their religious beliefs were particularly reviled by the public and the greater global community. Reports indicated that U. S. military personnel forced prisoners to appear nude in front of female soldiers, put women's underwear on their heads, and sexually humiliated them. According to a report in the *Washington Post*,

> One was attached to a leash and made to walk around the room and "perform a series of dog tricks." The report also notes the use of "gender coercion," in which women straddle a detainee or get too close to them, violating prohibitions for devout Muslim men on contact with women. Interrogators also threatened to tell other detainees that an individual is gay, according to the report. Detainees were posed in mock homosexual positions and photographed (White, 2005).

The outpouring of condemnation over these accounts threatened to redefine the enemy combatants as victims, which would have been an uncomfortable image for the war on terrorism to reconcile. Many believe that moving the prisoners back to the United States would provide more oversight of their treatment than the remote Cuban facility. These examples demonstrate that it is not always more law that is needed, but sometimes simply better agency regulation and supervision.

PLANNING FOR THE UNKNOWN

According to Yu (2009), there is evidence that crime concentrates in time as well as in space. This means that government and civic initiatives seeking to address crime in specific locations such as campuses, hot spots or other crime-prone areas (like socially disorganized neighborhoods), would need to be aware of the temporal aspects of crime and their implications. Daily, seasonal, or even long-term changes in patterns of activity may increase or decrease the need for law enforcement or other crime prevention strategies. Urban renewal, changing land use patterns, resident mobility, and the economy of neighborhoods all hold the potential to alter the urban landscape and its potential for victimization. It is possible then, that strategies appearing to be practical or necessary at one point in time are no longer feasible in another time, yet may still be mandated under policy or law. Unfortunately, laws are often passed in haste and the consequences of committing resources on a relatively permanent basis may make communities less responsive to new needs that arise.

Victims groups are a powerful political lobby. Organizations such as MADD, Parents of Murdered Children, and those representing other activist causes are able to evoke strong emotional responses to issues during elections and other significant government milestones. The demands made by these various interests consume disproportionate amounts of criminal justice research, training, and prosecutorial monies. The more politically-popular one victim is over another, the more poised that group will be to divert funds toward their causes. Still, there are some issues like campus crime and child sexual abuse, arising at just the right time in history, that seem to result in the passage of laws that are supported by a majority of victims, policymakers, and citizen groups alike.

References

Bailey, E., & Reza, H. G. (1994, October 26). Grandfather of slain girl lashes out at Lungren. *Los Angles Times.* Retrieved from *http://articles.latimes.com/keyword/tom-umberg*

Banda, P. S. (2007, September 22). A site "about remembrance." *Houston Chronicle*, A7.

Bronk, C. (2010, February 11). In new federal legislation, a victory for cybersecurity. *Houston Chronicle,* B11.

Fisher, B. (1995). Crime and fear on campus. *Annals of American Academy of Political & Social Sciences, 539,* 85–101.

George, C. (2007, October 13). Feds often yield to states in hate-crime cases. *Houston Chronicle,* B4.

Hurley, E. (2009). Overkill: An exaggerated response to the sale of murderabilia. *Indiana Law Review, 42,* 411–440.

In re Pellegrino 42 B. R. 129 (1984).

Kinkade, P., Burns, R., & Ilarraza Fuentes, A. (2005). Criminalizing attractions: Perceptions of stalking and the stalker. *Crime & Delinquency, 51,* 3–25.

Langford, T. (2009, September 26). CPS now must give details on victims. *Houston Chronicle,* B1.

Marquez, J. (2007, September 18). Goldmans to seek Simpson memorabilia. Associated Press. Retrieved from http://news.yahoo. com.

McShane, M., & Williams, F. P., III (1992). Radical victimology: A critique of the concept of victim in traditional criminology. *Crime & Delinquency, 38,* 258–271.

Pennsylvania Department of Public Welfare et al. v. Davenport et ux, 495 U. S. 552, 110 S.Ct. 2126, 109 L. Ed. 2D 588 (1990).

Potter, D. (Associated Press) (2009, November 8). Victims, relatives await sniper's execution. *Houston Chronicle,* A25.

Vaughn, M., & del Carmen, R. (1996). Legal issues: V. Constitutional issues in prison operations In M. McShane & F. P. Williams, III (Eds), *Encyclopedia of American prisons* (pp. 289–298). New York: Garland Publishing.

White, J. (2005, July 14). Abu Ghraib tactics were first used at Guantanamo. *Washington Post,* A1.

Discussion Questions

1. Is the politicizing of victims' issues unavoidable? How can victims be insulated or protected from the negative effects of the political processing of their needs?
2. Discuss the factors that seem to make some issues move to legislation faster than others. Also what factors seem to make some pieces of legislation more effective than others?
3. How can more transparency in government work to the advantage of victims?
4. Look at your campus' crime data, what trends if any are apparent? How would you characterize crime on your campus? When was the last time you received notice of a crime on your campus and how did you receive it?

Books You May Want to Read

Pierce-Baker, C. (2000). *Surviving the silence: Black women's stories of rape.* New York: Norton.
Krakauer, J. (2003). *Under the banner of heaven: A story of violent faith.* New York: Doubleday.
Wilson, B. (1991). *Wouldn't it be nice: My own story.* New York: HarperCollins.

Movies You May Want to See

The Burning Bed (1984)
A Mighty Heart (2007)
Shake Hands with the Devil (2005)

Web Links

http://www.securityoncampus.org/
http://www.e2campus.com/
Sex offender registry laws:
    http://www.ojp.usdoj.gov/smart/pdfs/so_registry_laws.pdf
National Center for Missing and Exploited Children:
    http://www.ncmec.org/missingkids/servlet/PublicHomeServlet?
    LanguageCountry=en_US

CHAPTER 5

The Victim in Court

INTRODUCTION

Victims are often the focal point in legal proceedings and, with the extensive media coverage of cases today, the audience is easily caught up in the raw emotions that are exposed. According to labeling theory, societal reactions form the basis of our beliefs about the worthiness of any particular victim, a factor that may weigh significantly on the outcome of any offender's criminal trial. This chapter will cover a number of issues related to victims who come to the courts everyday, including legal orders protecting victims and potential victims, notification of case progress, participation and consultation in criminal prosecutions, and decisions about restitution and compensation. Although there is some variation between jurisdictions, federal initiatives and court rulings have clarified the role of the victim in criminal trial testimony and have even evaluated the use of victimization as a defense against future criminal conduct. Although some have argued that the variety of syndromes advanced today seems like an attempt to avoid responsibility for one's actions, it is also possible that the complex and long-term effects of victimization require more humanistic approaches.

In addition to pursuing criminal charges, many victims and family members of victims choose to bring civil suits for injuries or wrongful death against a suspected or convicted defendant. Generally, these may result in monetary damages for pain and suffering and, in the case of homicide victims, financial compensation for the earnings that may have come to the family over a lifetime career. After reading this chapter, the reader should understand that the role of a victim in court is not limited to testimony but includes a number of contributions to our legal system, from philosophy to everyday policies and practices.

VICTIM PARTICIPATION AND VICTIM PROGRAMS

Victim Testimony

Physical, emotional, and sexual abuse can have serious negative effects on victims, many of whom may be given special consideration when testifying in court. In many instances these protections may help ease the trauma of recounting a victimization. To facilitate the prosecution of child sexual abusers, laws in many states have been reformed to allow measures such as reducing the size of the courtroom audience, rearranging the courtrooms for less intimidating décor, eliminating the competency requirements for children, using screens and partitions to reduce direct exposure to alleged perpetrators, and allowing children to testify remotely by video conferencing or using taped depositions instead of appearing on the stand. Although defendants have challenged such practices on the 6th Amendment's right to confront one's accuser, courts have generally ruled that the special needs of the youngest child victims outweigh any possible defense limitations (Hamill, Graham, Thomason, & Huerta-Choy, 2001). There are other techniques for reducing stress on child victim/witnesses including taking the child to the courtroom prior to trial to become familiar with the physical surroundings of the court. Many advocates also alert the child to the various actors and their respective physical positions in the court. Research has also indicated that children fare much better under the stress of court testimony when their mothers are supportive advocates (Lipovsky, 1994), which may be less likely to occur when a boyfriend or stepfather is the alleged perpetrator.

Victims of sexual abuse and or domestic-violence survivors are generally called to testify against their abusers in criminal proceedings. The reality is that a tiny percent of sexual-abuse cases ever go to trial. There are several reasons to explain this: lack of evidence due to reporting after seventy-two hours (the body begins to heal itself and evidence of sexual assault is difficult to obtain), lack of victim cooperation, the prosecutor may not feel the case is strong enough to bring charges against the accused, etc. Even so, those few cases that do go to trial may be very difficult and traumatic for victims. The victim has to recount the events several times to varying sources. The victim may lose wages for time off from work to appear in court. Issues of transportation, child care, social support, counseling, and timely notifications of court proceedings may compound the stress and pressures of victim testimony. However, many states provide direct services to victims through offices in county and local governments. Usually the programs are tied to immediate needs and are coordinated with the district attorney's office overseeing the case. Common services include referrals to social service agencies, counseling, transportation for victim and family members to court proceedings, sexual-assault advocate support, notification of victim rights, information about the case and court proceedings, aid in requesting funds for restitution, and completing the paperwork for victims' compensation.

Although it may not always be in the best interests of the victim to do so, most victim-compensation programs require that the victim participate in cases selected for prosecution. The testimony of victims is often a critical part of the prosecution and studies show that cases with multiple forms of evidence (a previous similar charge, witnesses, confessions, etc.) are more likely to result in formal charges. Research also indicates that victims experience greater safety and empowerment when cases are successfully prosecuted and that child victims experience less stress when there is corroborating evidence presented (Walsh, Jones, Cross, & Lippert, 2010).

Victim Compensation and Victim Assistance

Most states have modeled their victims' compensation, assistance and services programs after the federal Crime Victims Fund established under the Victims of Crime Act of 1984 (VOCA). Under this model, federal offenders contribute money that is collected by the U. S. Attorney's Office, Federal Courts, and the Federal Bureau of Prisons in the form of fines, forfeited bail bonds, penalties, etc. Under the USA Patriot Act of 2001, the fund is also eligible to receive gifts, bequests and donations. Although there is a cap on how much money can go into the fund, that cap can be lifted by Congress, as has been the case several times in the last few decades.

The federal government keeps a portion of these funds for use in the federal court system and for projects and programs and distributes part of the money to the states in the form of grants. In 2007, states received over $1 billion for the roughly 4,000 programs available nationwide (Walker, 2011) . In exchange for underwriting these efforts, the government dictates the states' use of funds according to specified criteria. In order to be eligible for victims' compensation/assistance, victims must report the crime to law enforcement within three days of the offense and file the claim within a fixed period of time. All private sources of health care or insurance must be exhausted before one is eligible to receive victims' compensation from these funds. States usually distribute their monies through public and nonprofit organizations that provide victim-related services at the local level.

Victim compensation usually includes medical costs, funeral and burial costs, psychological services, lost wages or support, and repair of eyeglasses, prostheses, or dental work. Money may also be available for crime-scene clean-up but does not cover property damage or loss. Victim assistance on the other hand, may include a variety of services such as crisis intervention, emergency shelter or transportation, and the provision of advocacy representation in the criminal justice system.

Victim-Impact Statements

One of the most common forms of victim participation in the criminal justice process is the victim-impact statement (VIS). Victim-impact statements are generally used in court to communicate society's concern for victims and to have justice reflect sensitivity toward the harms they have endured. Although there are some differences between practices at the state and federal level and between states, at a minimum every state allows some form of victim-impact statement and almost all states include a written VIS as part of the presentence investigation report. These may be used to make decisions about bail or pretrial release as well as later awards of restitution. The use of oral statements or an allocution is most often found at the sentencing phase of the criminal court process and is made by the victim, survivor or a close family member (Karmen, 2001). The Victims of Crime Act of 1994, (VOCA) was the legislation insuring that victims of violent crimes, such as sexual assault, now had the right to make a statement at the sentencing phase of federal trials. Further, some states allow various forms of statements to be presented at other phases of the process including at parole hearings.

Victim-impact statements can take various forms; they may be oral, written, electronic, and, in some cases, drawings. The use of drawings is often important in cases where the victim is a small child. The Child Protection Act of 1990 addressed this issue, insuring that child victims of federal crimes would be able to submit victim-impact statements using means that are "commensurate with their age and cognitive development," which could include drawings, models, and other visual representations.

According to the National Center for Victims of Crime (NCVC) website, the victim impact statement (VIS) usually describes the negative impact that the offense has had on the victim, including details of the financial, physical, psychological or emotional effects suffered, an explanation of the harm to family relationships, descriptions of medical or psychological treatments needed by the victim or the victim's family stemming from the crime, and the nature of the need for restitution. In each state, the law might outline the specific information that should be detailed in the statement, or it may call for a more general "description of the impact of the offense." Although more legally controversial, many states allow victims to render an opinion about what would be an appropriate sentence.

Mothers Against Drunk Driving (MADD) is one of the largest victims advocacy groups in this country and much of their efforts focus on providing direct assistance to the families of those harmed by drunk drivers. Their mission includes explaining victim's rights and the court processes involved in prosecutions of drunk drivers, accompanying victim family members to court if they request and helping in the preparation of victim-impact statements. MADD has constructed a workbook that offers advice for constructing a good victim-impact statement. They suggest that statements do not repeat evidence that has already been discussed at trial but should instead focus on the emotional, physical and financial effects of the crime on the victim, specifically addressing how the survivor's life is different since the crash (DWI). The statement should be three-to-five minutes long and should be simple and descriptive.

Although victim-impact statements give victims an opportunity to participate in the criminal court process, in many states, the accused party is afforded the opportunity to challenge the statement. *Booth v. Maryland* (1987) and *South Carolina v. Gathers* (1989) questioned the constitutionality of the victim-impact statement in the sentencing phase. In both cases, the question was whether or not there was a violation of the 8th Amendment. In *Booth v. Maryland*, the U.S. Supreme Court ruled that a victim-impact statement could not be used during the sentencing phase in death penalty cases given that the use of the statement interfered with the offender's right to due process. Further, in *South Carolina v. Gathers*, the U.S. Supreme Court ruled that information about the victim in a death penalty case should not be allowed during the sentencing phase in a death penalty case. However, *Payne v. Tennessee* (1991) overruled both *Booth v. Maryland* and *South Carolina v. Gathers*. In *Payne v. Tennessee*, the U.S. Supreme Court found that victim-impact statements were not a violation of the 8th Amendment. Further, victim-impact statements could be allowed in the sentencing phase of death penalty trials. Payne argued that the use of the victim-impact statement during the sentencing phase was a violation of the 8th Amendment as it resulted in the death penalty. Payne was convicted of attempted murder and two counts of capital murder for stabbing to death a mother and her two-year-old daughter. A three-year-old son was also stabbed, but survived. The statement offered insight into the psychological effects of the attack on the young boy and was presented to the court by the survivor's grandmother:

> He cries for his mom. He doesn't seem to understand why she doesn't come home. And he cries for his sister Lacie. He comes to me many times during the week and asks me, Grandmama, do you miss my Lacie. And I tell him yes. He says, I'm worried about my Lacie.

Trial or Tribute?

As we have indicated, the victim-impact statement is a fairly recent addition to the criminal trial process. However, in a number of cases, the prosecution has already been accused of manipulating the presentation of this material from a personal account to a professionally-produced media event. The use of music videos featuring the victim and highlighting their character at the punishment phase of the trial has been examined closely to the courts. And to date, there has been no clear signal to rein in these embellishments.

The use of media-enhanced victim-impacts statements was at the center of appeals in the cases of *People v. Prince, People v. Zamudio, Salazar v. Texas* and in *People v. Kelly*. Overall, the courts have noted that there must be limits and have attempted to separate some types of photo-video presentations as acceptable and others as not. In *Salazar* it was found that the 17-minute photo-montage set to the music of the movie *Titanic* may have crossed the line of what would be permissible. In that case, the Texas Court of Criminal Appeals ruled that the defendant's claim of prejudice could not be dismissed and the case was remanded for consideration of the potential harm resulting from the video. In *Zamudio*, the appeals court found that the use of the 118-picture-video only, without the audio/musical part being allowed was permissible as the narrator was given instructions as to a more objective presentation of the material. In *Kelly* the court found that, although not all of the video was immediately relevant, it was not overly emotional and represented facts in the victim's life. It was determined that if there was in error in the use of this material, it was harmless. Similarly, in *Prince* the court cautioned that juror reactions should be monitored but in this case, the video testimonial consisted of content previously recorded by the victim in a neutral interview studio and had not been constructed for the purpose of the trial. In general, the courts have indicated that "…a criminal trial is not a memorial service for the victim. What may be entirely appropriate eulogies to celebrate the life and accomplishments of a unique individual are not necessarily admissible in a criminal trial" (*Salazar v. Texas*, p. 36).

Orders of Protection

Protection orders are filed through the courts to protect a person from harm and/or contact with an abuser. The orders are filed through a civil court; the person requesting protection is the petitioner and the respondent is the person for whom the petition is filed. Generally, the process of obtaining an order of protection begins with requesting a temporary order. Temporary protection orders generally last two weeks. Subsequently, the petitioner appears before a judge; the judge then makes the determination to approve or deny the order of protection. Orders of protection typically apply for one year. If the order of protection is granted by the judge, both the petitioner and respondent are given certified copies of the order. Local law enforcement agencies are also provided with a copy of the protection order. If a respondent violates an order of protection, the petitioner must inform law enforcement and contact the court to file a motion to have the petitioner held in contempt of the order.

One obvious concern with an order of protection is the issue of transportability which arises whenever victims of abuse relocate to escape an abuser. Victims groups and womens' advocates have lobbied to insure the orders granted by a judge in one state will be recognized in another state. Using the constitutional concept of Full Faith and Credit, legislation on this subject was signed into law by President Bill Clinton on September 13, 1994. Full Faith and Credit stipulations from the *Violence Against Women Act* (VAWA) require courts of one state to honor and subsequently enforce an order of protection issued by another state. Under the VAWA it is a federal crime to cross interstate lines with the intent to, and purpose of, violating an order of protection. Information disseminated through the National Crime Information Center (NCIC) allows law enforcement agencies to access information from federal, state, and local law enforcement agencies nationwide (Sims & Zaorski, 1998). Also, law enforcement agencies can access existing orders of protection through information provided by civil and criminal courts. Though almost all states have enacted their own full faith and credit laws recognizing the reciprocity of restraining orders between states, there is tremendous variation between the states in the way they handle violations of restraining orders as the Box 5-1 illustrates.

Because there is no standardized form for restraining orders, Arrington and Lutz (1998) suggest that orders of protection should be constructed in a manner that will "enhance the confidence of law enforcement to act in good faith on the order, and will provide an enforcing court with the information to provide the full faith and credit that the issuing court intended" (p. 66). The authors also offered some suggestions for preparing orders of protection:

- include name and contact information from the issuing court and statutory citation,
- provide more information than is required by the NCIC,
- indicate the type of protection order, and
- indicate that the respondent has been served.

Box 5-1. How Protective Orders Vary by State

An individual who violates a protective order in Indiana commits invasion of privacy, which is considered a misdemeanor offense. Entering a building in violation of the terms of a protective order is construed a first-degree criminal trespass in Connecticut. Pennsylvania's Supreme Court found a violation of a protective order to be partial grounds for a burglary charge. Some states, such as Utah, treat a domestic violence protective order violation either as a misdemeanor or as criminal contempt and a separate domestic violence offense. State courts in California, Kentucky, Minnesota, New Mexico, and Texas have held that finding a defendant guilty of criminal contempt does not preclude a subsequent prosecution on the grounds of double jeopardy. A few states require anyone who violates a protective order to serve a minimum term of confinement. In Hawaii, violators of protective orders entered in domestic violence and harassment cases must spend at least 48 hours in jail for a first violation and 30 days for any subsequent violations. In Iowa, the mandatory minimum sentence for the violation of a no-contact order is seven consecutive days. Illinois's requisite 24-hour imprisonment for a second or each subsequent protective order violation is less stringent.... Colorado law provides that any sentence imposed for a violation of a protective order must run consecutively (following) and not concurrently (at the same time) with the sentence imposed for the crime giving rise to the order.

Source: National Center for Victims of Crime, *Enforcement of Protective Orders*, Legal Series Bulletin, #4, Office of Justice Programs, Washington DC, January 2002.

Further, the petitioner should make the best possible effort to distribute copies to all area law enforcement agencies and carry a copy of the protection order at all times. In essence, orders of protection are only as useful as the information provided to those who must endorse and certify the orders. Given the importance of protection orders, all parties should exert the most effort possible to ensure that victims of violence and the threat of violence are protected from harm.

LIABILITY FOR VICTIMS

The Duty to Protect

A landmark case in 1984, *Thurman v. City of Torrington,* directly addressed the outmoded 'mind your own business' attitude concerning instances of domestic violence between married persons. In the lawsuit, Tracey Thurman alleged that she had sought protection from her abusive estranged husband Charles Thurman, Sr. on many occasions with minimal response. As the litigation stipulated:

> On June 10, 1983, Charles Thurman appeared at the Bentley-St. Hilaire residence in the early afternoon and demanded to speak to Tracey. Tracey, remaining indoors, called the defendant police department asking that Charles be picked up for violation of his probation. After about 15 minutes, Tracey went outside to speak to her husband in an effort to persuade him not to take or hurt Charles Jr. Soon thereafter, Charles began to stab Tracey repeatedly in the chest, neck and throat. Approximately 25 minutes after Tracey's call to the Torrington Police Department and after her stabbing, a single police officer, the defendant Petrovits, arrived on the scene. Upon the arrival of Officer Petrovits at the scene of the stabbing, Charles Thurman was holding a bloody knife. Charles then dropped the knife and, in the presence of Petrovits, kicked the plaintiff Tracey Thurman in the head and ran into the Bentley-St. Hilaire residence. Charles returned from within the residence holding the plaintiff Charles Thurman, Jr. and dropped the child on his wounded mother. Charles then kicked

Tracey in the head a second time. Soon thereafter, defendants DeAngelo, Nukirk, and Columbia arrived on the scene but still permitted Charles Thurman to wander about the crowd and to continue to threaten Tracey. Finally, upon approaching Tracey once again, this time while she was lying on a stretcher, Charles Thurman was arrested and taken into custody.

Tracey Thurman's well-documented history of calls to police suggested that, prior to that incident, she was virtually ignored by several City of Torrington police officers even though she had followed all of the legal procedures under the restraining order. In fact, some beatings were even witnessed by officers responding to her calls. Still, Charles Thurman, Sr. was allowed to live and work in the City of Torrington.

The district court of Connecticut found that police officers have the responsibility to provide equal protection under the law to all persons, including spouses and children. Tracey's unprecedented award ($1.9 million) was instrumental in clarifying the nature of police responses to domestic violence, set the stage for implementing mandatory arrest policies and encouraged municipalities across America to buy liability insurance to protect against bankruptcies in the face of similar judgments. The case of *Thurman v. City of Torrington* soon became a made-for-television movie, and perhaps serves as a reminder of what the term "duty to protect" really means.

The Duty to Warn

Another controversial legal issue involving crimes of violence is the role that third parties may play in preventing or attempting to prevent victimization. *Tarasoff v. The Regents of the University of California (1976)* is a case that was instrumental in clarifying the concept of the duty to warn. It involved the murder of a University of California graduate student, Tatiana Tarasoff, at the hands of Prosenjit Poddar. Poddar had dated Tarasoff and, at some point, began to resent and disapprove of her dating other men. Various accounts from the literature suggest that Poddar, an Indian immigrant, was not completely aware of dating as defined in Western culture. He revealed a plan to a university psychologist to purchase a gun and shoot Tarasoff. The psychologist alerted campus police who interviewed Poddar. He was subsequently released when he promised to stay away from Tarasoff. The psychologist in charge of the university clinic destroyed paperwork relative to Poddar's interview with the police. Tarasoff was later stalked and stabbed to death by Poddar. Tarasoff's parents sued the university health services, university police, and California regents on the grounds that Tarasoff's death might have been prevented if she had been informed as to the nature of Poddar's visit with the university psychologist and interview with police.

Although the case was dismissed in the lower court citing that a doctor has a duty to the client, not a third party and the appeals court agreed, the California Supreme Court found that a therapist has a responsibility to alert a potential victim of danger. The court ruled that overt threats to specifically named individuals require that therapists alert those individuals of the risks posed by their client. The court further noted that law enforcement agencies should be alerted to protect potential victims. This case has been one of the most controversial challenges to the therapist-client relationship and for over thirty years has been interpreted and reinterpreted throughout the profession for its implications for psychological services.

Parental Liability and Wrongful Death

Parental liability laws are not frequently used but have been conceived as a means to compel parents to address the gang, gun and drug behaviors of their children. Under strict liability laws, parents may be held liable for shoplifting or property damage caused by their children although most states cap that amount at about $2000. In most cases, this includes damages caused by a child driving without a license. While most cases are pursued as civil matters or torts, criminal charges against the parents may be allowed in some states if the parents conduct is so negligent that it would grossly depart from normal societal standards. However, courts are more often focused on getting parents into classes or under supervision so that future delinquency in their children might be prevented. One of the most controversial cases involving parental liability, and one that has shaped the legal context of this issue in recent years, is that of the Columbine High School shootings.

April 20, 2009, marked the ten-year anniversary of the massacre that occurred at Columbine High School in Littleton, Colorado. Students Dylan Klebold and Eric Harris shot 12 students, one teacher, and injured over twenty others. The two eventually committed suicide in the high school after many hours of a stand-off that was captured on film and televised around the world. The two were armed with homemade bombs, weapons, and ammunition.

In the wake of the tragic event, a number of lawsuits were filed. Parents of the victims sued the parents of the perpetrators. Parents and survivors of victims also sued the companies, including Nintendo, Sega and Sony, that produced violent video games popular with the two young killers. They also sued the men who illegally sold the weapons used as well as a young female friend of the two gunmen who provided the weapons to the teens. Some families sued the school district to allow religiously-themed memorials to be included on the property. And, there was some discussion of holding victims' families responsible for cutting down two trees that had been part of the memorial because they had been representative of the two young men who committed the crimes and took their own lives (Crosson, 1999; CanWest Interactive, 1999; Midland Independent Newspapers, 2001).

Following the Columbine murders a number of lawsuits were also filed against the Jefferson County Sheriff's Office. There were allegations that deputies failed to address earlier threats made by the gunman. The parents of one of the killers also filed notice of intent to sue the Sheriff's Office for failure to warn them of the violent tendencies of the other young killer. Finally, lawsuits against the department focused on delays relative to their response on the day of the 1999 shootings. Although individual officers were not deemed responsible, ranking officers or commanders were criticized for their lack of action that may have led to the preventable death of teacher Dave Sanders. Law enforcement officers waited for the S.W.A.T. teams to arrive before responding to the scene despite a sign hanging from one of the classroom windows saying "1 bleeding to death." A settlement was reached in the amount of $1.5 million dollars paid by the Jefferson County Sheriff's Department's insurance company (Nicholson, 2004). A second settlement with the Jefferson County

Sheriff's Department was also reached involving $117,500 to survivor Patrick Ireland. Many can remember the dramatic and heart-stopping escape of the boy in the window who crawled to safety after being shot. The department was again criticized for failing to act, although a number of additional claims by other survivor and victim families had been dismissed by the court (Nicholson, 2004).

VICTIMIZATION AS A DEFENSE

In the past, the courts have been accused of not being sensitive to the plight of the victim and of even using the legal process to further victimize those who have been subjected to criminal harms. Over the last three to four decades, concern about this second victimization resulted in many reforms relative to the status and treatment not only of victims but also of offenders with a history of victimization. These reforms have not been without controversy and some may argue that we have gone too far in considering the background of an individual and its effect on future conduct, particularly criminal conduct. A few examples of the types of issues that have significantly changed over the years are highlighted here.

Battered Woman Syndrome

Battered woman syndrome was developed from research conducted in the late 1970s by Lenore Walker who took strong exception to early assumptions that abused women received consolation from domestic abuse, felt a need to be punished, or sought out abusive treatment in adult intimate relationships (Koss, et al., 1994). Further, Walker proposed learned helplessness to explain why women experiencing physical assault from their partners find it difficult to leave abusive relationships.

Victims of intimate partner violence exhibit a variety of psychological symptoms that are similar to those of other trauma victims. The more a woman is assaulted, the more psychological distress she experiences. If a battered woman perceives the danger to be life threatening, she may take what she sees as necessary lifesaving actions, including killing the batterer, that she would not take under ordinary circumstances. She will likely do this without thinking through the consequences. Her only goal in this mental state is to stop the actual or anticipated violent attack (Walker, 1995). A woman's mental state during an assault on her abuser can be determined by her immediate reaction to a perceived danger or by post traumatic reactions that stem from prior abuse (Dutton, 1994). The perception of danger makes subsequent abuse more vivid.

Criminal courts in all states accept expert witness testimony on battered woman syndrome (Walker, 1995) . Testimony can be offered to assist the judge and/or jury in understanding the battered woman's perceived threat of danger at the time of the act, as well as her response to that threat (Dutton, 1994). Individuals who qualify as expert witnesses on battered woman syndrome are usually accepted because of their professional training or work experience (Merlo & Pollock, 1995). Expert testimony on battered woman syndrome has been admitted in cases where the imminence of danger was clear. The testimony acknowledges that the circumstances of a woman who is repeatedly battered may be outside the knowledge of the average juror. Expert witnesses are allowed to tell jurors about the psychological impact of repeated battery and its effect on a woman's ability to perceive imminent danger (Swisher & Wekesser, 1994).

One of the landmark cases for admitting expert testimony on battered woman syndrome occurred in New Jersey in *State v. Kelly* in 1984. In one of the first decisions of its kind, the court held that expert testimony could be heard to determine whether the defendant's belief that the regular pattern of serious physical abuse, combined with the prior threats to kill her, formed a reasonable basis upon which she could determine that her life was in danger (Swisher & Wekesser, 1994). The court found that expert testimony was relevant to the case because the defendant believed she was in imminent danger of death.

Defense attorneys most often use expert testimony on battered woman syndrome in cases involving women who kill their abusers (Knudsen & Miller, 1991). Defense lawyers have a hard time explaining to jurors the shame, isolation and emotional dependency that bind victims to their abusers. According to Swisher and Wekesser (1994, p. 265), Many lawyers say it is virtually impossible to defend a battered woman without some expert testimony about the effect of the syndrome over time. Some critics argue that such testimony allows attorneys to stretch the rules governing self-defense.

Battered woman syndrome has been used in a variety of legal proceedings, including criminal prosecutions of batterers, criminal prosecutions of women who have attacked their batterers, and divorce and child custody proceedings (Crowell & Burgess, 1996). The fact that battered woman syndrome has been used as a rationale for self defense in homicide cases suggests that the act was reasonable and necessary because the accused "reasonably believed she was in imminent danger of serious bodily harm or death and that the force she used was necessary to avoid that danger" (Swisher & Wekesser, 1994, p. 299).

Child Sex Abuse Accommodation Syndrome

In the evolution of the defensive use of syndromes, child sex abuse accommodation syndrome followed closely on the heels of the acceptance of battered womens' syndrome. Although it is not used as a defense, per se, it is often used to explain why an accusation or claim against a defendant may take so long to be officially reported. It is often used to detract from a defendant's claim that the failure of a child to report sexual abuse in a timely manner should undermine the veracity of an accusation. The use of child sexual abuse accommodation syndrome was a response to the recognition of the problem of gaining convictions when children are too frightened to tell anyone about their abuse. These cases largely depend on the believability of the child victim as perpetrators go out of their way to make sure there are no witnesses (Shiu, 2009). In addition, medical evidence was not always clear. In trying to explain why some children might retract or deny that sexual abuse occurred, experts developed profiles of what appeared to be typical behaviors that fit a syndrome explaining how children adjust or adapt to sexual abuse as a coping mechanism. Summit (1983) outlined the traits as secrecy, helplessness, accommodation, delayed disclosure, and retraction as common features of the behaviors and expressions of the sexually abused child victim.

In addition to the symptoms of child sexual abuse accommodations, psychiatrists also identify depression, adjustment disorders, self-destructive behaviors and the ability to form meaningful relationships in adulthood with past abuse (Patterson, 2002). For example, it wasn't until two adult brothers heard about the sexual abuse of other boys at the hands of parish priests that they realized they were not the only ones abused and that their experiences, prolonged exposure to attacks by a close family friend, were often an underlying cause of mental health problems later in life (Patterson, 2002).

As the above example indicates, children victimized by priests have been cast into the framework of child sexual abuse accommodation syndrome. Many accounts over the years have detailed how parents' disbelief and support for their religious leaders have facilitated children's retractions. Further, feelings of anger and betrayal building for years may also explain why so much later, some victims would be motivated to attack their perpetrators. One alleged victim appeared at the home of a Baltimore priest who had been placed on involuntary leave in another case of abuse allegations, and shot him. Dontee Stokes believed that his accusations had not been taken seriously and he attempted to talk with the priest who refused to see him. Stokes then fired upon Maurice Blackwell, seriously wounding him before surrendering to authorities (MediaNews Group, 2002).

Child sexual abuse cases demonstrate the wide range of victim issues from persons falsely accused of child sexual abuse to children attempting to adjust to the complex fears associated with abuse to perpetrators killed at the hands of distraught survivors and avenging zealots. How the justice system chooses to investigate and prosecute these cases and how jurors are instructed on these issues from both a legal and a scientific standpoint will be influenced by our perceptions of how accurate diagnoses such as child sexual abuse accommodation syndrome really are.

Battered Persons' Syndrome

As with child sex abuse accommodation syndrome and battered womens syndrome, the development of a viable battered persons syndrome has been used to explain not only why an abused person might not report their victimization but also why they might recant it (O'Keeffe, 1993). More modern gender orientations recognize that men as well as women may be exposed to violence in patterns conducive to post-traumatic stress. The maturing social conscience of the court means that we are more likely today to refer to a "battered persons syndrome," endowing the symptoms with a more gender-neutral designation. Military courts in particular are facing more cases where defenses such as the battered persons syndrome are being raised.

Coercion and Duress

The use of the defense of duress or coercion is also complicated and must meet a number of legal criteria. According to Finkelstein (1995, p. 254) the defendant must be under threat of an illegal and imminent harm that rises to the level of death or serious bodily injury and have no reasonable means of escape. The defendant must also be acting on a specific order or demand from the coercer. Further, the person cannot have placed themselves into a relationship where such coercion would have been normally expected to have occurred such as joining a gang or an organized crime syndicate. Although it seems that it would be difficult to mount a successful defense based on coercion, these are often the circumstances described by drug couriers who claim that they or their family members would have been killed had they not cooperated in drug smuggling activities.

Stockholm syndrome

Stockholm syndrome is generally defined as a group of psychological symptoms experienced by victims under tremendous emotional and physical threat in situations of captivity. It is mainly viewed as a coping mechanism which manifests itself as an emotional bond with captors. Stockholm syndrome is so named by psychologist Niles Berjerot who used term to describe the emotional state of hostages of the Sveriges Kredit Bank in Stockholm, Sweden. In August 1973, prison escapee Jan-Erik Olsson and Clark Olafsson attempted to rob the bank. In a stand-off with police, the bank robbers held four employees hostage for over 5 days (131 hours). The hostages established an emotional bond with their captors and began to sympathize with them.

As previously described, Stockholm Syndrome typically results when captives begin to view their captors as human beings as opposed to the enemy. This view allows hostages to identify or, rather, rationalize the behavior of the captor and is a response to the perceived threat of death or violence. When rescue attempts were made to release the hostages of Sveriges Kredit Bank, many initially refused and some refused to testify at the trials of the bank robbers. Most surprisingly, hostages raised money for the defense of the bank robbers and publicly spoke in support of their captors. One hostage became the love interest of a captor. Carver (2009) suggests there are four components to explain why hostages empathize with their captors:

1. The presence of a perceived threat to one's physical or psychological survival.
2. A perceived small kindness from the abuser or captor.
3. Isolation from perspectives other than those of the abuser or captor.
4. The perceived inability to escape.

Patricia Campbell Hearst, better known as Patty Hearst, is most often used as an example of Stockholm syndrome. In 1974, the heiress was kidnapped from her home in Berkeley, California by the Symbionese Liberation Army (SLA). Hearst was held blindfolded and nude in a closet and was continuously physically and sexually abused by her kidnappers. The SLA requested millions of dollars and sent numerous audio and video tapings of Patty Hearst wearing SLA regalia and pledging allegiance to the organization. In several accounts, Hearst communicated that she changed her name to reflect her loyalty to the SLA. Approximately two months after her capture, Hearst went on-air citing her refusal to leave the SLA and her intent to support the organization. On April 15, 1974, Hearst was seen on videotape wielding a rifle and, apparently, a willing participant in the bank robbery of Hibernia Bank in which one person was fatally wounded. Hearst was arrested in September 1975; Stockholm syndrome was used by the defense in the criminal trial. On March 20, 1976, after hundreds of hours of psychiatric testimony, security videotape, and audiotape, the jury found Patty Hearst guilty of felony robbery with the use of a firearm.

Today it is not uncommon for us to see internet images and televised videos of prisoners of war in various countries forced to give false statements condemning their own countries or admitting to acting as a spy. However, back in the late seventies, people were more prone to believe that what was captured on camera was true; thus, Hearst was sentenced to seven years in prison. After serving approximately twenty-two months in prison her sentence was commuted to probation by then President Jimmy Carter in 1979 and she received a pardon by President Bill Clinton in 2001. The brainwashing theory used by the Hearst defense team suggested that her participation in SLA terrorist activity was not of her own will but as a response to long captivity and the psychological anguish sustained while she was held as a kidnap victim.

Stockholm syndrome has also been recently used to explain the actions of Elizabeth Smart when she did not escape her captors when given several opportunities. In June 2003, then 14-year-old Elizabeth Smart was kidnapped from her Utah home by Brian David Mitchell. Reports indicated that Smart denied her true identity and evaded questions when initially approached by law enforcement officials. However, police continued to question the young girl who donned a wig and large sunglasses. Smart was held by her abductors for approximately nine months before being reunited with her family. Her captors Brian David Mitchell and Wanda Barzee have been deemed mentally unfit to stand trial but it appears they will be charged with aggravated kidnapping, aggravated, burglary, and aggravated sexual assault.

Although many of the kidnap victims we see and hear today do not suffer from Stockholm syndrome, they admit to being worn down, capitulating to the demands of their captors by the duration and long-term abuse they suffer. Journalist Roxana Saberi was held for four months in an Iranian prison. Under severe psychological pressure and distress, she erroneously confessed to being a spy. She explains what happened:

> The first few days, I was interrogated for several hours, from morning until evening, blindfolded, facing a wall, by up to four men, and threatened...that I would be put in prison for 10 to 20 years or more or even face execution. And I was in solitary confinement for several days. The really difficult thing was they didn't let me tell anyone where I was. ...in the past, one of the ways that people get out of these kinds of situations is to make a confession, and even be videotaped making this confession, even if this confession is false. And so, under

pressure, I did the same thing. After I realized that nobody knew where I was, I was very afraid, and my interrogators threatened me and said, "If you don't confess to being a U.S. spy, you could be here for many years—10 years or 20 years, or you could even face execution" (http://www.npr.org/templates/story/story.php?storyId=104612989).

The irony of using duress and self-defense as a justification for one's criminal conduct is not only that past victimization now plays a role in another person's victimization but that it is used to undermine the defendant's accountability. In recognizing the effects of trauma on victims, we also inherit the consequences of those effects. In the quest for justice, the courts must continually balance the current science of victimology against some of the most basic instincts for vengeance, retribution and revenge.

CAN THE COURTS DO BETTER?

Even though the avenues for recognizing victims' rights and encouraging participation in the court system have steadily increased over the years, research seems to indicate that many victims do not fully understand their rights in court, and do not participate as often as might be expected. In some cases, state assistance programs seem to be more oriented toward witness assistance than victims' assistance (Walker, 2011) . On the website of the organization Parents of Murdered Children (POMC) writers decry the stressfulness of their position in the criminal justice system. They claim that victims are stereotyped as angry, vengeful, bitter and hateful and that even members of the prosecution fear their involvement as potentially prejudicial to a fair trial. To some members of that organization, the adversarial orientation of the law, operating with the presumption of innocent until proven guilty, seems to minimize the victim and their plight. Part of the challenge for modern victimology is to examine and reflect on the role of the victim not only in our courts, but in our society today.

References

Crowell, N. A., & Burgess, A. W. (1996). *Understanding violence against women.* Washington DC: National Academy Press.

Dutton, M. A. (1994). *Validity of battered women syndrome in criminal cases involving battered women.* Retrieved from http://www.ojp. usdoj.gov/ocpa/94Guides/Trials/Valid/

Finkelstein, C. O. (1995). Duress: A philosophical account of the defense in law. *Arizona Law Review, 37,* 251–283.

Hamill, S., Graham, E. S., Thomason III, E., & Huerta-Choy, R. (2001). Current practices in the use of televised child testimony: Questions of constitutionality and personal biases. *Criminal Justice Policy Review, 12,* 4, 282–294.

Karmen, A. (2001). *Crime victims. 4th Ed.* Belmont, CA: Wadsworth.

Knudsen, D. D., & Miller J. L. (1991). *Abused and battered.* New York: Walter de Gruyter.

Koss, M., Goodman, L., Browne, A., Fitzgerald, L., Keita, G., & Russo, N. (1994). *No safe haven: Male violence against women at home, at work, and in the community.* Washington, DC: American Psychological Association.

Lipovsky, J. A. (1994). The impact of court on children. *Journal of Interpersonal Violence, 9,* 238–257.

MediaNews Group, Inc. (2002, May 14). Priest shot by alleged sex abuse victim. *Long Beach Press-Telegram,* A1.

Merlo, A. V., & Pollock, J. M. (1995). *Women, law & social control.* Needham Heights, MA.: Allyn & Bacon.

Nestruck, J. K. (2003, August 25). Inmate to be charged with killing priest. *National Post* (Canada) A3.

O'Keeffe, R. B. (1993). Uses of battered person evidence in courts-martial. *Army Law,* 3–14.

Patterson, M. (2002, April 10). Doctor explains brothers' delay in suing cleric. *Newark, Star-Ledger,* 20.

Payne v. Tennessee 501 U.S. 808 (1991)

People v. Kelly 42 Cal 4th 763 (2007)

People v. Prince 40 Cal 4th 1179 (2007)

People v. Zamudio 43 Cal 4th 327 (2008)

Rogers, B. (2010, April 15). Pair must show good-faith restitution. *Houston Chronicle,* B2.

Salazar v. Texas No. 2180-01

Shiu, M. H. (2009). Note: Unwarranted skepticism: The federal courts treatment of child sexual abuse accommodation syndrome. *Southern California Interdisciplinary Law Journal, 18,* 651–676.

Swisher, K. L., & Wekesser, C. (1994). *Violence against women.* San Diego, CA: Greenhaven Press.

Tarasoff v. The Regents of the University of California (1976) 17 Cal. 3d 425; 551 P.2d 334; 131 Cal. Rptr. 14; 1976 Cal. LEXIS 297; 83 A.L.R.3d 1166

Thurman v. City of Torrington (1984) 595 F. Supp. 1521; 1984 U.S. Dist. LEXIS 22524

Walker, L. (1995). Understanding battered woman syndrome. *Trial, 31* (2). Retrieved from LOUIS: InfoTrac OneFile database.

Walker, S. (2011). *Sense and nonsense about crime, drugs, and communities.* Belmont, CA: Wadsworth.

Discussion Questions

1. How much weight should be given to past victimization when defendants who have a history of abuse are tried for criminal acts? Does it matter if the act is committed directly against the perpetrator of their abuse?
2. Is there any threat to justice when some victims prepare and deliver more dramatic and emotionally compelling victim impact statements than other victims? Should there be attempts to "equalize" the process? Why or why not?
3. There are many possible lawsuits that may emerge after a highly publicized crime. Should the litigation be curbed or restricted in any ways? What ways and why or why not?

Books To Read

Cullen, D. (2009). *Columbine.* New York: Twelve Pub.

Moore, Rebecca (2009). Understanding Jonestown and People's Temple. Westport, CT: Praeger.

Movies To See

Notes on a Scandal
The Accused (1988) Jodie Foster
Taken in Broad Daylight

Web Links

http://www.enditnow.gov/dv/flash.html
http://www.law.northwestern.edu/wrongfulconvictions/
http://www.ncvc.org/vb/Main.aspx
http://www.courtinfo.ca.gov/programs/collab/dv.htm

CHAPTER 6
Victim Advocates and Agencies

INTRODUCTION

The study of individuals, organizations and agencies who interface with victims on a routine basis is an important aspect of victimology. Those most inspired to work with victims are often victims themselves. Some victims may seek employment in a field that allows them to use their insights and experiences with victimization to assist others. Some victims may join local groups that offer support and fellowship to help them with coping and adjustment. Though less common, some victims are driven to establish their own groups and organizations to address what they believe are unmet needs. Sometimes there is a single mission or goal for that group, while in other cases efforts become multifaceted and grow from local grassroots activities to national movements.

This chapter will look at a number of professional agencies that provide services to victims. Some are private and some are government operations. It will also examine a number of specific activist groups that consist mostly of volunteer networks. When comparing the roles of activists, advocates and agencies it is possible to see how the different viewpoints of individuals and organizations might affect the services offered by each and the policies they follow. Another important topic to be discussed is the trend today where agencies form partnerships or networks that allow victims to transition to related programs. In this way, smaller organizations are able to link clients to a broader range of services and to insure that victims do not fall through the cracks of bureaucracy,

Today more and more victim-service agencies are moving from volunteer to paid staff positions (Dunn & Powell-Williams, 2007).

111

Concerns over legal liabilities, increased standards associated with accreditation, certification, and funding have made it more practical and defensible to have educated and trained professional employees. Torts or civil lawsuits may be brought against agencies when it is found that employees have acted in a manner that is negligent or involves malpractice. Normally, in such cases three elements are argued 1) that there is a duty owed by the professional to the plaintiff or the general public, 2) that the professional failed to perform a duty according to a required standard of care the 3) the injury or harm that resulted to the client was a direct result of that breach of duty.

Despite the progress made in developing professional agency staff, the role of an advocate may not be clearly defined or interpreted. For example, many who work with domestic violence victims find themselves frustrated by promoting a client's independence and choices and then accepting that the victim chooses to return to an abuser or not press charges against him. The standards of professional relationships may necessitate that one respects his or her clients, yet personally, the advocate may not respect the choices that the client is making. While activists are generally promoting an issue or a cause, the role of the advocate is tied to the individual client, in this case, the person who is also a victim. In the close personal relationship of advocacy, there are often ethical and moral challenges that must be confronted as clients move through the various stages associated with victimization.

Victimization Stages and Needs

The National Organization of Victim Assistance theorizes that the experience of victimization is characterized by movement through a series of predictable stages (Geberth, 1992). This means that studies of victims have found patterns in the way individuals adjust to the trauma of victimization. Although there is variation from case to case, these are general observations that may aid in working with victims through the criminal justice process and in the provision of treatment and services. The stages are:

$ denial
$ protest or anger
$ despair

$ detachment
$ reconstruction of life

Denial is as much a coping mechanism as a response and is common in the families of murder victims. Relatives will often speak of the victim in the present tense or keep the victim's room or possessions ready as if the deceased will return. Protest and anger may be enhanced by experiences in the criminal justice system, perceived injustices or lack of information about the case can also trigger agitation. Despair may be marked by sleeplessness, loss of appetite and the inability to maintain work and home-life routines. As with detachment, survivors may stop attending social groups, church or professional functions. Studies characterize the responses most commonly seen in members of homicide victims' families as follows (King, 2004, p. 194):

They are wracked by turmoil, then numbness. They become preoccupied with the horror of the suffering of the victim, needing to know the details of the death.... They become restless, are plagued by insomnia, and have trouble concentrating. They fear for their own lives or the lives of other family members and have flashbacks to the moment they received the death notification. Some consider suicide. Many are angry with the victim for dying, which produces extreme feelings of guilt.... The survivors' self-confidence and sense of control over their world is severely compromised. They lose their ability to trust, and many lose their religious faith....

The needs of victims cannot be stereotyped as they vary between individuals and with different crime scenarios. In some cases, professionals must attempt to separate layers or needs and to prioritize certain services in order to facilitate recovery. Victimization from one set of circumstances, may trigger subsequent circumstances that make an individual more vulnerable to crime. For example, victims of Hurricane Katrina in 2005 lost homes, loved ones and jobs. Being out on the streets, traveling to relatives or shelters placed them at risk for further victimization. Looting, ransacking, scams and fraudulent schemes were common as offenders attempted to benefit from the influx of emergency federal relief funding. In such circumstances, advocates attempt to minimize subsequent victimizations by quickly and effectively addressing primary needs so that the risk of further exposure to harm is reduced.

A Social Problems Analysis of Victim Groups

As the social problems literature explains, special interest groups work to advance their issues in a very dynamic and competitive environment. Experts are used to verify the scope and seriousness of a social problem and employ data and research in ways that best positions the problem for attention and resources. Resources may be in the form of legislation, political lobbying, grants, funding, and services. For example, *FocusDriven* is an advocacy group for people who have lost a loved one to an accident caused by a distracted driver, primarily those who are texting. This group campaigns for certain types of law changes and for government funding to be devoted to studying and improving the safety issues that they concerned with.

With limits on which issues can be most effectively addressed, an organization such as *FocusDriven* would compete for attention and resources against groups such as MADD, Parents Against Tired Truckers, and, perhaps, Kidsandcars.org. In this process, theorists explain, groups may attempt to highlight media focus on potential worst case scenarios, misinterpret data that exaggerates a problem and generate what is referred to in the literature as a "moral panic" over their issue. At one time, the FocusDriven group could be lobbying to have laws passed that would require car manufacturer to install devices that would disable phone service that is not run through a hands-free device. The MADD organization might ask for a law mandating interlock devices be installed in all vehicles so that no one under the influence could start a car. At this same time, Kidsandcars.org would be seeking legislation that would require car makers to install backup sensors to insure that children are detected when a car is in reverse. As this example illustrates, car manufacturers would similarly flex their lobbying power to insure that they were not required to install any additional devices that might negate the competitive pricing of domestic autos.

Effective use of the media is one of the ways advocacy groups strengthen their impact. It is reported, for example, that distracted drivers cause 200,000 crashes per year, killing almost 6,000 people per year and injuring another 515,000 (Webber, 2010). The groups aligns itself with the Secretary of Transportation who calls the problem "an epidemic" and creates a website, Distraction.gov. The use of victim stories in testimony and on billboards humanizes the issue and makes it difficult for policymakers to separate not funding programs or sponsoring bills from not caring about these families. The cause also enlists the support of Oprah Winfrey who launches a "No Phone Zone" campaign (Webber, 2010).

Another example of the competitive nature of causes, The Memorial of Perpetual Tears, is also a good example of the emotional push behind the politics of advocacy efforts. Sonja Britton lost her 30 year old son in a drunk driving crash in Colorado. After years of grieving, Britton who lived in New Mexico, began efforts to establish a four acre memorial for DWI victims. The donated land has a number of stone walls, sculptures, benches and plaques, some symbolic steel art and a commemorative display of grave markers made from steel plates with tears carved down the sides. There are over 800 of the headstones spread across a field representing victims of DWI from New Mexico from the past five years.

Britton began her organization with a board of directors and a set of bylaws. From there, she obtained non-profit charitable status and began raising money. Although many small donations and a few larger gifts were obtained, the memorial has been mostly funded by taxpayers. In fact, more than $1,105,000 of federal, state and local tax revenue has been the major source of financing. And just recently, Britton's Congressional Representatives have sponsored legislation to insure that the memorial will be legally recognized as the first and only "National DWI Victims Memorial" (Springer, 2010). Some may wonder why a rural and remote site (pop. 1,800) came to be the national memorial, and why other venues were not allowed to compete for such a project. It is also worth considering what alternative DWI-related projects could have been funded with $1.1 million. What types of school-based programs, interventions, services, treatments, equipment, enforcement or training might have been undertaken or provided for this $1.1 million of taxpayer funds?

PROGRAMS AND AGENCIES

In 2008, The National Crime Victimization Survey reported that U.S. residents of age twelve or older were the victims of approximately 21 million crimes, and almost one quarter of those were violent offenses. Programming and services to address the various needs of crime victims, particularly survivors of violent crimes often involve a network of stakeholders including law enforcement and institutional and community corrections officials. Some of the duties and services are required by law, others are a mix of policies, traditions and specially funded activities. Optimally, those programs that demonstrate scientifically validated benefits are retained and those that don't are revised or discontinued. Program and policy evaluation, therefore, is an important part of the consideration of which services to provide to whom and under what conditions.

Wrap Around Programs

One of the latest trends in victim programming has been the expansion of the services arc to include the victim in the pre-release planning phase of the offender in the department of corrections. Wrap Around Programs, as they are called, recognize that for some victims, critical needs may emerge with the pending release of their offender, particularly when the neighborhoods or communities of both overlap. As Hurley (2009) explains, while restitution and engagement in other support services may have already been addressed early in the process, notification needs, updates on the status of the offender and the creation of a safety plan are tasks that arise long after sentencing has occurred. When an offender is pending release into the community following a term of incarceration, the victim may feel more comfortable after a third party delineates geographic conditions or boundaries that would best fit the needs of the offender and the safety needs of the victim. In some cases, a service worker will examine the victim's home to identify and address crime prevention needs including whether a civil protection order is needed.

Restorative Justice Programs

Restorative justice programs represent a broad array of practices designed to address the more personal context of the victim-offender relationship, a reality that exists beyond the legal intervention of the state as the aggrieved party. Elements of the programs may include restorative conferencing and victim-offender mediation which bring the parties face to face to work on resolving issues that go beyond simple restitution. This community-based treatment intervention is aimed at empowering victims by having the offender address questions they may have about why they were targeted and how they have been harmed by the events. Still, the methods seek to provide less punitive and more rehabilitative program components.

Reparative justice is also a concept used to describe these voluntary community practices. This term implies a more comprehensive "repair" model that is more than just material compensation. Instead it implies that emotional and psychological healing must be facilitated and the victim should feel "whole" again. In most cases, individuals are referred to restorative justice programs through offices of the court, judges, prosecutors or victim services. According to Van Ness and Heetderks Strong (2010) every victim and offender should be offered the opportunity to participate in restorative justice and that the experience should allow both to more smoothly reintegrate into the normal functioning of society.

The National Institute of Justice reports that there are almost 300 victim offender mediation programs currently operating in this country. Most professionals who provide victim services believe that it is a valuable experience and believe that programs should be available in all jurisdictions. The American Bar Association officially endorsed victim offender mediation as an option to bring about healthful resolutions to conflict and stress-related disputes. The structure and formality of the process provides a safe and controlled environment for the victim and allows them to explore feelings and issues that are not always relevant to court or criminal proceedings. According to a study of juvenile offender victim mediation programs by Umbreit (1994), almost all of the mediation sessions produced a viable restitution agreement. In addition, when victims and their offenders met with a trained mediator, the victims reported more satisfaction with the criminal justice system than similar victims going through the traditional court process. Further, the mediated victims subsequently reported being less fearful of revictimization.

It is important to note that mediation and other restorative options are not suited for all victims, offenders or types of crimes. Most have strict preconditions and exclude a significant number of offender/crime scenarios. Having both the offender and the victim benefit from the process requires that they be healthy, willing, and prepared to commit to the program. Most experts will agree that offenders must mature to the point where they are not only accountable for their crimes, but have expressed remorse to the extent that reparation work is the next step in realizing the full extent of the consequences of their actions. To prepare for this, many offenders have participated in correctional treatment based on cognitive behavioral therapy.

Cognitive behavioral counseling methods have been one of the more successful trends of the last twenty years and they have been associated with "what works" in drug and alcohol, anger management and sex offender treatments. The goal of this approach is to have offenders become sensitized to the effects that their actions have on victims. It is hoped that offenders develop empathy towards those they have hurt and that they discover and practice alternative behaviors that avoid causing harm to others. These objectives are important because program funding is most often results-based or outcome-driven. Evaluations are also used to determine best-practices in the field.

Child Protective Services

Child Protective Services is the agency responsible for investigating reports of child neglect and abuse where the custodial parent or guardian is the alleged perpetrator. While the criminal justice system is the reporting agency for claims of stranger or acquaintance abuse of children the two agencies often work together when formal charges appear to be substantiated and cases are processed as crimes. As would be expected, cases that come to the attention of CPS through mandatory reporters such as teachers and hospital personnel are more likely to be substantiated than those that come from tip lines or from calls by other nonprofessionals.

Unlike other justice related functions, child protection services developed at the local level rather than from federal sponsorship or initiatives. And, up until 1935 many of the agencies responding to claims of abuse were privately run organizations. At that time, some publicly funded child welfare programs became available under the Social Security Act (Myers, 2008). As more and more government regulations were implemented, it became less feasible for private agencies to engage in programming and treatment in this area.

Throughout the child abuse literature there are concerns that Child Protective Services agencies are underfunded, understaffed, undertrained and undersupervised. In 1980 over one million cases of suspected child abuse were reported and by 2000 that number was three million (Myers, 2008). Among CPS workers, turnover is high, decision-making is inconsistent and there are often critical time delays in the processing and transferring of information (Weibush, Freitag & Baird, 2001). Even when cases are substantiated, there is often a lack of consensus about what measures should be taken, whether children should be removed from the home or whether the court should pursue termination of parental rights.

ADVOCACY ORGANIZATIONS

This section provides examples of victim-support or services groups. The examples used here demonstrate the various ways that advocacy organizations come about, the types of agendas they develop, the work they engage in and some of the impact they have been able to have.

Survivors of Incest Anonymous

Survivors of Incest Anonymous (SIA) (http://www.siawso.org) was founded in 1982 as a self-help group for victims of childhood incest. This non-profit provides low-cost resources to former victims of incest who must be at least 18 years of age to participate. SIA uses a broad definition of incest that is not limited to physical penetration but includes any physical and/or emotional behavior in which a child feels violated. SIA follows a 12-step treatment method (similar to that of Alcoholics Anonymous and Narcotics Anonymous). The SIA website specifically explains that board members do not allow perpetrators to attend meetings. Safety—in a sense that victims must feel free to express their stories of victimization and legal issues mandating the reporting of issues related to abuse are rationales for this policy. SIA members appear to recognize that they are a self-help group and do not purport to provide therapy or treatment. The group specifically encourages members to seek professional help in resolving the serious issues, symptoms and effects of incest.

Survivors Network of Those Abused by Priests

The Survivors Network of Those Abused by Priests (SNAP (www. survivorsnetwork.org) was founded in 1989 in Chicago. SNAP claims to be the largest, oldest, and most active organization devoted to helping victims of priest abuse. The organization is a non-profit organization that operates in 60 United States cities. The group views sexual abuse by priests as a pervasive problem within the Catholic Church and not as isolated incidents.

SNAP was founded by Barbara Blaine who was abused by the assistant pastor of her church from the age of 13 until her senior year of high school. Blaine went on to earn a master's degree in social work and worked in a Catholic shelter before founding SNAP. The organization began as a small activist group and has grown into a victim support group. The group works to help victims deal with abuse suffered at the hands of nuns, priests, ministers, and bishops, and also works to develop strategies to prevent abuse. Across the country, efforts have been directed toward passing legislation that would extend the statutes of limitations for prosecuting child sexual abuse. This is particularly important for victims of clergy abuse as children may have been threatened not to tell their parents and parents did not suspect abuse from trusted church leaders. To a child, priests and bishops may appear as too dominant a force to challenge.

SNAP offers over 20 leaflets for dissemination, an elaborate website with a digest of links of news reports and media coverage. This information is also available in Spanish. The archive list is available online for 12 months. SNAP has an Internet support group named Survivors of Abuse in Religion (SOAR) which provides victims the opportunity to communicate with other victims of priest abuse. Of course, abusers are not allowed to become members of the support group. This may exclude a number of potential members as some victims have been forced to victimize others or have engaged in acts that mimic their abuse. Still, the website specifically states that perpetrators are not allowed to participate.

One of the primary tools that SNAP believes will help combat abuse is the concept of a "civil window" that allows victims to bring forward cases, with civil or criminal charges that otherwise may not be considered viable because of the statutes of limitation in different jurisdictions. Although a number of states allow victims of child sexual abuse to come forward many years following the crimes, and even into adulthood, many had a very short, one year time period from when the victim reported having been abused to when formal charges had to be filed. These restrictions, SNAP believed, allowed the church to stonewall providing information on alleged perpetrators so that it was less likely that prosecutions would be successful. SNAP has dedicated a considerable amount of effort towards encouraging a broader "window" of time in which to pursue cases, which to date, has been supported by legislation in several states.

Using an international media platform, the organization has broadened its scope to provide information about not only predators and suspected predators, but those who enable them. The hope is that fear of liability and widespread media exposure will prompt those who have knowledge about abuse cases to cooperate with authorities. Their website hosts a database of priests who have been publicly accused of child molestation within the United States. The database can be searched via name of the priest, state, or diocese. The goal is to reduce the hiding and shielding of perpetrators by the Church and to encourage more proactive prevention measures by those who supervise clergy members. What may be controversial about this practice is that unlike sex offender registries that identify persons who have been convicted, this list publicizes those who have been accused. This may result in those who are truly innocent being publicly denounced in a media forum. Repercussions, such as vigilantism may cause harm to those who have been falsely accused.

Parents of Murdered Children

The Parents of Murdered Children (POMC) was established in 1978 by the parents of a 19-year-old who was murdered by her ex-boyfriend. The organization today has 100,000 members in 300 local and regional chapters and a national headquarters in Cincinnati. The website for POMC explains their mission as one of providing emotional support, advocacy, prevention strategies as well as educational programs that promote awareness of the plight of parents of murder victims. The purpose of POMC is to work within support groups to achieve these goals. The Speakers' Bureau gives informative presentations often as training for law enforcement, social work, media and religious professionals as well as for community leaders. They sponsor a Murder is Not Entertainment program that protests and boycotts media products they feel are distasteful and disrespectful of co-victims or those loved ones left behind by the murder victim. Examples of media they have targeted include murder mystery dinner theatres and VH1's Music Behind Bars series.

Groups of POMC regularly sponsor Grief Weekend workshops for the self-help development of coping skills for survivors. The organization also has helped to promote a national "Day of Remembrance" that has been initiated locally in many communities. Along those lines, a memorial wall of victims display recognizing loved ones has also been established. Besides a newsletter for publicizing various issues, annual awards highlight the service of dedicated volunteers as well as justice professionals who stand out in their dedication to victims' rights. Finally, it is noted that the POMC were active in campaigning for the Amber Alert system and had an active presence at the 9/11 site.

Truth in Sentencing measures have also been an area of concentration for POMC. They worked toward the establishment of legislation tied to truth in sentencing and operate a Parole Block Program that circulates petitions on the web to gain signatures to be used at upcoming parole hearings to oppose the release of murderers as their cases are scheduled. One of the ironies of this position is that parole is often the only chance that the public has to insure that offenders will be supervised very strictly in the community following their incarceration. Without parole, many will fully discharge their obligations to the state and be released without any monitoring or tracking mechanisms that might also be beneficial to society. The structure and sanctions provided under parole may insure a more disciplined adjustment for offenders. Although POMC may view parole as a benefit or perk that the offender should not be afforded, the truth is that many offenders on community supervision find conditions more unpleasant and restrictive than prison (Petersilia, 1990). One of the potential problems with activism, then, is that often, members of the group do not really understand the system well enough, or are not detached enough to weigh the merits of policy based on relevant information and research.

Advocacy in Action: The Justice for All Act 2004

The Justice for All Act of 2004 is an excellent example of the way advocates struggle to advance their issues into law. The politics and use of media as well as the work of countless volunteers blogging, sending out newsletters and engaging civic resources to pass measures related to victimization is illustrated in this Act. The comprehensiveness of this measure is evidenced in its attempt to involve the victim in every phase of criminal justice decision-making.

The Justice for All Act is a sweeping array of measures that apply to victims of federal offenses, crimes prosecuted in the federal judicial system. The Act extends some former laws and incorporates a number of new piecemeal bills that had been generated within the system over a number of years. For example, it extends the 1990 Victim's Rights and Restitution Act of 1990 and adds The Scott Campbell, Stephanie Roper, Wendy Preston, Louarna Gillis and Nila Lynn Crime Victims' Rights Act, The Debbie Smith Act and the Innocence Protection Act as well as the DNA Sexual Assault Justice Act.

The Debbie Smith Act would enhance the use of DNA testing and attempt to overcome the problems of backlogged rape kit analysis which would assist in identifying rapists faster and insure higher conviction rates. The Innocence Protection Act would also involve improved DNA analysis, particularly for insuring that innocent persons are not convicted because of faulty testing or insufficient databases for comparative sampling. Additional provisions of the legislation enforce formerly identified rights including notification, input, privacy, protection and restitution.

Administration of Victim Organizations

The administration of victim-based organizations often grows more complex as membership grows and projects and goals become more diverse. For most, staffing needs include accountants and bookkeepers familiar with non-profit administration and compliance with all funding regulations and reporting systems. Most need a full-time grant writer and fundraiser as well as someone familiar with media, newsletters, publicity. Administrators must be able to train, schedule and monitor volunteers as well as engage in public speaking to raise awareness for the organization and its needs.

Budgeting for all of the programs and services an organization wants to provide consistently is difficult when it is unclear whether existing sources of money will be available in subsequent funding cycles. In most cases, the price of goods and services, like utilities, continues to rise and emergencies like building repairs or computer failures exhaust any savings. Donors are unpredictable and economic hard times reduce charitable contributions.

One organization, HEAL a domestic violence program for Lincoln County, New Mexico, is typical in its attempts to service a high-needs population in uncertain economic times. They market products such as pasta sauce and a cookbook in many area stores to raise money. They hold golf tournaments and schedule fundraisers at local dinner theaters, concerts and charity auctions. As their website explains the cost of maintaining a 28-bed shelter for victims of domestic violence is expensive. Unlike many shelters, the NEST, is advertised by address which is probably more realistic in a rural area where it is difficult to conceal a location. The facility's first $20,000 was spent on a security system with components listed below.

- Intruder Detection and Reporting System
- Computerized Security Surveillance Program
- Fire and Security—Visible Strobe and Sound Alarms
- 17 Cameras—Inside Facility and On Perimeter
- Audio-Video-Intercom System at Entry to Shelter

- Card-Swipe Security for Resident Entry Into Shelter Courtyard
- Monitored by Staff and First Alarm and Security of Ruidoso
- Emergency 911 Pendants for Staff on Duty
- Lexan Glass throughout Shelter—Bullet Resistant
- Five Emergency Escape Doors
- Panic Buttons throughout Facility and Office

In addition to the security system, the NEST was built with 18-inch walls and steel doors, something which adds to the capital outlay for construction (www.helpendabuseforlife.org).

ADVOCACY IN AN INDUSTRY OF TROUBLED PERSONS

The role of a victim advocate continues to unfold as new social problems are recognized and addressed. For example, just recently, changes were made to upgrade the status of the advocate used in the U. S. military and to provide more protections within the victim-advocate relationship. These improvements were spearheaded by the mother of a murder victim who believed that the military does not take violence against service members, by service members, seriously. She argues that the death of her daughter, Marine Lance Corporal Maria Lauterbach, could have been prevented.

In 2007, Maria Lauterbach told Naval investigators that fellow marine, Cesar Laurean raped her. Laurean was never charged with sexual assault by military or civilian authorities although Maria had the military equivalent of a restraining order against him (Wehrman & Carr, 2008). The subsequent murder of Lauterbach and her unborn child and the discovery of her body buried at Laurean's home has led to reforms in the U. S. Military's response to victims of sexual assault. The "Improved prevention and response to allegations of sexual assault involving members of the Armed Forces" bill is Section 567 of the National Defense appropriations bill of 2010. Through the efforts of Maria's mother Mary Lauterbach, the new law will grant privileged communication status to conversations between an alleged victim and an advocate. The legislation also specifies that victim advocates are full time positions, report outside the normal command structure and require certain training. Lauterbach's family has also filed a wrongful death suit against her accused attacker (Ka, 7, 2010).

Researcher and womens' advocate Donileen Loeske refers to domestic violence services as an industry of troubled persons. Much the same can be said for any of the related victim-service programs. While it is evident that it takes special people to work effectively in this field, they must have the proper authorization, tools and policies at hand in order to best service their clients. In the study of victims, we often fail to examine the agencies and organizations, the volunteers and professional staff that work with very traumatic circumstances every day. The stress of victim work mirrors that of criminal justice in the emotional toll it takes and the way it often changes the outlook of those who encounter people pain on a regular basis.

References

Bureau of Justice Statistics (2008). *Criminal Victimization in the United States*. Washington, DC: U S. Department of Justice. Retrieved from http://www.ojp.usdoj.gov/bjs/abstract/cvusst.htm.

Dunn, J., & Powell-Williams, M. (2007). "Everybody makes choices": Victim advocates and the social construction of battered women's victimization and agency. *Violence Against Women, 13,* 977–1001.

Geberth, V. J. (September 1992). Secondary victims of homicide. *Law and Order, 40*(9), 91–96.

Hurley, M. H. (2009). Restorative practices in institutional settings and at release: Victim wrap around programs. *Federal Probation, 73,* 1. Retrieved from *http://www.uscourts.gov/FederalCourtProbation PretrialServices/FederalProbationJournal.aspx*

Kay, L. (2010, June 2). Lauterbach legislation in Senate. Jacksonville, NC. Retrieved from http://jdnews.com.

King, K. (2004). It hurts so bad: Comparing grieving patterns of the families of murder victims with those of families of death row inmates. *Criminal Justice Policy Review, 15,* 193–211.

Loseke, D. R. (2003). *Thinking about social problems: An introduction to constructionist perspectives*. New York: Aldine.

Myers, J. E. B. (2008). A short history of child protection in America. *Family Law Quarterly, 42,* 449–464.

Petersilia, J. (1990). When probation becomes more dreaded than prison. *Federal Probation, 54*, 23–27.

Springer, C. (2010, July). A mother's driven spirit. *Enchantment: The voice of New Mexico's Rural Electric Cooperative, 62*(7), 10–11.

Umbreit, M. (1994). *Victim meets offender: The impact of restorative justice and mediation.* Monsey, New York: Criminal Justice Press.

Van Ness, D. W., & Heetderks Strong, K. (2010). *Restoring justice: An introduction to restorative justice (4th Ed.).* New Province, NJ: Lexis Nexis.

Webber, R. (2010, June 6). Stop texting behind the wheel. *Parade*, p. 14

Wehrman, J., & Carr, R. (2008, April 20). Civilian, troop sexual assault allegations may spur legislation. *Houston Chronicle*, A1.

Wiebush, R., Freitag, R., & Baird, C. (2001, July). Preventing delinquency through improved child protection services. *Juvenile Justice Bulletin* (NC 187759). Washington, DC: Office of Juvenile Justice and Delinquency Prevention.

Discussion Questions

1. Is the *Justice for All Act* typical of legislation or is it perhaps just typical of victims' legislation. What makes this law different from others we have discussed?
2. What do you think are the characteristics of a good victims advocate? Should advocate volunteers be screened? If so, what type of criteria should be used?
3. Do some online research looking at programs nationwide and attempt to answer this question: "What type of program or services related to DWI could you develop and operate for $1.1 million?" Compare your results with other students and see which efforts appear to be the best use of limited funds and explain why.

Books you may want to read

Lefkowitz, Bernard (1998). *Our guys: The Glen Ridge rape.* Berkeley, CA: Vintage Books

Movies you may want to see

The Brave One. Jodie Foster

Weblinks

http://www.usaonwatch.org/
http://americasmissingadults.com/
http://www.citizensagainsthomicide.org/
http://www.justice.gov/dea/resources/victims_crime.html

CHAPTER 7
Special Victims

DESIGNATING VICTIMS AS SPECIAL

This chapter explores some of the possible explanations why certain victims are designated as special, as well as the effectiveness of measures taken by the criminal justice system on their behalf. A special victim would be one who is given particular attention in case processing. This status is usually based on perceptions about the victim's ability to protect and defend him- or herself. Historically, women and children were considered deserving of preferential or differential treatment both within society and within the criminal justice system. Offenders who harmed members of these groups seemed to receive more severe sentences as judicial and jury sentiments supported the use of affirmative measures because of their presumed vulnerability. Over time, the rise in violent juvenile crime as well as women's struggles for equality in social, political and economic positions served to decrease social perceptions of vulnerability. As a result, special treatment became less viable.

Cultural influences and special-interest groups, as well as the popularity of notorious cases, have all affected the way some victims are evaluated as more "special" than others. Victimology textbooks traditionally recognize the concept of special victims and often discuss, in addition to the categories of women and children, the categories of the mentally-ill and the physically- or developmentally-disabled. In this chapter we will look at additional categories of special victims as identified by media coverage, legislatures, and funding initiatives as well as some of the more recent and active special-interest groups. The reader may find it interesting to consider other special populations who may be in need of similar considerations or predict which groups may qualify for that status in years to come.

THE UNBORN CHILD

In 1993 John George Brewer was the first inmate executed in Arizona using lethal injection. His case was also one of the first in which prosecutors considered pursuing the death of the fetus carried by his slain fiancé. The prosecution's decision to seek the death penalty solely based on the death of the adult female highlighted the weaknesses in existing laws that would make any other option unfeasible. In fact, the court ruled that, under existing Arizona law, the definition of homicide did not allow for charges in the case of the unborn child (*State v. Brewer*). Today in some states, defendants may be charged with murder of a fetus but not manslaughter, a barrier many prosecutors find daunting as intent to kill is much harder to establish in cases where the fetus is the secondary victim— meaning that the woman is the intended victim of the attack.

To many, a fetus represents perhaps the ultimate vulnerable victim. Our social value-system affirms that all pregnant women have a responsibility to get prenatal care, eat nutritious foods, and refrain from any behaviors that can cause harm to the unborn child. However, attempts to prosecute pregnant women for behavior deemed unsafe have resulted in controversy and debate among advocates for women and children. Some have claimed that the criminalization of specific actions will result in "pregnancy policing," driving more at-risk women away from critical prenatal care. Others argue that scientific evidence of the effects of certain chemicals or activities is not advanced enough to warrant prosecution. Most are concerned that poor, minority women will bear the brunt of the criminalization process even though they are not the only ones engaging in risk-taking behaviors.

The Crack Baby Panic

One example of the construction of a social problem leading to calls for more legal intervention in pregnancy was the crack-baby phenomenon. In 1989 (July 30) *Washington Post* columnist Charles Krauthammer predicted "The inner-city crack epidemic is now giving birth to the newest horror: a bio-underclass, a generation of physically-damaged cocaine babies whose biological inferiority is stamped at birth." His sentiments reflected the social panic created by the myth of 'crack babies' as he predicted "Theirs will be a life of certain suffering, of probable deviance, of permanent inferiority." Crack cocaine, readily-available in the United States in the early 1980s, was a cheaper alternative to the more expensive powder cocaine. Crack addiction became associated with the urban drug problem in poor, minority neighborhoods. Although powdered cocaine and crack cocaine are pharmacologically the same and both are metabolized by the body the same, crack cocaine has been given a more negative social image.

In the criminal court system, possession of powdered cocaine continues to carry much shorter sentences than crack cocaine suggesting that there is a moral stigma attached to its use. Although crack-addicted mothers were singled out for criminal prosecution, research was never able to tie their substance abuse directly to any specific negative outcomes. Much more was known, for example, about effects of fetal-alcohol syndrome, but that avenue may have been deemed more difficult to pursue with criminal charges. Indications are, experts say, that a child exposed to the troubled upbringing of a mother's drug-addicted lifestyle presents many variables that can be harmful to children aside from one specific substance. "Genetics, the birth mother's other habits, prenatal health care and home environment play a role" (Vargas, 2010). Many of the 22,000 babies left at hospitals, often by mothers fearing prosecution, have become successful high school graduates thriving in foster care and adoption. One such baby, adopted before the age of one, did not find out about his past until middle-school. He explains (Vargas, 2010):

"Honestly, I had the perception that crack babies were born messed up, that they went through their life having problems," said Jeff, who was a B student in high school, played sports and has worked part time since he was 14. He works at Starbucks and attends Howard Community College, aiming for a degree in accounting. "I don't see other kids doing things that I don't see myself capable of doing."

Understandably, media and politicians have consistently focused on the mother's role in the abuse of an unborn child perhaps because it is such an emotionally-charged issue. Because the mother-child bond is a core value of our society, we seem to have great social consensus on the need to condemn violations of that relationship.

However, the fetus can also be victimized while in the womb through harm caused to the mother by another. In many cases, pregnant women who are assaulted or murdered are assaulted at the hands of a husband or boyfriend. There are many explanations as to why significant others would harm their pregnant partner and unborn children. Jealousy, escape, control, finances, and fear are among the factors that may motivate these individuals.

Prenatal Violence

Rae Carruth, a former NFL player, stunned the nation when he was charged with hiring a person to kill his pregnant girlfriend. On November 16, 1999, Cherica Adams was driving behind Carruth's vehicle after an evening out. After being shot by someone in a car that pulled up behind her, Adams was able to call 911 and place Carruth and an unknown accomplice at the scene in the incident. Although Carruth maintains his innocence, he was convicted of conspiracy to commit murder and sentenced to 18 years in prison. Adams died as a result of the attack but her son was delivered 10-weeks-premature by C-section. The surviving son has cerebral palsy as a result of the loss of oxygen to his brain following the shooting. Although his caretaker grandmother won a $5.8 million judgment against Carruth, there are no assets available for her to access (St. George, 2004).

The circumstances facing Cherica's mother are not uncommon. Data indicate that poor, less-educated, younger, minority women who did not intentionally become pregnant are more likely to be victims of domestic abuse. In addition, Black women are more likely than White women to be murdered when pregnant (Flavin, 2008). According to a *Washington Post* study of 1,367 pregnant or postpartum women who were killed, the children left behind face not only health struggles and financial difficulties but usually the removal of or abandonment by the surviving parent and the inheritance of a legacy of violence. In one state, Virginia, St George reports, "68 children were left behind after the killing of their pregnant or postpartum mothers since 1990." In one year, 2002, there were 62 children born under these circumstances nationwide. One grandmother explained the deep pain she is left with this way: every birthday for the child is a reminder of the death day of his mother (St George, 2004).

After the remains of a pregnant Laci Peterson and her unborn child washed up on the shores of San Francisco Bay, her mother was committed to changing the way the law viewed these cases. Laci's husband Scott Peterson was subsequently charged with first-degree murder in the death of his wife and second-degree murder in the death of his unborn child Connor. On March 16, 2005, Scott Peterson was found guilty by a jury of his peers and sentenced to death. Sharon Rocha, Laci's mother, campaigned for federal legislation that would prosecute both the pregnant woman and the fetus as separate murder counts (Rocha, 2006). Laci and Conner's law, the *Unborn Victims of Violence Act* was signed by President Bush on April 1, 2004. While this bill applies only to federal criminal cases, many states have developed their own fetal-homicide statutes that provide for charging offenders in a similar manner.

As a result of current legal trends, one could technically argue that the pregnant woman does not quite fit into a special-victim category; nor does the fetus, because someone guilty of this offense now faces the same penalties as for the murder of any other child covered under existing penal statutes. Still, there have been significant legal changes in this area since John Brewer murdered his pregnant fiancé in 1987.

THE HOMELESS

For the last two decades researchers and activist groups have attempted to get an accurate census count of the homeless in America in hopes that proportional funding and services might be made available. Current estimates place the number of homeless in this country anywhere from 600,000 to 2.5 million (Congressional Research Service, 2005). While the average length of time a person may remain homeless is about eight months, programming emphasis has been placed on the chronic, long-term, homeless person who may be displaced from housing afforded under mental health residential care, or substance abuse rehabilitation, or veterans' temporary services.

Research indicates that the homeless may be at higher risk of victimization, particularly juveniles who may have fewer resources and experiences to prepare them for life on the streets. Substance abuse and other high-risk behaviors, histories of sexual abuse and neglect, and post-traumatic stress disorder seem to be related to higher levels of victimization among the youthful homeless population at the hands of both strangers and acquaintances. Survival strategies such as prostitution, dumpster diving and panhandling also seem to increase risk of violent victimization for both adults and teens (Simons, Whitbeck, & Bales, 1989; Tyler, Melander, & Noel, 2009; Tyler, Whitbeck, Hoyt & Cauce, 2004).

Theories of Homelessness

There are numerous reasons for which individuals may become homeless. Some are veterans of war suffering from post-traumatic stress disorders, some are former prisoners, alcohol and/or substance abuse addicts, and some are dealing with mental illnesses of various types. Many have experienced economic crises and have lost access to even temporary residences. Some are fleeing domestic violence, particularly mothers who leave their abuser with children in tow. Zorza (1991) suggests that over half of all homeless women and children are domestic violence survivors.

Conflict theory would suggest that competition for goods and services allows the wealthy to control the economy to their own benefit, thus creating groups who are disadvantaged. Industrial change results in surplus populations as workers are displaced by improved technology. The "have nots," as Karl Marx referred to the powerless workers, are not able to access the skills necessary to stay employed. In short, a form of "planned skills obsolescence" serves to keep competition for jobs high and insures a group of unemployable and low-skilled individuals, some of which will become homeless.

Social disorganization theory would argue that homelessness is caused by the deterioration of the social environment and, thus, the homeless are victims of environmental circumstances. Certain communities suffer in the absence of meaningful services and programs causing a breakdown in social cohesion and support. Many areas in which the homeless are found are considered dilapidated and uninhabitable, breeding fear, inequity and deviance.

Victimization of the Homeless

Given contemporary theorizing on homelessness, it would be reasonable to assume that victimization of this group is less likely to come to the attention of the criminal justice system. The homeless are a marginalized group within society who are closely identified with deviance both by physical space and the inability or unwillingness to conform to the norms of society. Generally, the homeless are located in transient, crime-prone areas and, given their exposure on the streets, are a vulnerable population. They may dwell in areas with limited or infrequent law enforcement patrol, and commonly in places that are dimly-lit and close to bars, as well as other venues known for criminal activity.

According to the National Coalition for the Homeless (2009), between 1999 and 2008 there were approximately 900 acts of violence against the homeless documented by advocacy groups and organizations. Homeless victims of violence may be less likely to report attacks against them because of fear of law enforcement, concerns that they will not be believed, fear of reprisal, or they may perceive that their victimization will be viewed as secondary to their homeless status. Violent victimization of this group has come to the attention of state legislatures prompting the addition of hate-crime protections for the homeless.

Video exploitation has also been used as a means to violate and humiliate the homeless. *Bumfights.com* was created by six skateboarding teens to entice homeless individuals to attack each other for money and alcohol. The videos featured Rufus Hannah and Donald Brennan, both San Diego military veterans. Brennan, a two-time-decorated Vietnam War veteran, was paid $200 to have the word 'bumfight' tattooed to his forehead.

Initially used as a tool for suburban, middle-class youth to exploit the homeless for profit, it is aimed at a teen audience as the videos are generally enhanced by popular music. Because of the success of bumfights, several copycats have emerged to exploit the homeless for profit. Such acts included paying the homeless to perform stunts, pull out their teeth with pliers, set themselves on fire, defecate on the streets, smash their heads through windows and fight other homeless individuals (Lyman, 2002). Doward and Deen (2004) report that

> ...one gang, known as the Three Eleven Boys, based in Las Vegas, filmed a series of late-night fights that ended with several participants being taken to a hospital. In Australia a group of teenagers who had watched the bumfights video killed a tramp when they set fire to his shelter, burning it to the ground.

Charged with conspiracy, solicitation of a felony, and illegally paying people to fight, the youths have since served community service sentences. Still, Ryan McPherson, the 19-year-old producer of the films sold the rights to the series for an alleged $1.5 million, giving rise to the term "thug entrepreneur." According to an official from the National Health Care for the Homeless Council, the offenses seem to illustrate "the generally dismissive public attitude toward homeless people" (Lyman, 2002).

Intervention and Prevention for Homeless Victims

Pressure from activist groups, highlighting states' lack of services and programs for the homeless, resulted in the passage of federal legislation in 1987. The *McKinney-Vento Homeless Assistance Act* funded a broad array of initiatives, many of which have been refunded by subsequent legislatures. There is the Education for Homeless Children and Youth Program, the Emergency Food and Shelter Program and the Projects for Assistance in Transition from Homelessness. There is also a Consolidated Runaway and Homeless Youth Program, Street Outreach Program and a Homeless Veterans Program.

　　　Although homelessness was long considered a problem that individual states and jurisdictions could address on their own, laws that would create protections for this group were slow to evolve. In 2004, California enacted a law that required police training on hate crimes against the homeless and, in 2006, Maine legislation allowed judges imposing sentences to consider the homelessness of the victim as an enhancement to an offense. In 2008, Alaska passed a law that officially designated the homeless as a vulnerable population. By 2009, a number of states had added the homeless to the list of groups protected under the umbrella of hate-crime statutes (National Coalition for the Homeless, 2009).

ELDER ABUSE

The term "granny battering" was first used around the 1970s. Prior to this time, elderly victimization was virtually ignored. Granny battering brought to light the many issues of victimization and violence against the elderly. Even so, a standard definition of elder abuse has yet to be formulated. Defining and identifying elder abuse is critical for serving the needs of the more than 36 million persons in this country who are now 65-years-of-age and older. By 2030, that number is expected to double (Bulman, 2010). And, if reported rates of elder abuse remain constant at just under 2%, there would be 1.2 million victims.

In 1988, Pillemer and Finkelhor estimated that one-in-fourteen elderly individuals may be a victim of domestic abuse. Between 1986 and 1996, however, The National Center on Elder Abuse (NCEA) (2005) estimates that one to two million elders have been abused but that only one-in-fourteen cases will be reported. As with other forms of crime, attempts to increase reporting have been made through educational and awareness campaigns and the passage of mandatory reporting laws. The majority of elder-abuse victims in domestic settings were female. However, there was no significant gender difference between the perpetrators as males (47.4%) and females (48.9%) committed the crime at about the same rate. According to Payne (2005), adult children are the most likely perpetrators of elder abuse and, as the NCEA (2005) adds, spouses and other family members are the second-most-likely perpetrators.

Although most elder abuse occurs at the hands of family members, not all family members are equally responsible for the protection of their elderly relatives. Examining the court ruling in *People v. Heitzman* (1994), it was obvious that California statutes did not adequately identify who could be held responsible when neglect of the elderly led to death. In that case, daughter Susan Heltzman may have known that her father was suffering from dehydration, malnutrition, and bed sores that led to septic shock, and perhaps she even had the duty to report his condition while he was living with her brothers, but because she was not his legal caretaker, she could not be held accountable for his death.

Still, resources and services designated specifically for elderly victims are sparse, as this group did not historically appear to have as great a need for domestic violence intervention as their younger couple counterparts. Thus elderly domestic-violence victims are more likely to remain in abusive relationships due to financial need, shame, and family loyalty (Nelesen, 2003).

Although bruising is one of the indicators of abuse in these cases, medical analysis must differentiate carefully between accidental bruising to which the elderly are prone and intentionally-inflicted injuries. Experts indicate that abusive bruises are often larger, with most measuring two inches or larger in diameter. And, as one study determined, victims of physical abuse "were much more likely to have bruises on the head and neck, especially the face, and on the posterior torso. Researchers also noted significant bruising on the right arm, perhaps because people raised their arms in an attempt to block an attacker" (Bulman, 2010). Although physical neglect and financial exploitation promptly come to mind, institutional abuse is also relatively common (Payne, 2005, p. 6).

Institutional Abuse of the Elderly

Today, almost two million people live in nursing homes nationwide. This figure represents about 7.4% of all Americans who are seventy-five-years-of-age or older (Nasser, 2007). Although the rates now are somewhat lower than previous years, many more individuals are in alternative forms of supervised care—elderly day-care centers, assisted-living and hospice arrangements—that mean that they are being cared for by individuals other than family members. With this industry growing every year and with population trends showing America aging, it is important to have clear-cut standards and definitions that would identify abuse and allow for its prosecution.

In addition to physical, sexual, and emotional abuse, elder abuse includes verbal abuse, material abuse as with theft and fraud, and various caretaker abuses such as over-medicating, withholding medication, and improper discipline or punishment. In long-term care situations, inappropriate use of physical restraints can also take place. Research has indicated that a significant portion of elderly who report abuse say that multiple forms of abuse were taking place (Post, et al., 2010).

It is generally understood that the majority of elderly-abuse cases go unreported. Even when discovered by an institution, officials rarely report these incidents to police. A CBSNEWS report (Sims, 2001) suggested that one-in-three elderly residents are abused in nursing homes. Almost a third of the 1600 nursing homes included in the study were cited for some form of abuse, be it sexual abuse, physical abuse, or death (Sims, 2001). In one quarterly report from 2000, twenty-six percent of nursing homes received violations for instances of poor record keeping and failure to implement practices that would control abuse (Associated Press, 2002).

In taped testimony shortly before she died, Helen Love, a then 75-year-old grandmother, described how she was pummeled by a staff member because she soiled herself while a resident at a Sacramento, California nursing home. She was choked and her neck, wrists and hands were broken. The perpetrator plead guilty to elder abuse and served one year in jail for the fatal assault (Associated Press, 2002).

According to the NCEA (2005), which has been collecting data on reports of elder abuse since 1986, it is very difficult to track elder victimization as there is no uniform reporting system in place and, further, there is no national center for data dissemination. Still, interest in this area of crime prevention has been growing. The University of California at Irvine has instituted an Elder Abuse Forensic Center and San Bernardino County, California has been operating an Elder and Dependent Adult Abuse Prosecution Family Violence Unit in the District Attorney's Office since 2000 (Berson, 2010).

BULLYING

Bullying is generally defined as an aggressive behavior that, over time, physically, emotionally, and or psychologically harms another. Bullying is typically classified as a behavior that occurs between school-aged children in which a perceived weaker student is taunted and or physically harmed by a perceived tougher student. Most often these instances are understood as developmental phases that one will most likely experience, and with age, most likely ceases. However, bullying has been transformed from typical school-yard behavior to an area of high-need responsiveness. This may be because bullying has the potential to become deadly as significant numbers of students report either owning a gun or having access to a gun, carrying guns to or near schools, and the weapons available are most likely to be automatic and semi-automatic handguns (Nofziger, 2001).

The literature suggests that bullying can be classified into three types: verbal, physical, and emotional. While verbal and physical bullying are fairly obvious, emotional bullying is further defined as consistently or purposefully denying a victim's wishes, withholding friendship and ostracizing or excluding one from activities and making gestures or faces designed to hurt feelings (Nofziger, 2001). According to a national study on school-safety indicators, about 32 percent of children in the age group 12–18 indicated that they were bullied at school in 2007. This included being made fun of, being the target of rumors, being threatened, having their property destroyed or being publicly excluded from certain activities (Dinkes et al., 2009).

The 1999 Columbine school shootings in Littleton, Colorado provide an example of such retaliation. The Columbine massacre spurred a national response to bullying in the United States. Dylan Klebold and Eric Harris were the students who killed and wounded several students at Columbine High School. The two were allegedly bullied and subsequently avenged an attack that resulted in the murder-suicide of both students. Since Columbine, several policies, strategies, and programs were created to address the issue of bullying.

Cyberbullying occurs when an electronic device is used to "taunt, insult, threaten, harass, and/or intimidate a peer" (Raskauskas et al., 2007, p. 565). The use of electronic means to torment others presents a challenge to authorities because discipline is traditionally associated with the monitoring and control of physical space. Cyberbullying, on the other hand, allows for anonymity of the perpetrator and occurs in text messaging and emails, chat rooms, and interactive game sites. Webpages provide a forum for cyberbullies to embarrass, defame, harass, and humiliate their victims. According to the Cyberbullying

Research Center's data on 6,000 preteens and teens, almost one-third have been a victim of cyberbullying. More than half of the attacks take place in chat rooms and the type of abuse seems to vary by gender. Hinduja and Patchin explain that "Girls tend to spread rumors. Boys will say bad things online or post hurtful or embarrassing photos or videos." The researchers also have found that the reasons given for cyberbullying include revenge as well as "just for fun."

For 16-year-old Rachel Neblett, the "fun" turned deadly. She took her own life in October of 2006 following a period of being cyber-stalked through her MySpace account. As the textbox below indicates, a number of teen suicides have been tied to this new bullying trend. These cases suggest that, as internet use becomes more integrated into daily life, so does its potential abuse. By 2010, the broadband penetration rate in this country was over 74% (Nhan, 2010). About one-third of young people have internet access in their own bedrooms and the average 8-to-18-year-old spends more than 7.5 hours per day hooked up to smart-phones, computers, and other electronic devices. It has also been determined that the heaviest users of electronic media are more likely to report being depressed, getting into trouble, doing poorly in school and not getting along with their parents (Lewin, 2010).

Prevention strategies to address bullying in schools have taken several forms. Many programs focus on alerting education profession-als to the warning signs of bullying. Some programs seek to identify bullies and offer strategies for these individuals to avoid harassing behaviors. Other approaches have been used to help victims of bullying deal with their emotions and vulnerabilities. Experts remind us that parents of identified bullies should be included in bullying prevention, thus bullying should be viewed as a community concern rather than an issue that only affects one specific victim and bully.

Mean Girls: Cyberbullying Blamed for Teen Suicides
by Yunji de Nies, Susan Donaldson James & Sarah Netter
Jan. 28, 2010

Massachusetts girl, 15, (Phoebe Prince) was reportedly bullied online before taking her life.... Friends say the Irish immigrant, who moved to South Hadley just last year, had been the recipient of nasty online messages and e-mails. "Someone told her to go hang herself, and I don't really know who that was," student Jessica Chapdelaine said. "But she was getting bullied by some people, because there were people talking about her and I guess she just didn't like being hated."

In Lewisville, Texas, a 9-year old boy hung himself in the nurse's bathroom at his elementary school 11-year-old Carl Joseph Walker-Hoover hung himself with an extension cord after bullies repeatedly called him gay.

In 2006, Megan Meier killed herself after the mother of a former friend created a fictitious profile to harass the Missouri 13-year-old. Three years earlier, 13-year-old Ryan Patrick Halligan of Vermont hung himself after he'd been bullied online.

Currently, 41 states and the District of Columbia have anti-bullying measures and 23 have statutes against cyberbullying. Massachusetts is not one of them. Massachusetts' House Bill 483, sponsored by the Anti-Defamation League of New England, would require schools to have anti-bullying training and procedures in place. It would also require districts to produce an annual report citing incidents for the state legislature and the department of primary and secondary education.

http://abcnews.go.com/GMA/Parenting/girls-teen-suicide-calls-attention-cyberbullying/story?id=9685026

CREATING VICTIMS IN POSITIONS OF TRUST

From daycare and Little League to Girl Scouts and church, parents find it necessary to rely on outside agencies and activities for a significant portion of their children's lives. In doing so, they assume employees and volunteers in positions of trust have been carefully screened and have no history of criminal behavior. One of the mechanisms that businesses and services use to make checks on prospective staff is the National Crime Information Center's (NCIC) background check. The FBI's database collection that makes up the NCIC receives five million police inquiries per day and yet many operations either don't check or don't follow up on reports of suspicious actions by staff members. It is also possible that when offenses are detected, they are the first reported for a perpetrator, so no record would have been found in a background investigation even when employers are diligent.

Typically, workers in child-care services and day-care centers are low-paid and turnover is high. Likewise, criticisms of foster-care systems and child protective services point to overworked staff and unmonitored caseloads that seem to tolerate and exacerbate child abuse. In Texas, three children's deaths that could have arguably been prevented were blamed on faulty supervision by the office of Child Protective Services (CPS).

According to newspaper reports, the Houston Region CPS alone averages over 21,000 investigations each year involving over 35,000 alleged victims. Still, neglect or abuse was substantiated for only about 6,000 of those children (Langford, 2009). Plans to improve operations include more drug monitoring of parents, hiring more investigators and teaming caseworkers with trained law enforcement investigators when making repeat calls to homes with a CPS case history. CPS is also altering policies that required children to be in a direct emergency situation before they could be removed.

The death of Jabriel Walder is an example of the need for such protections. Despite the fact that a number of professionals including doctors, nurses, child-care workers and law-enforcement officers indicated that he was being abused, CPS failed to take action. Although the 3-year-old's death resulted from a blow that severed his pancreas, post-mortem findings also indicated 56 non-accidental scars on his 25-pound body (Associated Press, 1999). While many are resigned to the likelihood that government agencies will be ineffective in stopping child abuse, parents continually claim to be blindsided by the violations of trust they and their children suffer from close family associates like teachers, coaches, club leaders, and clergy.

From Local Churches to the Vatican: Sex Abuse Scandal

Paul Richard Shanley has become the infamous figure behind the Catholic Church sex-abuse scandal that received nationwide attention in early 2002. Shanley worked with wayward juveniles, often in the streets of Boston in the 1960s and 1970s. The Boston Archdiocese was aware of Shanley's questionable psychiatric status, yet he was recommended for senior positions within the Catholic Church and was eventually moved to California. At least 25 victims have come forward to claim that they were sexually assaulted by Shanley (Lavoie, 2008).

News accounts of sex abuse by clergy have focused on young boys, as they appear to represent four times as many victims as girls. Nonetheless, reports indicate that girls who are victims of clergy abuse are younger at the time of the offenses (Wingert, 2010). Although only about two percent of Catholic clergy are represented in child sexual-abuse cases, a study at John Jay College of Criminal Justice and funded by the United States Conference of Catholic Bishops, found that between 1960 and 2002, almost 4,400 clergymen, mostly priests, were accused of sexually abusing 10,667 victims. The scandal has caused many to question celibacy within the Catholic Church and, most importantly, the Archdiocese cover-up of sexual misconduct. Many of the child victims, now adults, have publicly-revealed histories of child sexual abuse. Other victims have declined to do so. One father of a child victim suggested that he failed to report details of abuse because of "disbelief, fear of scandal, love for the church and for his son, and a desire to shield him from future harm" (Wakin, 2002).

Although the number of allegations against priests has begun to decline, the financial settlements are just beginning to be tallied up. According to the John Jay study, in 2008, the Church paid out $324 million in payments to victims (Associated Press, 2010). In 2009 that figure was $55 million but that did not include: "attorney's fees (almost $29 million), support for clergy offenders including therapy, living and legal costs (almost $11 million), and therapy for victims not covered by settlements (another $6.5 million)." In addition, the diocese also paid $21 million for a range of child protection, training and education services, including background checks. The "safe environment" curriculum will be integrated into the faith's private school and other religious education programs' lesson plans (Associated Press, 2010).

HUMAN TRAFFICKING

Human trafficking is not a new term. In fact, the practice can be traced to the African slave trade and even further back to biblical times. Although the motive, exploiting others for economic gain, remains the same, the methods and types of trafficking have become more sophisticated. Human trafficking affects all countries and has no age limit or boundaries. Officials estimate that somewhere between 600,000 to 800,000 persons are trafficked each year. About 90 percent of the victims in sex-related trades are female and about 15,000 enter the U.S. every year. In modern times human trafficking was thought to be a problem of neighboring countries and continents, as the perpetrators are often the same nationality as the victims (IFC International, 2007). However, today's human trafficking has become an issue of global proportions and, with the support of advocates, agencies, and organizations, federal legislation was created to address and respond to issues relating to sex-trafficking victims. The Trafficking Victims Protection Act of 2000 (TVPA) was signed into federal law by President Bill Clinton. The TVPA provides resources to investigate and prosecute known or suspected human-trafficking organizations, to provide information about the dangers of human trafficking for those deemed at-risk for victimization, to protect and provide economic and outreach support for women and children victims of human trafficking, and to train criminal justice personnel to identify, respond, and enforce potential instances of human trafficking.

Human trafficking has been called modern-day slavery, although many of those abused by the practices do not view themselves as victims (Newton, Mulcahy & Martin, 2008). Because they may have paid some initial fees for transportation, victims may feel culpable and believe that they will be arrested if the scheme is exposed. Some traffickers may be sending a small stipend to the victims' families in order to compel their continued participation. Still others may be forced into committing offenses like transporting drugs and have been threatened with being reported to law enforcement agencies if they renege on their tasks (Logan, Walker & Hunt, 2009). Many who are forced into work are underpaid or unpaid laborers in domestic services and agriculture. Often, nail salons and massage parlors are a front for the sex industry. Some victims have their identities taken away, some are tortured, others still are deprived of their liberties. Family members back in their countries of origin may also be threatened. In many cases, victims fear deportation more than anything else (Clawson, Dutch & Cummings, 2006).

According to the National Sexual Violence Resource Center, approximately 100,000 children are exploited every year in the child sex-trafficking industry. Most of the children are sexually exploited by the age of 13 and most are introduced to the industry by way of supposed caretakers, boyfriends, or pimps (Shared Hope, 2009). Many uninformed parents are given promises of a better life for their children; adequate food, clothing, shelter, and education may be seen as a worthy cause to give up control of their children to others. "They yield their children because couriers dangle the promise of school like a diamond necklace" (Skinner, 2008, p. 8). Many women in poorer countries are lured by human traffickers with the promise of a job, thus providing support for the family in the homeland. However, when many victims arrive, they are greeted with prostitution, threats, violence, and forced labor. Among those victims trafficked for labor, most are Asian, are just as likely to be male as female, and tend to be younger than their abusers (Newton, Mulcahy, & Martin, 2008).

Most victims of human trafficking do not know how to seek help from, or are reluctant to contact, authorities even though they desperately need housing, shelter, medical care, and counseling, and legal advocacy assistance (Clawson, Dutch & Cummings, 2006). There are many reasons why victims do not come forward: fear of reprisal, ignorance of the law, fear of the United States, no access to the outside world, personal safety, cognitive immaturity, and other personal reasons.

THE SPECIAL VICTIM AND CONTEMPORARY LAW

As the examples in this chapter illustrate there are indications, perhaps on a global scale, that certain victims are viewed as deserving special consideration in the eyes of the law and the justice system. While there may be debate over which groups require the designation of "special," most agree that official mechanisms such as sentencing enhancements need to be available when those individuals are viewed as more vulnerable and at greater risk for victimization. The use of aggravating conditions or special sentencing provisions provide a rational and defensible approach to the plight of these victims, if for no other reason that their harm may diminish our status as a civilized society. Hate crime laws in particular recognize the way race, ethnicity, religion, and sexual orientation may increase the likelihood of one being targeted for violent crimes and the penalties for such offenses are much more severe.

As with other areas studied by victimologists, we run the risk of not meeting the needs of victims if we concentrate specifically on offenders by making punishments harsher and longer for them, yet doing nothing directly for the victims. While it is understood that special victims need special assistance with navigating and participating in the criminal justice process, it is also clear they will have other, non-criminal-justice-system needs that must be addressed. The use of advocates and support groups may be important steps in making the system responsive to the circumstances of special victims.

References

Associated Press. (2010, March 23). Report: Catholic clergy abuse claims drop in USA. *USA Today*, A1.

Associated Press. (1999, September 27). CPS reportedly found its efforts were lax before child was killed. *Houston Chronicle*, A19.

Associated Press. (2002, March 5). Abuse in nursing care focus of report. *Los Angeles Times*, A9.

Berson, S. (2010). Prosecuting elder abuse cases. *NIJ Journal, 265*, 8–9.

Bulman, P. (2010). Elder abuse emerges from shadows of public consciousness. *NIJ Journal, 265*, 4–7.

Clawson, H. J., Dutch, N., & Cummings, M. (2006, October). *Law enforcement responses to human trafficking and the implications for victims: Current practices and lessons learned.* Fairfax, VA: ICF International (for National Institute of Justice)

Congressional Research Service (2005). Homelessness: Recent statistics, targeted federal programs, and recent legislation. Washington, DC: Library of Congress.

Dinkes, R., Kemp, J., Baum, K., & Snyder, T. (2009). *Indicators of school crime and safety: 2008.* Washington, DC: Bureau of Justice Statistics, National Center for Educational Statistics, Institute of Education Sciences.

Doward, J., & Deen, S. (2004, May 16). Outrage as TV plans to screen brawling tramps. *The Observer,* 11.

Flavin, J. (2008). *Our bodies, our crimes: The policing of women's reproduction in America.* New York: NYU Press.

Hinduja, S., & Patchin, J. W. (forthcoming). Bullying, cyberbullying, and suicide. *Archives of Suicide Research.*

IFC International (2007, April). *Evaluation of a comprehensive services for victims of human trafficking.* Washington, DC: National Institute of Justice.

Krauthammer, C. (1989, July 30). Children of cocaine. *Washington Post.*

Langford, T. (2009, September 5). State launches review of CPS. *Houston Chronicle,* A1.

Lavoie, D. (May 29, 2008). A former priest seeks new trial. *Boston Globe.* Retrieved from http://www.boston.com/news/local/ articles/ 2008/05/29/a_former_priest_seeks_new_trial/

Lewin, T. (2010, January 24). Researchers shocked at kids' online time. *Houston Chronicle,* G8.

Logan, T., Walker, R., & Hunt, G. (2009). Understanding human trafficking in the United States. *Trauma, Violence, & Abuse, 10,* 3–30.

Lyman, R. (2002, September 26). 2 arrested over video of homeless. *The New York Times,* A1.

National Center on Elder Abuse (2005). *15 questions and answers about elder abuse.* Washington, DC: National Center on Elder Abuse.

National Coalition for the Homeless. (2009, August). *Hate crimes and violence against people experiencing homelessness.* Factsheet. Washington, DC: National Coalition for the Homeless.

Nasser, H. E. (2007, September 27). Fewer seniors live in nursing homes. *USA Today,* Retrieved from http://www.usatoday.com/ news/nation/census/2007-09-27-nursing-homes_N.htm

Nelesen, D. (2003, August 30). Violence in the home—unwanted guest. *San Diego Union Tribune,* A1.

Newton, P. J., Mulcahy, T. M., & Martin, S. E. (2008, September). *Finding victims of human trafficking.* Washington, DC: National Institute of Justice (NORC Report).

Nhan, J. (2010). *Policing cyberspace.* El Paso, TX: LFB Scholarly Publishing.

Nofziger, S. (2001). *Bullies, fights, and guns: Testing self-control theory with juveniles.* New York: LFB Scholarly Publishing.

Payne, B. K. (2005). *Crime and elder abuse.* Springfield, IL: Charles C. Thomas.

Pillemer, K., & Finkelhor, D. (1988). The prevalence of elder abuse: A random sample survey. *The Gerontologist, 28,* 51–57.

People v. Heitzman 886 P. 2d 1229 (1994).

Post, L., Page, C., Conner, T., Prokhorov, A., Fang, Y., & Biroscak, B. (2010). Elder abuse in long-term care: Types, patterns, and risk factors. *Research on Aging, 32,* 323–348.

Rocha, S. (2006). *For Laci: A mother's story of love, loss and justice.* New York: Three Rivers Press.

Sampson, R. (2009, May). *Bullying in school.* Washington, DC: Office of Community Oriented Policing (COPS).

Shared Hope (2009, May). *The national report on domestic minor sex trafficking.* Vancouver, WA: Shared Hope.

Skinner, B. E. (2008). *A crime so monstrous.* New York: Free Press.

St. George, D. (2004, December 21). Mending shattered childhoods: Newborns, siblings and substitute caregivers endure reminders of loss. *Washington Post,* A1.

Simons, R., Whitbeck, L., & Bales, A. (1989). Life on the streets: Victimization and psychological distress among the adult homeless *Journal of Interpersonal Violence, 4,* 482–501.

Sims, M. (2001, July 30). One in three US nursing homes cited for abuse. CBSNEWS report. Retrieved from http://www.cbsnews.com/stories/2002/01/31/health/main327668. shtml

State v. Brewer, 170 Ariz. 486, 826 P.2d 783 (1992).

Terry, K. (2010). *The nature and scope of the problem of sexual abuse of minors by Catholic priests and deacons in the United States.* New York City: John Jay College of Criminal Justice.

Tyler K., Melander L., & Noel, H. (2009). Bidirectional partner violence among homeless young adults: Risk factors and outcomes. *Journal of Interpersonal Violence, 24,* 1014–1035.

Tyler, K., Whitbeck, L., Hoyt D., & Cauce, A. (2004). Risk factors for sexual victimization among male and female homeless and runaway youth. *Journal of Interpersonal Violence, 19,* 503–20.

Vargas, T. (2010, April 18). Once written off, 'crack babies' have grown into success stories. *The Washington Post,* A1.

Wakin, D. J. (2002, May 31). Family says church know of allegations. *The New York Times,* B1.

Whitaker, B. (2001, July 31). Nursing home abuse increasing: Approximately 1.5 million U.S. seniors living in nursing homes. CBSNEWS. Retrieved from http:www.cbsnews.com/stories/2001/07/30/national/main304038.shtml.

Wingert, P. (2010, April 15). What about the girls? Boys aren't the only victims of the Catholic Church's sex-abuse scandal. *Newsweek.* Retrieved from http://www.newsweek.com/2010/04/14/what-about-the-girls.html

Zorza, J. (1991–92). Woman battering: A major cause of homelessness. *Clearinghouse Review, 25,* 421.

Discussion Questions

1. Should we continue to designate some victims as "special"? If so, how do we best address the needs of special victims? What else can be done in terms of prevention? Intervention? Or treatment?
2. What other categories of special victims do you think should be recognized and why? Are there any types of victims discussed in this chapter that you do not consider to be "special needs"? Why?
3. Who shares in the liability for victimization that is perpetrated by people in positions of trust and how would you evaluated the measures that have been taken to date to reduce victimization by those in positions of trust.

Books You May Want to Read

Salcido, Carmina (2009). *Not lost forever: My story of survival.* New York: William Morrow.

Warshaw, Robin (1994). *I never called it rape: The MS report on recognizing, fighting, and surviving date and acquaintance rape.* New York: Harper.

Movies You May Want to See

Enough (2002) Jennifer Lopez
Murder in Mississippi

Web Links

www.elderabusecenter.org
www.preventelderabuse.org
www.snapnetwork.org
http://www.usccb.org/nrb/johnjaystudy/

CHAPTER 8

Family Violence Victims

INTRODUCTION

The concept of family violence has been part of human history since the Bible recorded the fratricide of Cain killing Abel. Religious and cultural traditions historically favored the private and independent functioning of the family unit and, as governments developed, they did not interfere in matters of the home. In *State v. Oliver,* 1874, the North Carolina Supreme Court acknowledged that it was best "to draw the curtain," and to "shut out the public gaze" when husbands beat their wives, as long as "no permanent injury has been inflicted."

It is only within the last fifty years that the criminal justice system, particularly the police and courts, have become the primary arbiter of family-violence issues. Children killing parents, one parent kidnapping a baby from another parent, siblings battering and sexually assaulting each other, and elderly relatives being kept prisoners in their own homes have all generated challenges for our society. Unlike stranger-perpetrated crime, family violence typically involves histories of unhealthy and dysfunctional relationships. Complex arrangements in marriage, common law, and same-sex partnerships, as well as divorce and separation create not only nuclear families but blended and extended families. Social and criminal justice agencies often find it difficult to determine fault or verify many of the allegations involved in episodes of abuse. Sorting out the behaviors that most need to be addressed with formal interventions is also a challenge. This chapter will examine various forms of family violence but will focus on the two most commonly discussed, spousal battering and child abuse.

DOMESTIC VIOLENCE

Domestic violence is generally an act which occurs when gratuitous force is used by a partner to gain control over the victim. Each year approximately 1.5 million women are physically or sexually abused in an intimate partner relationship (Harding & Helweg-Larsen, 2009). Further, approximately 25% of all women will have experienced some form of intimate partner violence. Although spousal violence generally occurs in a situation in which the abuser is a man, it is well understood that there are instances in which the abuser is a female. Still, the majority of research and theory on domestic violence focuses on the women as the victim and the man as the abuser.

Currently, domestic-partner violence accounts for about seven percent of all homicides and three-quarters of those victims are female (Marcotte, 2009). Research by Marcotte (2009) reveals that, though there has been a significant decrease in the number of intimate partner homicides since the passage of the *Violence Against Women Act*, male victims have accounted for a disproportionate percentage of this decrease.

In many cases of mass murder, murder rampages or serial killings, family members are often included as victims. One example was drifter Henry Lee Lucas, one of the first to be labeled a "serial killer." Lucas confessed to, and allowed police to clear, over 600 murders across the country. However, authorities were unable to make a solid case in more than a few of these, including Lucas' alleged first murder, that of his abusive mother. In fact, mothers are often the targets of violence for the mentally-ill (Silver, 2001, p. 40). Studies indicate that "discharged patients living in chaotic family environments, where there is alcohol or substance abuse and an ongoing history of conflict among family members," are at greater risk of engaging in some type of violent response. Also, the mentally-ill who threaten violence often perceive their family members as hostile and attacking (Silver, 2001).

Multiple-murder scenarios can also involve family violence that continues into workplace violence. As Armour (2004) reports, episodes of workplace violence often begin with the killing of relatives at home. Mark Barton, a 44-year-old day trader who shot nine people at two Atlanta brokerage houses, first killed his wife and two children. Before forklift-operator Ramon Salcido killed his supervisor at a Glen Ellen

California winery, he brutally murdered his wife, two daughters, mother-in-law and her two daughters (Salcido, 2009). Another of his daughters, a three-year-old, survived to tell authorities, "Daddy cut me."

Swisher and Wekesser (1994) suggest that there are two characteristics distinctive of victims of domestic violence. These characteristics include those who are repeatedly subjected to coercive behavior by an abuser and those who have experienced at least two acute battering incidents. Research also indicates that about two-thirds of women who have been physically abused in a relationship have also been sexually abused (Taylor & Gaskin-Laniyan, 2007; McFarlane & Malecha, 2005).

The increase in reporting of domestic violence over the last two decades has been attributed to more public awareness and education on domestic violence as well as the creation of more outlets for reporting. The lessening of stigma related to abuse and the development of support groups and service agencies for victims has also increased the probability of reporting.

As might be expected, the likelihood of reporting domestic violence varies by race, income, and immigration status. Asian-American women are less likely to report or to use victim services. According to Bui (2004) cultural and economic isolation limits the options immigrant women believe they have, so they are less likely to jeopardize relationships that may lead to work, income and eventual legal residency.

Phases of Domestic Violence

Because of the large volume of case studies generated over the last few decades, experts have been able to develop a generalized picture of the dynamics of the abusive relationship. To some, the process appears to occur in a cycle composed of three phases: tension building, the acute battering incident, and the tranquil, loving or nonviolent phase (Swisher & Wekesser, 1994). During the first phase, physical violence may or may not be present, but when it is present it is regarded as minor. The victim works hard during this phase to keep her mate calm and to keep peace (Knudsen & Miller, 1991). During this phase, the woman commonly goes to excessive lengths to rationalize her mate's behavior and conceal the abuse from others, isolating herself from potential sources of assistance (Swisher & Wekesser, 1994). The severe battering incident occurs during the second phase. The man is perceived as being out of control and in a rage. No matter what the woman does or says, the batterer becomes angrier (Knudsen & Miller, 1991). The acute phase is remarkable for its savagery and uncontrolled nature. At this point, the woman feels psychologically-trapped. Her outwardly submissive demeanor functions as a defense mechanism, cloaking a sense of distance from the attacks and terrible pain (Swisher & Wekesser, 1994).

In the third phase, the batterer appears to be loving, warm and affectionate. He is generous and consumed by grief and remorse. He is full of apologies and promises (Knudsen & Miller, 1991). The couple experiences profound relief that the violence has abated. This final phase is the one in which the woman sustains the greatest psychological harm. The two parties exhibit their mutual emotional dependence—her for his caring behavior, he for forgiveness (Swisher & Wekesser, 1994). This is the phase that typically draws the victim closer to her batterer. It is known as the "honeymoon phase."

Power and Control

Batterers tend to want overarching power over victims and may use psychological abuse to lower self-esteem and devalue feelings of self worth. Victims of domestic abuse may be humiliated and verbally abused by their batterers. Batterers tend to blame their victims for the abuse. Domestic-abuse victims may rationalize their situation, citing that all relationships have problems, and some may even assume responsibility for the abuse, seeing it as a consequence of their inability to keep the intimate other happy and content. Although it may appear irrational, many domestic-abuse victims use these explanations as coping mechanisms. Domestic-abuse victims tend to stay in abusive relationships because they may receive other forms of relationship reinforcement during the honeymoon phase of the battering cycle. A number of victims may assume that the honeymoon phase truly marks the end of violence and that the situation will change for the better.

Domestic-abuse victims often lack the economic resources they feel are needed to live independent of the batterer. In some cases, the batterer may dominate the couple's finances and may not allow the victim to have money. Some batterers may not allow the victim to work, restricting not only her movement but her income. Abusers may also disrupt victims' work routines with absenteeism and confrontations on the job putting them at risk of being fired (Barnett, 2000). Many victims are deprived of a formal education as batterers try to limit access to information and knowledge. In some cases, victims grew up with domestic abuse in the home which may have increased their probability of living in a domestic-violence relationship themselves.

Batterers tend to discourage their intimate others from engaging in social relationships. Many domestic-violence victims will have limited communication and contact with family members and are isolated from friends and social venues. According to a number of experts, domestic-abuse victims suffer from learned helplessness. Typically, they accept their situation because they do not believe that they can do anything that will improve their life circumstances. As one victim, Patrice, explains (Nichols & Feltey, 2003, p. 792)

> Some people get themselves in this situation because they think that is the way it is supposed to be. Like when I, I thought that I was supposed to take it. I think that women need to be told that they don't have to take that abuse and stuff. That is what helped me, when people here started telling me that you don't have to take that, you don't have to live like that, you deserve to be treated better than that. You know you are a good person. I was always told the opposite by him, see. So they need to know.

Batterers may also threaten to harm themselves, consequently making it the responsibility and duty of the victim to sustain the relationship. The children may be used as a pawn to keep the victim in a relationship with the batterer. The batterer may threaten to withhold the children, harm the children, or kill the children if the victim were to leave the relationship. Consequently, fear is a major reason why some women remain in an abusive relationship. Many victims are afraid to report incidences of violence to agents of the criminal justice system because they fear retaliation (Tellis, 2010). Some victims have strong misgivings about the ability of the criminal justice system to protect them from future harm. Cultural traditions and family pressure to stay in a marriage may be exerted. Hoan Bui's (2003, p. 218) study of immigrant women in four cities detailed the feelings of the abused.

> I talked with my [Vietnamese] priest and my [Vietnamese] neighbors.
> My priest advised me to give him (her husband) time to change. My neighbors showed their sympathy, but when I asked whether I should call the police would he abuse me again, they just kept silent. I think no one wanted to intervene in other people's [family] business.
> My mother and my siblings told me they couldn't do anything about it (the abuse) because I was a married woman. My mother advised me not to make my husband angry, not to upset him

Concerns about the financial and home-life stability of their children cause others to tolerate abuse. Further, in some cases, the batterer may not be charged and thus the victim is again vulnerable to abuse. Some victims may fear the unknown while their abusive situations are, at least, familiar. Research suggests that many women who leave their abusive partners are eventually reunited. Approximately one-third of women return to their partners within three months of departing and many more return within one year.

Cycle of Violence

Although media and practitioners often refer to a "cycle of violence" this concept is less clearly established in research. What popular literature is attempting to describe is the way violent behavior patterns and responses to stress appear to be passed down from parents to children and then when they are grown, to their own children. In actuality, what is usually meant is that children may learn or model behaviors that they are exposed to. As learning theories tell us, the more frequent and prolonged the exposure to these behaviors, the more firmly they may appear to be engrained. In addition, rewards and reinforcements for aggressive actions will increase the probability that they will be repeated.

One of the problems for research on the "cycle of violence" is that much of the data is retrospective. This means that when someone is accused of violence, they go back into their past and recount incidences as victims of violence. These events may seem to be major influences although there may be a variety of different childhood experiences that they were exposed to, including happy and nurturing relationships. In addition, if samples of study participants are not drawn randomly, it is difficult to tell how many other nonviolent members of society also experienced abusive pasts which have not led to later episodes of violence.

In the most comprehensive research studies on the "cycle of violence" Cathy Spatz Widom (1992) found that childhood abuse increased the victim's risk of becoming involved in delinquency and adult criminality. In particular, abuse and neglect dramatically increased the chances of females being arrested later in life. Not all risk, it should be noted, was risk of specifically becoming a child abuser. In fact, a much more general concept of future violence is involved in this perspective. However, because so many other factors are often present in an abusing household, such as poor school achievement, mental health problems, and unemployment, it may be difficult to detect if any one factor could have direct effects at all.

Survey research appears to indicate that men and women are equally likely to report using violence in intimate-partner relationships. Men who report being a victim of battering in a relationship are also likely to report battering. That is, couples engaging in partner violence are more common than thought, although men are more likely to report women using weapons.

Women are also more likely to report more serious injuries than men and that they were responding defensively to anticipated violence from men (Buzawa, 2007). But, as Houry et al. (2008, p. 1042) summarize, "the violence in a sample of mutually violent couples was found to be low level, mild, gender neutral, bidirectional, and without injury."

Interventions for Domestic Violence

Attempts to reduce repeated incidents of domestic abuse have included mandatory arrest policies and use of "non-contact orders" issued by police when victims may be too intimidated to press charges or seek restraining orders. Critics of mandatory arrest argue that the loss of police discretion is a morale problem and leads to crowding in lockups. Others worry that police intervention may increase later domestic violence and cause batterers to retaliate against the victim. Some argue that such policies lead to greater arrest rates of poor and minority citizens and that it takes police resources away from fighting other forms of violent street crime. While feminists generally view the measures as necessary reforms that reduce the greater harm of errors introduced by predominantly-male policing bias, they are concerned about the resulting increase in female arrests. This occurs when officers are unable to determine fault or when injuries have been inflicted on both sides. Indeed, Darrell Steffensmeier related to one of the authors that research looking to explain an increase in female violent crime in Los Angeles found that most of the increase was a product of a new domestic-violence mandatory arrest policy.

Although most jurisdictions have adopted mandatory arrest policies, research on its effectiveness have been mixed. Few studies, though, show overall increases in battering or retaliatory effects. The deterrent effects of the policy seem to be limited to batterers who have more stakes in conformity (i.e., jobs, social status, and community leadership).

A number of studies have begun to look at the use of second-responders or social work counselors who follow up after police reports of domestic-violence incidents. The second-responder confidentially helps participants develop safety plans, contact service providers, and become educated on laws, policies and procedures related to domestic violence. While some practitioners were concerned that these home visits might increase violence, some analysts seemed to believe that the programs gave victims more confidence to call police and to engage services later on, which seemed to give the appearance of an increase in contacts following the program. As Davis, Weisburd, and Taylor (2008) concluded, the program did not increase or decrease the amount of family violence, it simply increased the likelihood that victims would contact authorities if it did recur. Thus, the main effect was to increase the number of reported incidences.

The lack of adequate numbers of shelter beds makes referrals for emergency housing problematic. For every woman accepted into a shelter, many more are turned away (Kindschi- Gosselin, 2003). Many shelters do not admit clients on the weekends, which is a high priority time for women attempting to escape violence. In order to determine which clients are truly serious about relocating, the shelters often make the acceptance process complicated and frustrating. Some facilities do not take children and most do not allow older children, particularly boys who have entered puberty. Women with mental health, drug or alcohol problems are also labeled unserviceable according to most shelter guidelines. Physical arrangements are likely to be crowded and residents must be able to adjust to and get along with a variety of personalities.

According to Loseke (1992), shelters, like other service agencies, rely on funding that is contingent upon successfully transitioning clients to independent living. Unfortunately, women with the highest risk and greatest need do not fit this profile and are turned down. Women who appear more motivated to adapt to a new, independent life are given priority. This means those accepted have employment skills, a good work history, and are motivated to follow through with the legal steps necessary to separate from the batterer. Also, shelter staff who are bilingual are rarely available so immigrants and other clients with language difficulties are routinely excluded. Ideal clients and their children are those considered the most adaptable and without serious medical or psychological problems or handicaps. And, because most shelters are not locally-situated and locations must be kept secret, children are required to leave their schools and wait for alternative education arrangements to be made.

CHILD ABUSE

The History of Child Abuse

Historically, children were deemed as property of the father and social concerns regarding their treatment generally stemmed from issues of inheritance, family status, and disobedience. Ancient Greece and ancient Rome had different legal systems but most subscribed to patriarchal, or father-centered, philosophies that were mirrored in later English common law. Infanticide, or the killing of babies, was practiced for a number of economic and "practical" reasons including illegitimacy, poor health and physical deformities. Girls were more likely to be viewed as a burden and children could even be sold as deemed necessary (Gosselin, 2003). These were some of the principles that influenced the development of early law in America.

The Massachusetts Stubborn Child Law of 1646 essentially made disobeying a parent an act punishable by death. This law governed the behavior of children and outlined the expectations of parents. The stubborn child law was born from Puritan principles that emphasized the moral institutions of the family, church, and community. The Puritans maintained that no individual was exempt from sin and it was the responsibility of moral institutions to train and educate children in the proper manner. Social concerns of child abuse were all but nonexistent as such issues were handled within the confines of the home. In other words, child abuse was not a social concern but rather a family concern.

After the Civil War, child abuse was soon recognized as a social problem. The impetus to a movement to recognize the plight of child abuse is traced to a young girl named Mary Ellen in 1873. Mary Ellen was a victim of child abuse and neglect in the state of New York who was, according to popular accounts, reported to the Society for the Prevention of Cruelty to Animals because there appeared to be no other agency to address the social services needs of children. Court documents on the case revealed a:

> ...pale, thin child the size of a 5-year-old, although it was later established that she was 9. It was a bitterly cold December day, yet the barefoot child wore only a thin tattered dress over one other ragged garment. A whip lay on a table, and the child's arms and legs bore many marks of its use. The saddest aspect, Wheeler reported, was written on the child's face, the face of an unloved child who knew only misery and the fearsome side of life.... She had scarcely any clothing—no shoes or stockings. She slept on a piece of old carpet on the floor in front of a window. She was not allowed to go outside or to play with other children. She could not remember any expressions of affection from Mrs. Connolly, only her whippings and beatings with a twisted whip—a rawhide—

almost every day. The whip always left black-and-blue marks on her body. The marks on her forehead, apparent in court, were made by Mrs. Connolly when she had struck and cut Mary Ellen with scissors. (The scissors were produced in court.) She did not want "to go back to live with mamma because she beats me so" (Costin, 1991, pp. 204, 207).

Subsequently, the Society for the Prevention of Cruelty to Children was created in 1874 in New York City to specifically address child abuse and neglect. The Mary Ellen case caused much public attention and highlighted the issue of child abuse in American society (Gelles, 1996, 1997).

Although child abuse was recognized as a social problem, the specific terms and their definition is what truly indicates that a problem is ready to be addressed by society. As Stephen Pfohl (1977) explains in his classic article, *The discovery of child abuse,* someone has to introduce the term, like "child abuse," and people must be ready to accept that parents are capable of battering their children and should be held accountable to the law for it. In this case, it was a radiologist who was in the best position to identify the phenomenon and to target parents as the cause. Working more behind the medical scenes, not directly with parents, who were the paying clients, a radiologist could examine broken bones and posit that their origin was not natural or accidental but the result of deliberate force or trauma. This "discovery" freed up others to respond and to acknowledge that this type of injury occurred and, as Pfohl (1977) relates, the process of confronting child abuse could officially begin.

Child Abuse Today

Today there are many offenses that can be construed as crimes against children and thus fall under the broad umbrella of child abuse. Child pornography, parental kidnapping, and exploitation of child labor all create child victims and responsibility for taking action has been delegated to one law enforcement or social service agency or another.

The courts today must continually strive to find a balance between parents' interest in raising their children according to their own personal and private beliefs and the states' need to protect children from harms resulting from those individual preferences. From a Constitutional standpoint, laws that regulate the conduct of parents must be the least restrictive means for accomplishing the goal of child safety. They must be clear in articulating what acts are required and which are prohibited and the benefit of their enforcement must outweigh intrusions on family privacy. Various court rulings over the years have helped refine the language of these child-abuse statutes. Judges have ruled for example, that "conduct detrimental" was too vague, as was "injurious environment" or what was meant by "acts causing pain" or a "proper home." On the other hand, phrases like "proper maintenance and care," "endangering without justifiable cause," and "cruelly and unlawfully punishes" have all been upheld as specific enough for interpretation.

The U. S. Department of Health and Human Services reports that, in 2008, child protective services (CPS) agencies in this country received 3.3 million reports of child abuse and neglect. And, according to the National Crime Survey, only about 45% of family violence is even reported to law enforcement. We know from trends in child abuse that girls and boys are equally likely to be abused but that the abuse of girls is more likely to be rated as being more serious. Despite this, boys are just as likely as girls to be removed from abusive settings.

Data on child abuse also tell us that mothers and fathers are equally likely to be abusers as well as almost equally likely to be the murderer of a child under five years of age. Still, fathers are more likely to be reported. Studies indicate that in dealing with their children, abusive parents use more punitive discipline rather than reasoning and simple directives. They also report that they are angry and disgusted with themselves after disciplinary actions.

Physical Abuse, Maltreatment and Neglect

The Department of Health and Human Services breaks down child abuse fatalities as being almost one-third physical abuse, one-third neglect and another third as some combination of maltreatment (2009). While all states have laws that prohibit these forms of abuse, each provides its own definition of the acts and there are varying sanctions for the offenses. Child maltreatment is generally used as an umbrella term to describe a child who is physically abused, sexually abused, emotionally abused, or neglected. Physical abuse may be defined as causing another physical pain through slapping, hitting, kicking, burning, punching, choking, and pushing. For some, physical abuse is any act of force used against a child. For others, it may be the appearance of bruises, scratches, or puncture marks on the skin. A review of the child-abuse literature will provide a range of definitions for physical abuse making it difficult to compare studies. The absence of exact severity, frequency, and duration are all common in most definitions.

Child neglect is generally defined as the failure of a custodial figure to adequately care for a child and is the most common form of child maltreatment. Neglect may be more passive than abuse as families living in poverty put children at risk in a variety of ways from low birth-weight and lack of shelter and medical care to learning problems and abandonment. Today, a record 22% of America's children live in poverty, nearly 18% live in homes with an insecure source of food, and up to 500,000 may be homeless in 2010 (Szabo, 2010).

Neglect is especially damaging because it can be difficult to detect even though it may co-exist with other forms of abuse. Victims of neglect may suffer from low self-esteem, depression, a negative sense of identity, and an inability to form and maintain positive relationships. Homeless juveniles including runaway and throwaway children often have histories of neglect.

The Missing Children's Assistance Act of 1984 (Pub.L. 98-473) specifically addressed this population when it provided for the collection of data that now known as the National Incidence Studies of Missing, Abducted, Runaway, and Thrownaway Children (NISMART) . Because there had been much controversy over claims made by advocacy groups, policymakers were attempting to assess not only the size of the homeless and missing population, but the number who are recovered as well. NISMART is a multi-agency undertaking, involving a periodic household survey sponsored by the Office of Juvenile Justice and Delinquency Prevention (OJJDP), the National Institute of Justice (NIJ), and the Bureau of Justice Statistics (BJS) . A NISMART report published in late 2004 that compared 1988 and 1999 surveys indicated that the number of lost or missing children significantly decreased. The rate dropped from about two per 1,000 to .5 per 1,000 in the ten-year period. Explanations may include clearer and more specific definitions of this term and the ability of law enforcement to better track and manage reports within this category. The data also indicated that cases in the most general categories of child abduction and running away had decreased. However, incidences of the types of cases that were of greatest concern to law enforcement, particularly parental abductions that were well-planned and involved identity-masking, were more stable and persistent (Hammer, H., Finkelhor, D., Sedlak, A., & Porcellini, L., 2004).

Child Sexual Abuse

Relatively speaking, the history of prosecuting cases of child sexual abuse is fairly recent. It wasn't until the 1970s that the definition of child maltreatment was extended to included sexual abuse and, thus, child-protection statutes were expanded. Prior to that time, sexual abuse was typically either denied or ignored by professionals. Sexual abuse is commonly defined as fondling, masturbation, digital penetration, oral intercourse, vaginal intercourse, and anal intercourse. Carnal knowledge, crimes against nature, forced sodomy, indecent liberties, and child pornography are the most common sex offenses committed against youth. It is well understood that girls are more likely than boys to be sexually abused. Also, disabled children are more likely to be sexually abused than their able-bodied counterparts. Increased vulnerability is a likely explanation for these two child populations. However, it should be duly noted that all children are at risk for sexual-abuse victimization.

Most instances of child sexual abuse are of a female child victimized by an adult male. Many perpetrators are known to the child as these individuals may be fathers, stepfathers, uncles, family friends, coaches, and teachers. Other pedophiles may be strangers and women may also be child perpetrators. In many cases, these offenders were once victims of child abuse themselves. Some studies suggest that female offenders had troubled relationships with their mothers and others cite histories of domestic violence (psychological and physical abuse) in their romantic relationships. Further, women sex offenders may co-offend with a male accomplice.

The kidnapping case of Elizabeth Smart is an example of a women sex offender acting as a co-offender. In June 2003, then 14-year-old

Elizabeth Smart was kidnapped from her Utah home by Brian David Mitchell. She was held captive by Mitchell and his wife, Wanda Barzee. Barzee, a former beautician, church organist, and mother of six was said to have spiraled into estrangement from her family, wandering the country with her mentally-ill husband. She recently pled guilty but mentally ill to the charges and received both federal and state sentences of 15 years, to be followed by a period of supervised release. She will remain registered as a sex offender for the rest of her life (Manson, 2010).

The child sex-abuse literature is consistent with the caveat that children rarely make false claims of this offense. A profile that has been developed for the child most likely to make a false claim is a bright adolescent with a grudge or vendetta against the defendant. This child is overly angry, and alleges vaginal intercourse, although no other actions or activities are involved. Also the alleged victim will describe overly bizarre behavior and acts that have little relationship to sexual stimulation.

False accusations of child sexual abuse are also noted in the psychiatric literature in cases of contested divorce and custody. The phenomenon appears to have such a predictable pattern that Blush and Ross (1990) refer to it as SAID Syndrome (Sexual Allegations In Divorce) . They note that it is often a female child around the age of 8, the parent making the allegations has a history of mental health problems, particularly hysterical or borderline personality disorder, and the charges do not surface until after the divorce proceedings begin.

Child Protection

All fifty states have mandatory reporting for child abuse and neglect. Mandatory reporting legally delegates responsibility to specific professionals to ensure the safety of children. Police officers and firefighters are public servants who have a duty to report suspicions of any child maltreatment they encounter. School personnel and daycare professionals, by nature of their employment, are also required to provide support to children in need of protection as are medical personnel who encounter suspicious illnesses and injuries. Child maltreatment cases are reported to Child Protective Services (CPS) agencies, who investigate suspected cases of maltreatment. CPS agencies are charged with protecting the interests of minor children. Although CPS agencies vary from state to state, they are generally alerted of potential cases of abuse and/or neglect via telephone hotline. Law enforcement officials, school officials, medical personnel, and anonymous callers may provide the initial information about a potential issue of child abuse and/or neglect. Depending upon the information reported, a file may be created and an investigator may look into the allegations. If there is sufficient information to suggest that a child is in need of services, CPS can take custody of the minor child. In many locations, CPS agencies are subjected to high turnover, case overload, and a lack of adequate staff. Thus, issues of child abuse or neglect may not be handled in the most efficient manner.

According to a 2009 study conducted by the national child advocacy group *Every Child Matters,* the state of Texas was rated number one in child-abuse deaths from 2001 to 2007 (Langford, 2009). In 2005, Texas allocated $248 million dollars to CPS thus creating 2,500 caseworker and staff positions and providing access to technology to aid CPS. At the end of the 2009 fiscal year (August 31), 189 Texas children had died as a result of child abuse. Further, virtually half of all child-abuse deaths involved a family member who was previously investigated by Texas CPS. On October 22, 2009, the *Houston Chronicle* published an article highlighting CPS abuse cases that resulted in child deaths. There were three recent cases highlighted in the article

Emma Thompson, 4, died after suffering a fractured skull and more than 80 bruises. The Spring [TX] girl was also sexually assaulted. Her mother tried to say her child had fallen. CPS was in the middle of an investigation into possible sexual assault of the girl after she tested positive for genital herpes. Because it can be transmitted in a nonsexual manner in rare cases, CPS let the girl stay with her mother. Three weeks later, Emma was dead.

In the case of Kati Earnest, the Vernon [TX] girl died after two previous investigations failed to verify the callers' complaints that she was neglected and possibly abused. Fifteen months after the second complaint, she was dead. Her mother said the girl drowned, but she was covered in bruises. Authorities say the mother finally admitted to beating her five times with a closed fist. She's now charged with capital murder.

And in Arlington [TX], CPS workers considered the mother of one-year-old Darrell Singleton "a pathological liar" and mentally ill from their prior visits, which included the removal of an older sibling because of abuse. But he remained in his mother's care. He died when he was left in a car all day while she worked in a nearby office (Langford, 2009).

Gaps in the provision of consistent field work and its administrative supervision have been blamed on staff shortages and lack of resources to more fully monitor and track cases. The ability of families to move frequently and the absence of interstate networks for managing clients has also been problematic.

WHEN THE FAMILY IS A VICTIM

Unlike other areas of criminal justice, feminist critics have argued that the focus of domestic violence has been on the victims, rather than on the perpetrators. From victims to survivors, the emphasis, and in particular media emphasis, has been on the changes that family members must make to flee, adjust, and adapt in order to reclaim their lives (Berns, 2004). For example, victims may be told how to avoid confrontations with their abusers or how to defend themselves against future attacks. The argument against this is that the system must hold family-violence offenders more accountable and address the behavior changes needed in batterers and abusers (which you might say is quite unlike other areas of crime and corrections we have studied so far). With stranger-perpetrated crime we seem to direct all of our energy and resources on punishing those guilty, while ignoring many of the direct needs of victims; in domestic abuse cases we may not be similarly motivated. Perhaps the preservation of the family and beliefs about the nature of family relationships changes the way we view crimes that take place in the home. Some question whether stranger and domestic crimes should be considered separate and what the consequences may be for doing so.

References

Armour, S. (2004, July 15). Some workplace killers start with their family members. *USA Today*, 2A.

Barnett, O. W. (2000). Why battered women do not leave, Part 1: External inhibiting factors within society. *Trauma Violence Abuse, 1*(4), 343–372.

Berns, N. (2004). *Framing the victim: Domestic violence, media, and social problems.* New York: Aldine de Gruyter.

Blush, G. L., & Ross, K. (1990). Investigation and case management issues and strategies. *Issues in Child Abuse Accusations, 2*, 1–3.

Bui, H. (2004). *In the adopted land: Abused immigrant women and the criminal justice system.* Westport, CT: Praeger.

Buzawa, E. (2007). Victims of domestic violence. In R. C. Davis, A. Lurigio, & S. Herman (Eds.). *Victims of crime,* 3rd Ed. (Chapter 4, pp. 55–74). Thousand Oaks, CA: Sage.

Clement, M. (2002). *The juvenile justice system,* 2nd Ed., Boston, MA: Butterworth/Heinemann.

Cook, P. W. (2009). *Abused men: The hidden side of domestic violence.* 2nd ed. Westport, CT: Praeger.

Costin, L. B. (1991). Unraveling the Mary Ellen legend: Origins of the "cruelty" movement *The Social Service Review, 65,* 203–223.

Davis, R., Weisburd, D., & Taylor, B. (2008, October 22). *Effects of second responder programs on repeat incidents of family abuse.* Washington, DC: National Institute of Justice.

Gelles, R. J. (1996). *The Book of David: How preserving families can cost children's lives.* New York: Basic Books.

Gelles, R. J. (1997). *Intimate violence in families.* Thousand Oaks, CA: Sage.

Hammer, H., Finkelhor, D., Sedlak, A., & Porcellini, L. (2004, December). *National Estimates of Missing Children: Selected Trends, 1988–1999.* Washington, DC: Office of Justice Programs.

Harding, H. G., & Helweg-Larsen, M. (2009). Perceived risk for future intimate partner violence among women in a domestic violence shelter. *Journal of Family Violence, 24,* 75–85.

Kindschi Gosselin, D. (2003). *Heavy hands: An introduction to the crimes of family violence.* Upper Saddle River, NJ: Prentice Hall.

Knudsen, D. D., & Miller, J. L. (1991). *Abused and battered*. New York: Walter de Gruyter.

Langford, T. (2009, October 22). Hundreds of children die despite CPS involvement. *Houston Chronicle*, A1, 6.

Loseke, D. (1992). *The battered woman and shelters: The social construction of wife abuse*. Albany, NY: State University of New York Press.

Malley-Morrison, K., & Hines, D. A. (2004). *Family violence in a cultural perspective: Defining, understanding, and combating abuse*. Thousand Oaks, CA: Sage Publications.

Manson, P. (2010, May 21). Barzee gets 15 years for Smart kidnapping. *The Salt Lake Tribune*.

Marcotte, D. (2009). *Intimate partner homicide: Using a 20-year national panel to identify patterns and prevalence*. Unpublished Dissertation, College Park, MD: University of Maryland.

McFarlane, J., & Malecha, A. (2005). *Sexual assault among intimates: Frequency consequences and treatments, Final Report*. Washington, DC: National Institute of Justice (NCJ 211678).

State v. Oliver, 70 N. C. 60, 1874.

Nichols, L., & Feltey, K. (2003). "The woman is not always the bad guy": Dominant discourse and resistance in the lives of battered women. *Violence Against Women, 9*, 784–806.

Pfohl, S. (1977). The discovery of child abuse. *Social Problems, 24*, 310–323.

Salcido, C. (2009). *Not lost forever: My story of survival*. New York: William Morrow.

Silver, E. (2001). *Mental illness and violence*. New York: LFB Scholarly Publishing.

Szabo, L. (2010, June 8). More than 1 in 5 kids in poverty. *USA Today*, A1.

Swisher, K. L., & Wekesser, C. (1994). *Violence against women*. San Diego, CA: Greenhaven Press.

Taylor, L. R., & Gaskin-Laniyan, N. (2007, January). Sexual assault in abusive relationships. *NIJ Journal, 256*.

Tellis, K. (2010). *Rape as a part of domestic violence*. El Paso, TX: LFB Scholarly Publishing.

U. S. Department of Health and Human Services (2009*). Child Maltreatment 2007.* Washington, DC: Administration on Children, Youth and Families, Department of Health and Human Services.

U. S. Department of Health and Human Services (2010). *Child Maltreatment 2008.* Washington, DC: Administration on Children, Youth and Families, Department of Health and Human Services.

Widom, C. S. (1992). The cycle of violence. *Research in Brief.* Washington, DC: National Institute of Justice, Office of Justice Programs.

Discussion Questions

1. As society changes, so do the dynamics of family violence. The way we view the roles of men, women and children in relationships will create differences in rates of certain types of domestic violence crimes. What changes to you see ahead and why?

2. What types of programs do you think would be important for intervening in family violence? Should batterers and victims be in programs together? Why or why not?

3. Do you think there is less emphasis on punishing the offender in cases of family violence than in other stranger perpetrated crimes? If so, how do you think this difference is perceived by victims? If this difference is not desirable, what specific changes do you think are needed in the justice system to equalize treatments?

Books You May Want to Read

Smith, Ashley (with S. Mattingly) *Unlikely angel: The untold story of the Atlanta hostage hero.* New York: HarperCollins.

Jeffs, Brent W. (2009) *Lost boy.* (with M. Szalavitz). New York: Broadway Publishing.

Goldman Family (1997). *His name is Ron.* New York: Avalon

Movies You May Want to See

Atonement
L. I. E. (2001)
Capturing the Friedmans

Weblinks

http://www.nccev.org/
http://www.pollyklaas.org/
http://www.positive-alternatives.org/teenrunaway.htm

CHAPTER 9

Places as Victims

INTRODUCTION

When Houston police officer Rodney Johnson was shot and killed by a suspect during a traffic stop, it was not long before the site at the cross streets became a makeshift memorial. A couple of years later, his sister and his widow visit the spot on occasion, particularly anniversaries to pray and connect to his spirit. Faded plastic flowers, police figurines, flags and religious crosses are still evident there (Bryant, 2007).

You see them all along the highway. Some are elaborate with wreaths, photos and assorted decorations. They commemorate where loved ones died, a place that draws attention to the victim of a car accident, the victim of a drunken driver or the victim of a hit and run. For sociologist Jeff Ferrell, the shrine reflects what he calls cultural space. He argues that they represent a "memorial to a life lost, salvaging something of the sacred from the profanity of noise and litter." Whether it is the place itself, the tragedy that occurred in the place, or the actual deceased that is being commemorated, the interpretation is perhaps up to the individual viewer. For Ferrell, it is all of these. He explains (2002, p. 187):

> As friends and family members affix toys, photographs, key chains, compact discs, work tools, and other personal memorabilia, each shrine also takes shape as a public display, a symbolic history of each individual victimized by automotive violence. And discovered day after day, mile after mile, these shrines have coalesced for me into something more; a road

map of sorrow and loss, a vast graveyard splayed out along the open road....

For one family who lost a son to a drunk driver, the erecting of a cross at the spot of the accident is about closure and the ability of a victim's family to have some control by establishing some permanent fixture (Bier, 2006). However, the establishment of roadside markers is not without controversy. Some believe that the public property of roadsides should not be monopolized by the families of the few and that beautification and scenery enjoyed by all should take precedent. Workers attempting to mow the roadside grasses are disrupted and burdened by the maintenance issues. Texas, through the Department of Transportation, has strict guidelines on the use of such markers meaning that even the spontaneous generation of personal feelings and needs related to grief must conform to state regulations (http://www. dot.state. tx.us/public_involvement/memorial_program.htm).

If the roadside shrine really is only about the person, then why aren't traditional grave sites enough? Some might argue that cemeteries and the private treatment of the remains of the dead are proper enough memorials and that roadside shrines are redundant or unnecessary. This leads us to ask, "What is the role of the exact place, rather than a traditionally designated place, in bringing attention to the victimization of a fellow human being?" Is there agreement that places elicit strong and painful reactions to events that happened there? If the emotions are bitter, angry and cause us to treat the area differently, perhaps condemn it or avoid it, or revere and enshrine it, then has it also not been altered by the events that transpired there?

In our discussion of human victims, it was noted that some appear more newsworthy and even more worthy of victim status than others. Depending on the circumstances and the sense of remaining risk, the site of human tragedy can be either a warning to avoid the location, or an attraction that draws visitors. Ciudad Juarez for example, has set recent records for violence and is, according to crime data, now one of the notorious murder capitals of the world (Olsen, 2009). The U. S. State Department has continued its travel alert for the area and, in a move the media unanimously proclaimed "unprecedented," the Texas Department of Public Safety warned that college students who ventured into the border areas between that state and Mexico for spring break would not be safe. While the annual event normally brings thousands of young, partying students and millions of dollars into the Juarez economy, it is also the same area that had 16,000 car thefts and 1,900 carjackings in 2009 (CNN.com, 2010). Comparing homicide rates, Houston and Dallas recorded approximately 13 per 100,000 residents in 2008, while that number exceeded 133 per 100,000 in Juarez. El Paso, Juarez' cross-border sister city, had a 2008 homicide rate of only 1.9 per 100,000 residents. Warring between drug cartels, government attempts to suppress drug trafficking, poverty, and global recession have all hit the city hard. As one researcher characterized the situation, "the city itself shows signs of weariness" (Olsen, 2009). Officials across the United States attribute the escalation of daytime combat violence to the use of automatic weapons and grenades randomly throughout the city centers.

On the other hand, the site of the Oklahoma bombing of the federal building in 1995, and the site of the World Trade Centers in New York that were attacked and demolished by terrorists in 2001 both draw millions of tourists. Places that were one day routine and of no special significance become symbolically-charged with ideological meaning, sentiment, and representative of some new mission or purpose. Would a place that seems to recover from its tragedy be less of a victim than one that continues to be plagued by a reputation for crime and violence?

Dictionaries often restrict our thinking about this topic by defining victims narrowly as persons. On the other hand, in criminal justice textbooks, victims are defined in terms of having experienced injury or loss, having suffered because of an accident, disaster, force of nature, disease, discrimination, crime or war. There is the implication that victims have been exposed to circumstances of abuse, exploitation, harm, destruction, unfairness or a violation of law (Karmen, 2001; Sgarzi & McDevitt, 2003). Still, in most these writings, traits are ascribed to a human, to a person. While this apparent consensus seems to provide a way to standardize victimology and define the boundaries of the subject matter, it also limits our consideration of the victimization experience.

When Hooker Electrochemical Company illegally dumped 21,000 tons of toxic waste into a field in Love Canal, New York, it would forever change the health and safety of the area (Clifford, 1998). As a result the town disappeared and the land will probably never be able to be used again, at least in our lifetimes. When an oil-tanker pilot off the coast of Alaska neglected his duties and ran the Exxon Valdez aground, spilling thousands of gallons of oil, he forever damaged the fragile coastline. While we know from these incidents that people as well as birds and marine life suffered, everyone also recognized that the ecosystem, the water and the land was dealt a crippling blow. While these examples represent actual physical damage to an area and specific environmental crimes that were committed directly against it, there is also the possibility that crimes against persons can taint a location as well.

Throughout this chapter we will consider a number of infamous places where crimes occurred. From the motel where Martin Luther King was assassinated to the spot where John Lennon was gunned down outside his apartment, policymakers are continually called upon to surrender areas to the sanctified realm of cultural landmarks and to dedicate and enshrine public spaces to the memory of horrific events. Such requests are an issue for public debate and discussion of the choices to be made as it becomes more difficult to preserve available land for no other purpose but its criminal legacy. In the very least, the victimization of people is tied historically to the locations in which those atrocities took place. It often stigmatizes and devalues a location. As labeling theory explains the concept of a master status, we can apply that to a place instead of a person. The master status of an area then would be those traits or characteristics that blind us to all other possible identities. Salem, Massachusetts would most likely draw to mind a place where witches were accused and burned. Hiroshima, Japan, where an atomic bomb was dropped during World War II. Chernobyl, Russia, was the site of a nuclear reactor break down and Bhobal, India, the site of a deadly chemical/industrial accident by an American manufacturer. The reputation of these locales are forever tied to the events that transpired there even centuries ago. As Foote explains,

> Landscape might be seen in this light as a sort of communicational resource, a system of signs and symbols, capable of extending the temporal and spatial range of communication. In effect the physical durability of landscape permits it to carry meaning into the future so as to help sustain

memory and cultural traditions. Societies and cultures have many other ways to sustain collective values and beliefs, including ritual and oral tradition, but landscape stands apart from these—like writing—as a durable, visual representation (1997, p. 33).

One could argue that given the magnitude of some events, individual people as victims do not seem to sustain the longevity that places do; perhaps places reflect victimization even better than people.

THEORIES OF CRIME AND PLACE

As criminologists have always argued, crime is not evenly distributed, but varies across time and across places. From the work of the early nineteenth-century social statisticians and cartographers we have understood how crime rates are differentiated by areas, climates and seasons. Researchers continually note the activity in "hot spots" that have absorbed disproportionate levels of law enforcement resources. In any city or town you can talk to realtors and police and they will tell you where the "bad" areas are. Their perceptions may be subjectively- or anecdotally-derived, but through advanced technology, geo-spatial analysts can demonstrate for us how each social problem or deficit accumulates across space.

As we discussed earlier, contemporary rational theories illustrate how multidimensional our thinking about crime has become. Instead of just focusing on offenders and how they violate laws, we now must consider how the environment or place influences the offender's decision-making. Still, all of our modern concepts of crime concentration can be traced back, at least to some degree, to the early Twentieth-century work of the Chicago School.

Social Disorganization

Perhaps the most prominent criminological theory associated with place is the concept of social disorganization offered within the Chicago School. Using the new science of ecology, theorists like Robert Park and Ernest Burgess (1925, p. 1), viewed the city as an organism, a dynamic environment that could, under adverse conditions exhibit pathologies and unhealthy symptoms of poverty and deterioration. As Park and his students mapped the social geography of the city, it resembled a set of concentric rings where rates of crime and delinquency dominated the zone of transition (which was the band directly surrounding the business district). With a population reflective of the newest immigrant nationalities, the zone was characterized by various cultural enclaves that experienced high rates of mobility as, over time, residents earned the money and thus the right to move away to better areas (Williams & McShane, 2010) .

For researchers Shaw and McKay (1942), delinquency statistics supported the premise that high crime rates persisted in areas despite relatively rapid and complete turnovers in racial and ethnic populations (Snell, 2001). While this notion contradicted more traditional explana- tions of crime, the focus on social disorganization and the study of neighborhood-level features and data continues to receive empirical support. The language of this research uses the concept of place in discussions of high crime areas. Findings often are expressed in ways that illustrate its status by using terms that sound very much like the descriptions of victims. Scrolling through headlines we see references to how "cities are suffering" from one crime problem or another. And, much like the discussions of the Chicago school, they seem to be areas where rates of poverty, joblessness, drug addiction and incarceration are high and rates of education, literacy, and two-parent households are low. These areas often make the news and, while the news is most likely about the people victimized there, the reports seem to typify the crimes as attached to the areas themselves.

Acres Homes and Dunbar Village

In a low income, predominantly-minority neighborhood in Northwest Houston, you can trace the victimization of a place through the last ten years of the city newspaper. The earliest articles talk about a strong community response to the drug war, of uniting to tackle problems through citizen action and empowerment. Over the years, stories evolve in episodes concerning abandoned homes, untended lots, illegal dump- ing, blight, prostitution and hourly rate motels and, finally, a string of serial murders that took several years to solve. "Garbage clogs the ditches along the quiet empty street" one report reads, "tire, bathtubs, beer cans, fast-food wrappers, dead animals" (Glenn, Moran & Stiles, 2007). Accounts of the rapes and murders concentrated in this area confirm what we have discussed theoretically about victim reporting. As one investigator noted, "surviving sexual assault victims have been reluctant to come forward because many of them have histories of prostitution and drug abuse—or both" (Wise, 2007). This community, often described as "depressed," is characterized by the classic social disorganization features described by the Chicago School.

Unlike the low-profile Acres Home and its enduring struggles, Miami's low-income housing project, Dunbar Village, was cast into an international spotlight when a young mother and her 12-year-old son were attacked in their home by a gang of young men who burglarized, raped and tortured the two victims for hours. Outrage of global proportions targeted the community, focusing on its rampant crime, unemployment, unsupervised youth and uncontrolled gangs. The war-zone imagery of the single mother's life was dramatically captured by the revelation that, gang-raped beaten and threatened, she was forced to engage in sex with her young son to the entertainment of her captors. Details of the experience grabbed headlines across the country describing how the victims were placed naked into the bathtub filled with various irritating chemicals in attempts to destroy DNA evidence. Dunbar Village became synonymous with the worst of evils, not just because of this particular event, but because of the residents' tired admissions that this wasn't shocking to them; it was just another day in their lives.

No doubt, crimes and their media interpretations color our perceptions of areas and form the basis of their image or reputation. Negative connotations impact the desirability of business and housing in a given area, lowering property values, leading to what theorists refer to as the "broken windows" syndrome. The appearance of graffiti and deteriorating buildings, they argue, seems to signal the decline of a community and fosters the process of spiraling into decay. High concentrations of unemployment, poverty and abandoned lots, just like toxic waste, undermines the health of the residents there and their ability to revitalize their surroundings. Government programs from the 1960s on have attempted to address these needs and range from the ambitious construction of a Great Society to more conservative Weed and Seed projects to more localized economic stimulation initiatives. Through these efforts the focus and unit of analysis has been the place and the people of that place, but uniformly, the place.

THE INTERPRETATION OF PLACES OF CRIME

According to social scientists, a number of outcomes are possible for notorious places and we will discuss three of them: sanctification, obliteration (Foote, 1997) and exploitation. Foote (1997) sees sanctification and obliteration at opposite ends of a continuum. Theoretically, events can be communally-endorsed as significant and worthy of preserving or they can be condemned as so shameful and scandalous as to need to be symbolically and literally destroyed. For example, the concentration camps Dachau and Auschwitz are now museums and centers for remembrance but the towns and communities in which they are located still bear the brunt of worldly anger and indignation, frozen in time, condemned to their ugly reputations.

Still, people are drawn to scenes of crimes, violence and suffering. Millions of pilgrims, flocking to the Holy Land, attest to the power and significance of standing in the space where Jesus was said to have been crucified. One of the websites offering information on Dachau reports that 800,000 people visit the site each year. Likewise, 2.5 million people per year visit the Alamo in San Antonio, Texas; the site of the slaying of a small band of mission defenders against the Mexican army of General Santa Anna in 1836. The line between historic site, crime scene, victim exploitation, tourism and venerable grounds are perhaps a matter of subjective interpretation. It is the official public designation of these spaces as meaningful that we will focus on in order to determine whether or not the place is, for all intents and purposes, a victim too.

History and the Politics of Sanctification

In complex democratic societies, there are no simple paths to the sanctification of spaces or any single interpretation of the victimization experiences they signify. Groups may argue about which events and sites warrant the status of sanctification and compete for the limited resources available to sponsor such designations. Even places as verifiable as Holocaust sites are challenged by those who deny the events ever occurred. Other sites such as Wounded Knee, Ruby Ridge and the Waco compound of David Koresh, are approached from a variety of perspectives depending on how one views the participants, the role of government and the veracity of reports received about these events. And, while there may not be consensus on what to do with a particular site, there is some agreement on what not to do. In the Ukraine, the site of Nazi atrocities has been the subject of a number of controversies related to how to best commemorate a victim place.

In 1941, in an area called Babi Yar, the Nazis launched one of the most horrific killings of the Holocaust, gunning down at least 33,771 Jews over the course of two days—the number recorded by the executioners. In the ensuing months, the ravine was filled with about 100,000 bodies, among them those of non-Jewish Kiev residents and Red Army prisoners of the Nazis (Danilova, 2009).

First, a writer who chronicled the massacre in a book called *Babi Yar*, Anatoly Kuznetsov, was persecuted and censored by the Soviet government—perhaps an indication of an official preference for obliteration. More recently, officials' plan to build a hotel at the site was internationally-rebuked and withdrawn. Finally, citizens of the area were able to erect a statue and honor all of the victims. An historic re-enactment has even been held on the anniversary of the event to call attention to the harms suffered by the citizens of that earlier time.

In years to come, the World Trade Center site will most likely undergo some challenges, including the controversial decision to build a mosque in the immediate area. While some argued that a religious education center focused on peace and tolerance was appropriate, others found that this might symbolize some type of victory for terrorist interests. Though the property seems to be a perfect candidate for sanctification, it remains one of the most valuable commercial properties in the country. The New York and New Jersey Port Authority and developer Larry Silverstein have been embroiled in disputes about what can be rebuilt at the "ground zero" site and who would be responsible for what costs. As reporter Charles Bagli (2010) explains:

The New York and New Jersey Port Authority is already building 1 World Trade Center, a $3 billion, 1,776-foot-tall skyscraper formerly called the Freedom Tower; a $3.2 billion transit center; a national memorial, and streets and utilities to serve the site. But there has been a 15-month deadlock on who will finance three additional office towers that Mr. Silverstein, who held the lease on the twin towers when they were destroyed on Sept. 11, 2001, has the right to build at ground zero. Unable to obtain corporate tenants (the city and Port Authority have agreed to rent space in one of the buildings) or construction loans, Mr. Silverstein insisted last year that the Port Authority, which owns the site, finance at least two of the towers.... the authority agreed to financially support Mr. Silverstein's first tower and said it would back the second one after he signed leases for about a fifth of the space...retail space would be erected on the land...the authority wants Mr. Silverstein to invest $300 million of his own money, while pooling all of the remaining insurance money from the terrorist attack and tax-free Liberty Bonds for construction of the two towers. It also wants Mr. Silverstein to continue paying full rent at the site until he exhausts the insurance money.

Officials appear desperate to "finalize an agreement that both protects the memories of those we lost and the overstretched taxpayers of New York and New Jersey" (Bagli, 2010).

Meanwhile, hotels across from the site appear to already be capitalizing on their proximity to the construction. Claiming to meet the needs of visitors, Cheryl Palmer, Vice President of the company opening the World Center Hotel, sees the marketing value of the views as does the Millennium Hilton also recently reconstructed nearby. Both consider their unique access to the location of the tragedy to be a selling-point. As they explain, many of the rooms have "floor-to-ceiling windows that look onto construction. Guests and members will have access to the restaurant patio with views of giant cranes, jackhammers and metal scaffolding" (Gross, 2010). Still, the Millennium's general manager admits that some guests have expressed regrets, saying that they would have changed hotels had they realized how close they were to ground zero. That all may change in 2011 when an estimated seven million people are expected to visit the memorial established in the renovated and reconstructed area (Gross, 2010).

The spot where the fourth plane hijacked by terrorists on September 11, 2001, crashed was different. While two planes hit the World Trade Center in New York City and one hit the Pentagon in Washington, DC, the fourth plane landed in an area of rural fields, and no one on the ground was killed. Eight years later, construction began on that Shanksville, Pennsylvania, farmland for a 3.5 square mile park memorial. Unlike the pricey real estate of downtown New York, this park will spread out over 2,200 acres and include a special garden that only the families of the victims will be allowed to enter. The victims names will be carved in a white stone wall and 40 chimes, representing each of the victims, will mark the entrance to a chapel. Still, the development of the plans for the $58 million memorial were contentious. Landowners and farmers were pressured into selling off their property and many are still bitter about the process today. Some argue that the design appears to honor the terrorists and their actions (Nephin, 2009).

Somewhere between sanctification and obliteration, then, there may be some room to rectify or reuse the officially-designated space. Foote (1997) explains that this is actually the most common outcome for former notorious locations. While few are really sanctified, more are simply designated or marked for historical purposes and then most likely, regenerated, often as its former self. For Foote, this is most likely to occur when an area has been the scene of a senseless tragedy or accident.

Most recently, we have seen the process of rebuilding as a natural step in the healing of a community or group of people. Cases of church arson, most often classified as hate crimes, have generated concern across the country over the last decade. The way the media highlights these events may make them appear more common than other types of property destruction. Because these crimes generally occur late at night when the building is unoccupied, they rarely result in death or individual victimization. In almost all cases, it is the church itself that is destroyed or damaged although the members report feeling the consequences personally. As one member explained "...it hurt terribly—like somebody setting your shoe on fire. The church is God's house...the pain and suffering; the agony" (Turner, 2010). The identification of church crime as a serious social problem led to many of the traditional benefits of legislative intervention, increased sanctions and the provision of resources dedicated to the prevention and prosecution of this crime. Responding to a series of 66 church fires impacting predominantly black congregations in an 18-month period, the *Church Arson Prevention Act* was passed in 1996 (Public Law 104–155). The language specifically characterizes the problem of one of threats to basic freedoms.

1. The incidence of arson or other destruction or vandalism of places of religious worship, and the incidence of violent interference with an individual's lawful exercise or attempted exercise of the right of religious freedom at a place of religious worship pose a serious national problem.
2. The incidence of arson of places of religious worship has recently increased, especially in the context of places of religious worship that serve predominantly African-American congregations.
3. Changes in Federal law are necessary to deal properly with this problem.
4. Although local jurisdictions have attempted to respond to the challenges posed by such acts of destruction or damage to religious property, the problem is sufficiently serious, widespread, and interstate in scope to warrant Federal intervention to assist State and local jurisdictions.

The additional classification of the offense under hate-crime statutes also allowed for the enhancement of punishments for those found guilty of these newly-designated crimes. The Sixteenth Street Baptist Church in Birmingham, Alabama, bombed during the height of civil rights tensions in 1963 was finally designated as an historical landmark by U. S. Attorney General Gonzales in 2006. Referring to the Klu Klux Klan attack that killed four young girls, Gonzales called the church "a catalyst for the cause of justice." "We protect this place for them," he said. In this sense, the church becomes a proxy victim, the lasting physical link to the young girls who lost their lives there.

In cases of church arson, the sentiment is most often to rebuild and recover. In the late 1990s, The National Council of Churches was able to raise over $4 million to rebuild churches victimized by suspicious fires (Turner, 2010). However, churches will likely remain attractive targets for arsonists. Churches are empty at night, the arsonists' preferred time frame, and are usually set back off the street away from routine traffic and patrols. Poor churches have no security or surveillance as they are not insured or designed as businesses. Following a fire at Dover Baptist church in Tyler, Texas, one trustee admitted they only had a "dummy," inoperable camera "because the church couldn't afford real video equipment" (Dixon, 2010).

To some survivors or relatives of the most prominent human tragedies, like the World Trade Center attack, it may never seem appropriate to do anything on this property, and many may feel to do so diminishes or trivializes those who died there. Places that are stigmatized or sanctified by horrific events also face the possibility of being commercialized or exploited for their ability to provide emotionally-evocative experiences for visitors.

Celebrity and the Exploitation of Crime Places

On August 20, 1989, Erik and Lyle Menendez murdered their wealthy parents in their $3.4-million home on 722 N. Elm Drive in Beverly Hills. The dozen or more gunshot wounds fired into the couple left a grizzly scene and the home was subsequently gutted and rebuilt, an example of Foote's rectification. The real estate market would argue that the lost value of a home involved in a notable crime or death is a form of victimization for the property. The stigma and for many, revulsion attached to the site can be a source of sorrow, hardship and loss for owners or an attraction or curiosity for others. In 2006, *U.S.A. Today* published a story about infamous-death real estate that discussed the stigma of crime-scene property. One expert on the issue explained that it usually takes two to seven years longer to sell a building associated with a notorious crime. State laws vary on disclosure requirements for the sellers and buyers vary in their degree of super-stition about owning such a property. Owners have options such as renovating the structure, as was the case for the O. J. Simpson condo, or razing the entire building, as was done with the apartment where Jeffrey Dahmer murdered and dismembered young victims.

According to a number of historical-tour websites, visitors to some cities like Los Angeles, San Francisco or Chicago are invited to go on famous crime site excursions. For example, one website (http://www.weirdchicago.com/) for tours in Chicago boasts,

> This chilling tour visits the city's grisliest and most haunted crime scenes and takes visitors on a haunting trip back to revisit crimes from Chicago's pass—from the St. Valentine's Day Massacre to the "Murder Castle" and Beyond! This is the REAL "Bloody Chicago Ghost Tour."

And,

> Join us for a "Ghosts of Gangland" tour as we explore Al Capone sites, death scenes and haunted crime spots throughout the Windy City! See places that you've only read about from Al Capone's house, Eddie O'Hare's death site, Capone hangouts, mobster murder scenes and much more.

In fact, it has been argued that American's fascination with crime, rather than any particular loyalty toward victims, is the motivation behind the crime-scene tour industry. The sites on these tours are more in line with Foote's clarification of events that are lesser known; certainly they have been rectified, perhaps not even marked, but still perhaps having some effect on people's value of the location before it fades into anonymity and a chance for a willing entrepreneur to make a buck.

Obliteration

Many historic sites of victimization risk obliteration because of the intense desire by many to forget or diminish the accounts of atrocities or painful civil strife. As one young man found out in his journey to visit the concentration camp at Dachau before it became an historical site and now perhaps even a sanctified location.

...I made my way to the Autobahn and hitchhiked north towards the infamous destination. Drivers who picked me up would ask where I was going. When I replied "Dachau", the response was uniform; the conversation quieted to silence. In retrospect, the response shifted from awkward embarrassment to naked shame. I had to walk the last 2 or 3 kilometers to the entrance, as it was far away from any settlement. There was no commerce or residence in the area. The day was very gray, and it was as if the whole countryside was sterile. As I approached, there was a very long border of high wire fence. Walking through the entrance I found no one in attendance. I moved in turn through all the buildings and the displays. I never found a soul the entire day, at least none that were living (http://www.scrapbookpages.com/Dachauscrapbook/KZDacha u/DachauLife01A.html).

Obliteration is a very deeply emotional purging. As one American visitor to Dachau wrote,

I felt so many emotions today as I rode into town. I kept looking around at all the shops and beauty parlors and got angry. Why didn't they burn this place to the ground and salt the earth? (http://www.scrapbookpages.com/Dachauscrap book/KZDachau/DachauLife01A.html).

As strong as the desire may be to rid the area of any trace of the crimes that occurred there, others see the need to educate and learn from the experiences of the past as much more critical.

PREVENTING THE VICTIMIZATION OF PLACES

Protecting meaningful public places is a task designated to various law enforcement agencies under the umbrella of homeland security. When threat risks are considered elevated, officials consider closing public parks, national monuments and historic venues in order to avoid potential terrorist attacks. The notion that terrorists might consider destroying significant places is testimony to the theory that places represent symbolic value and, as national images, they serve as a proxy victim for the people. In an interview, National Park Service spokesman, David Barna, indicated that they had contingency plans to close "five of the nation's most popular 'icon' tourist sites: the Statue of Liberty, the Washington Monument, the White House, the St. Louis Gateway Arch and the Liberty Bell pavilion in Philadelphia. The five sites were closed to all visitors for a time after the Sept. 11 terror attacks" (Shenon, 2003). However, reopening and bringing visitors into these attractions is viewed as a symbolic victory, a triumph over terrorism.

One could argue that the prevention of the victimization of people in public places is a way to prevent the tainting or stigmatizing of the places as well. Reducing robberies and thefts in the French Quarter of New Orleans is a priority for police in a city that depends on tourism for its very survival. The engineering and design of more crime-resistant environments have been studied by criminologists and social ecologists for years and these ideas have been used by contemporary urban planners to create defensible spaces.

Crime Prevention Through Environmental Design

Both crime-victim surveys and expanded police reports have offered researchers a wealth of information about the context of crime incidents. Collecting details of crime events such as time, place, and surrounding conditions has helped planners, policymakers and security personnel better prevent victimization by manipulating the environment to enhance safety and reduce risk. The study of environmental design focuses on three aspects of the potential victimization incident, the presence of a willing or motivated offender coming into contact with a suitable or even "attractive" target and the absence of capable guardians or impediments to the successful completion of the crime.

In Table 9–1, we see how Cornish and Clarke have addressed these concepts by directing efforts in five directions, all of which support rational theory principles. The first is to increase the effort that it would take from an offender to commit a crime which is based on the rational premise that too much effort would discourage the offense entirely. Second is increasing the risk that the offender would be seen or caught,; third is reducing the rewards that might be garnered from the crime.

Table 9–1. Updated 'Twenty-five Techniques of Situational Crime Prevention' by Cornish and Clarke (2003).

Increase the effort	Increase the risks	Reduce the rewards	Reduce provocations	Remove the excuses
1. Harden Targets immobilizing devices in cars, anti-robbery screens, tamper-proof packaging	6. Extend guardianship Go out in groups, carry phone, neighborhood watch, leave signs of occupancy	11. Conceal targets gender-neutral phone books, off-street parking, unmarked armored trucks	16. Reduce frustration & stress efficient waiting-line set ups, soothing lighting /music, expanded seating	21. Set rules rental agreements, hotel registration, distribute printed rulebooks
2. Control facility Access alley-gating, entry phones, electronic card access	7. Assist natural surveillance improved street lighting, neighbor-hood watch hotlines, defensible-space designs	12. Remove targets removable car radios, pre-paid public phone cards, refuges for women	17. Avoid disputes fixed cab fares, reduce crowding in pubs, separate rival soccer fan areas	22. Post instructions 'No parking', 'Private property'

Table 9–1 (Cont'd). Updated 'Twenty-five Techniques of Situational Crime Prevention' by Cornish and Clarke (2003).

Increase the effort	Increase the risks	Reduce the rewards	Reduce provocations	Remove the excuses
3. Screen exits tickets needed to get out, electronic tags for libraries	*8. Reduce anonymity* taxi driver ID's, 'how's my driving?' signs, school uniforms	*13. Identify property* property marking, vehicle licensing, cattle branding	*18. Reduce emotional arousal* controls on violent porn, ban pedophiles from childrens' areas, limit cursing, fan taunting at games	*23. Alert conscience* roadside speed display signs, 'shoplifting is stealing,' roadside speed indicators
4. Deflect offenders street closures in red-light district, separate toilets for women	*9. Utilize place managers* train workers to prevent crime, support whistle blowers, CCTV on public transportation	*14. Disrupt markets* checks on pawn brokers, licensed street vendors, control internet solicitations	*19. Neutralize peer pressure* 'idiots drink and drive,' 'it's ok to say no,' disperse troublemakers at school	*24. Assist compliance* litter bins, public lavatories
5. Control tools/weapons toughened beer glasses, photos on credit cards, restrict spray paint	*10. More formal surveillance* speed cameras, CCTV in tourist areas, more burglar alarms	*15. Deny benefits* ink merchandise tags, graffiti cleaning, speed bumps	*20. Discourage imitation* rapid vandalism repair, V-chips in TVs, censor details of offenders' methods	*25. Control drugs /alcohol* breathalysers in pubs, alcohol-free events, wrist-bands for age groups

Fourth is removal of provocations that might motivate a crime and fifth is reducing the ability to excuse criminal actions by making their prohibition clear.

Consider the case of twenty-year-old Adam Espinoza who was isolated and trapped. He was shot and killed in his vehicle at a rest stop on Interstate 10 in Anthony, New Mexico. Many items that were part of his cross-country move were stolen from the vehicle (Meeks, 2010).

State Police Captain Rich Libicer offered that this type of crime is unusual in that, although law enforcement does patrol the vicinity, rest area victimization "has not come up on our radar." Despite evidence from decades of environmental design research as well as data on the escalating gang violence problems in this particular town, Libicer concluded that the crime could have happened anywhere and that the place was not particularly significant. Further, having implemented better investigative resources, they were able to solve the crime in nine days with the arrests of three area gang members. "Some places" he added, perhaps concerned about potential lawsuits,

> ...are dangerous because there's dangerous people there and this young man was, unfortunately, in the wrong place at the wrong time.... I don't know that there's anything he could have done to prevent that the people he came across were bound and determined to commit a crime (Meeks, 2010).

THE PERCEPTION OF PLACES AS DANGEROUS

The extensive research that has been done on fear of crime has already determined that people rely on a variety of information sources when evaluating the safety of one place over another. Many of the views that people have about the relative safety of places is inconsistent with what we know from empirical research. For example, subways and mass transit systems are statistically much safer than people believe. The New York City subway which covers an extensive area has less than 3% of the city's serious crime (Kenney, 1987). In addition, several studies on light-rail expansion further out from the city center have found that crime did not gravitate out to these study areas (one in Los

Angeles and one in Jersey City, New Jersey) as many opponents of the projects had feared (Liggett et al., 2003; Seldelmaier, 2003).

The recognition that motivated offenders intersect in time and place with likely victims has led to a significant amount of research that attempts to identify those high-risk times, places and people. Certain types of establishments in public spaces such as grocery stores, pawn shops, liquor-licensed premises and convenience stores may increase the probability of crime, while others like banks and hotels with their own security forces seem to deter crime (Yu, 2009). Areas that offenders select for activity are usually within their comfort zones and are often referred to as "hot spots." Cornish and Clarke (2003) have also indicated that the probability of a crime occurring increases when those at high risk for repeated victimization, or "hot dots," are participating in activities in hot spots. Rap stars murdered outside or in the vicinity of popular nightclubs, pizza-delivery people, revelers who venture outside the perimeter of the New Orleans French Quarter and professional athletes who drive high-profile vehicles are all attractive targets or hot dots.

In order to expand what we know about places that are disproportionately associated with victimization, researchers have relied on geospatial analysis and sophisticated computer software that is able to code and illustrate crime in a multidimensional framework. Better prediction of where and how crimes occur will help us develop more effective prevention strategies. We are also assisted in this goal by technological advances in equipment that screens and interprets the environment to enhance surveillance and response times so that places we enjoy frequenting do not end up creating victims and these places themselves do not become victims either.

References

Adams, K. (1981). Former mental patients in a prison and parole system: A study of socially disruptive behavior. *Criminal Justice and Behavior, 10*, 358–84.

Bagli, C. (2010, March 5). Trade center financing rift still wide as deadline nears. *The New York Times,* A24.

Bier, C. (2006, March 9). Marking memories: Magnolia family leads program to honor victims of car crashes. *Houston Chronicle.*

Bryant, S. (2007, September 21). Struggling to let go: Family marks a difficult anniversary. *Houston Chronicle*, B3.

Clifford, M. (1998). *Environmental crime*. Gaithersburg, MD: Aspen Publishing.

CNN (March 2010) Texas police warn spring breakers: Stay out of Mexico border towns. Retrieved from http://edition.chron.com/ 2010/TRAVEL/03/04/Mexico.spring.break/index.html.

Cornish, D. B., & Clarke, R. V. (2003). Opportunities, precipitators and criminal decisions: A reply to Wortley's critique of situational crime prevention. *Crime Prevention Studies, 16*, 41–96.

Danilova, M. (2009, September 29). Kiev marks its own Holocaust tragedy. Associated Press in the *Houston Chronicle*, A14.

Davies, G. (2006). *Crime, neighborhood, and public housing*. New York: LFB Scholarly Publishing.

Dixon, S. (2010, February 10). ATF blames series of fires at churches on serial arsonist. *Houston Chronicle*, B1.

Ferrell, J. (2002). Speed kills. *Critical Criminology, 11*, 185–198.

Foote, K. E. (1997). *Shadowed ground. America's landscapes of violence and tragedy*. Austin, TX: University of Texas Press.

Glenn, M., Moran, K., & Stiles, M. (2007, September 27). A call to action in Acres Homes; After recent deaths, residents want city to clean up area and offer better protection. *Houston Chronicle*, A1.

Gross, S. (2010). New ground zero hotel is marketing 9/11 tragedy. *Houston Chronicle*, A6.

Karmen, A. (2001). *Crime victims. 4th Ed*. Belmont, CA: Wadsworth.

Kenney, D. (1987). *Crime, fear and the New York City subways*. New York: Praeger.

Liggett, R., Loukaitou-Sideris, A., & Iseki, H. (2003). Journey to crime: Assessing the effects of a light rail line on crime in the neighborhoods. *Journal of Public Transportation, 6*(3), 85–115.

Meeks, A. (2010, January 24). Police advise caution after killing. *Las Cruces Sun News*, A1.

Nephin, D. (2009, November 8). Shovels turn in honor of Flight 93's sacrifice. *Houston Chronicle*, A3.

Olsen, L. (2009, October 22). Ciudad Juarez passes 2,000 homicides in 2009, so far. *Houston Chronicle*, A15.

Park, R., & Burgess, E. W. (Eds.) (1925). *The city*. Chicago: University of Chicago Press.

Sedelmaier, C. M. (2003). *Railroaded: The effects of a new public transportation system upon local crime patterns*. Dissertation. Newark, NJ: The State University of New Jersey, Rutgers.

Sgarzi, J. M., & McDevitt, J. (2003). *Victimology: A study of crime victims and their roles*. Upper Saddle River, NJ.: Prentice Hall.

Shaw, C., & McKay, H. D. (1942). *Juvenile delinquency in urban areas*. Chicago: University of Chicago Press.

Shenon, P. (2003, March 6). Threats and responses: Protecting Institutions. *The New York Times*, A16.

Snell, C. (2001). *Neighborhood structure, crime, and fear of crime*. New York: LFB Scholarly Publishing.

Turner, A. (2010, February 14). Ring of déjà vu from 7 church blazes: An East Texas pastor recalls suspicious fires. *Houston Chronicle*, B1.

Williams, F. P., & McShane, M. (2010). *Criminological theory, 5th Ed*. Upper Saddle River, NJ: Prentice Hall.

Wise, L. (2007, August 6). Killings probe grows colder; At least 3 men are to blame in Acres Homes serial case. *Houston Chronicle*.

Yu, S. (2009). *Bus stops and crime: Do bus stops increase crime opportunities in local neighborhoods?* Unpublished Dissertation, Newark, NJ: State University of New Jersey-Rutgers.

Discussion Questions

1. How do you view the victimization status of places? What criteria would you use for evaluating the harm or injury to a place?
2. How do you balance the needs of victims who want to see a crime place set aside for memorial purposes with those who would like to continue normal public land use? What concessions should be made under what circumstances? Would it make a difference that, for example, the place was farmland that had been owned by a family for generations?
3. Describe the characteristics of a crime-prone area, how you would determine which areas are crime-prone and what can be done to reduce crime in those areas.
4. Which techniques for preventing crime could best be done by victims and what are the various costs and constraints of the various methods suggested. To what extent do any of these

measures impact either positively or negatively on the daily lives and activities of individuals?

Books you may want to read

Rubin, L. (1986). *Quiet rage: Bernie Goetz in a time of madness*. New York: Farrar, Straus and Giroux Publishing.

Thibodeau, D. (1999). *A place called Waco: A survivor's story*. New York: HarperCollins.

Gibbs, L. M. (1998). *Love Canal: The story continues*. Gabriola Island, British Columbia: New Society Publishers.

Movies you may want to see

Schindler's List
Erin Brockovich
Silkwood

Web Links

Crime site tours:
    http://www.weirdchicago.com/
    http://www.sfrichmondreview.com/archives/richmondreview/2004
    ditions/Aug04/crimetour.html
Property Stigma:
    http://www.usatoday.com/news/nation/2006-08-06-
    murderhouses_x.htm
Neighborhood watch:
    http://www.usaonwatch.org/
Crime prevention through environmental design:
    http://www.cpted.net

CHAPTER 10
Animals as Victims[1]

INTRODUCTION

In the news today one cannot help but notice a great deal of attention paid to crimes involving animals. Reports of dog fighting and cockfighting in particular have inflamed public opinions, sharply dividing cultures and generations, those who see the fights as defensible traditions and those who only see animal abuse. Similarly, one of the major arguments behind the banning of aerial fireworks in many jurisdictions and the adoption of what are often referred to as "Safe and Sane" policies on pyrotechnics was the way they scared animals and caused undue stress in dogs. And at times, plans for the establishment of dog parks and the designation of "dog beaches" have generated more heated debate in local newspapers than the war in Iraq.

In Harris County, Texas, Brandon Gregory plead guilty to the taking of a wildlife resource without landowner consent. The felony charge arose after the decapitated body of a tame and popular park deer, "Mr. Buck" was found in a wildlife sanctuary where it interacted with visitors, even allowing them to pet him. What led to this particular charge was not just that Gregory trespassed into a fenced area and stabbed the deer in the heart, but that he later used a bone saw to sever the deer's head, which was found in his freezer. Prosecutors called the defendant "dark in the heart" and his own attorney claimed "In all my years practicing law, I have never had a client who was so disliked by

---

[1] An earlier version of this paper was co-authored by Barbara Belbot and Frank P. Williams III and presented at the 2008 annual meeting of the Pacific Sociological Association. Portland, OR.

the whole community.... He is hated" (Rogers, 2010). The question raised at the trial was, if it is legal throughout the state to hunt and kill deer, why does this incident result in a felony prosecution? Is there a true difference in legal facts, or is it the way the media creates and relates the story?

The media's focus on some of these sensational animal-abuse cases leads to heightened public sensitivity and in some areas, serial reporting and investigations. When there are repetitive postings of a number to call if you suspect a neighbor of abuse or hoarding, it seems to inevitably lead to the discovery of more cases. "Victims" who appear particularly vulnerable, such as animals, generate increased activity by special-interest groups and general public empathy toward more punitive approaches to solving the problem.

In a public education campaign the advocacy group Dogs Deserve Better (DDB) has schoolchildren across the country create valentine cards. DDB subsequently sends these cards to persons identified as neglecting or isolating dogs in crates or on chains for long periods of time. The message is to "Have a Heart for Chained Dogs" and the organization's mission includes not only re-educating owners about options for more healthful dog care and assisting them in constructing or arranging care services, but also rescuing, transporting, fostering and re-homing animals. As Gilbert (2010) explains,

> Denying them interaction or frequent human contact and comfort, impeded by a sentence to a life of confinement, causes enormous mental and physical suffering.... They also suffer from constant exposure to the elements of weather, dying from heat stroke or freezing to death. They become entangled in chains, causing choking or fatal hanging, and suffer extreme physical damage or death from embedded collars and chains.

In debating whether an animal should be considered a victim and a subject of interest to victimologists, we would first need to analyze the role that animals play in society and their importance in cultural rituals as well as everyday survival.

AN HISTORICAL LOOK AT THE ROLE OF ANIMALS

In early times some animals were viewed as deities and were revered for their spiritual qualities. Others like the wolf were vilified as demons and were characterized as "threatening and malevolent metaphors." Their image as an analogy for evil, Kamil (2006, p. 5) writes, justified torturing, slaughtering and driving the species to the brink of extinction. An example of the deification of animals can be found in India where the cow is sacred to the Hindu religion.

> Some trace the cow's sacred status back to Lord Krishna, one of the faith's most important figures. He is said to have appeared 5,000 years ago as a cowherd, and is often described as bala-gopala, "the child who protects the cows." Another of Krishna's holy names, Govinda, means "one who brings satisfaction to the cows." Other scriptures identify the cow as the "mother" of all civilization, its milk nurturing the population (NPR http://www.pbs.org/wnet/nature/holycow/Hinduism.html).

Likewise, Christian narratives such as the story of Noah, connect the survival of mankind to the continued propagation of all species. Fables and folklore imbue the animal, such as the tortoise and the hare with humanlike qualities to teach moral lessons.

By the late 1800s many people, sensitized in part by the works of Darwin and other naturalists, were more inclined to acknowledge scientific links between man and animals. As our empirical analysis of life became more sophisticated, we were able to detect commonalities at the microscopic level which made it more difficult to ignore evidence of comparative intelligence and the thinking and feeling of many animal species. It is this evidence, Singer (1999) tells us, that leads philosophers to argue for some moral responsibility and protection of animals. Even in the late 1700s, British philosopher Jeremy Bentham (1789) argued,

> ...a fullgrown horse or dog is beyond comparison a more rational, as well as a more conversable animal, than an infant of a day, or a week, or even a month old. But suppose they

were otherwise, what would it avail? The question is not, Can they *reason*? nor Can they *talk*? but, Can they *suffer*?

Early American social reformers long decried the abuse of work animals, the whipping of emaciated and lame horses in busy market streets and thoroughfares. There was an SPCA (Society for the Prevention of Cruelty to Animals) before there was a SPCC (Society for the Prevention of Cruelty to Children). This coincides with the infamous report of an abused foster-child, Mary Ellen, being rendered at the SPCA, as there was no other agency for reporting abuse. This account is a staple in practically every contemporary criminal justice and juvenile justice textbook today.

THE ROLE OF ANIMALS IN SOCIETY TODAY

Arguably, we could distinguish our current era as one of unprecedented attention and care for animals. There are pet therapists, "big box" chain stores for animal supplies, pet spas and doggie day care centers. In Wisconsin, legislation has been proposed that will guide divorce law settlements involving pets. In some jurisdictions pets can be covered under restraining orders and many allow trusts to be set up in the interests of the pet, as for instance the $12-million settlement Leona Helmsley left to her Maltese. The pampering of pets by the wealthy, or anyone who simply chooses to spend their money that way, is a market that many companies have jumped to exploit. Honda specifically designed one of their vehicles, the Element, with dog-friendly options and the luxury Intercontinental Hotel which had always prohibited pets, now offers a deluxe Royal Pooch Package that can be added to a reservation for approximately $250 per night

> Your pooch will receive: Welcome amenity of organic dog biscuits; Bow Wow Bag; Rubby Buddy Pet Massager; Use of elegant Wetnoz Metro line dual feeders and a "Bolt" interactive laser toy. For you, the $25.00 per night pet fee is waived when booking the hotel's Royal Pooch Package (http://www.ichotelsgroup.com/intercontinental/en/gb/location s/experience-more/newyork-thebarclay).

According to an article in the *Los Angeles Times* (Huffstutter, 2007), by the year 2007 Americans were spending almost $41-billion per year on the care of their pets. Pet care appears to be a recession-proof market too, as expenditures are growing despite the economic hardships in the current fiscal crisis. In 2009, the amount was $45.5-billion, up 5.4 percent over 2008 ($43.2-billion)(Berkowitz, 2010). Although experts project that less than a quarter of what is spent on pets is actual veterinary services, the pet veterinary insurance industry is currently operating at $271 million and is "projected to grow to $500 million by 2012 (Berkowitz, 2010). What this means is that when pets are valued in nontraditional ways, there is the possibility that laws, and law enforcement, may also be used in nontraditional ways to support the status of pets and to protect them from harm or victimization. To find evidence of this shift, one need look no further than our television news programs and other mainstream media sources.

Animal Planet, a television channel devoted exclusively to animals, provides hours each day to the "reality show" coverage of animal-control operations. No doubt this programming is marketed to what is perceived of as a growing popularity of animal rights and interests in our society. And in turn, these programs have no doubt sensitized the public to the role of law enforcement in protecting pets and wildlife, as well as highlighting some of the worst-case scenarios. More recently, national attention has been drawn to the topics of cockfighting and dogfighting as many jurisdictions have enacted new laws, enforced existing laws and prosecuted some high-profile cases such as the dogfighting and cruelty charges against National Football League star, Michael Vick. Although our athlete icons are no strangers to criminal charges, the irony may be that wife-beaters, illegal drug users, bar-room shooters, rapists and fan attackers, DUI offenders too numerous to count, and pregnant girlfriend contract-killers seem to draw less serious sanctions and less public outcry than someone found to be abusing animals. Following the Vick controversy, Harris County Texas passed a dogfighting statute that made it a Class A misdemeanor to attend a dogfight, with punishment up to a one-year jail sentence. Sponsoring illegal dogfights may finally be seen as the chink in the armor of league, teammate, manager, and sports-apparel company support (Henry, 2007).

For law enforcement, aggressive pursuit of dogfighting operations may also yield fruitful international networks of organized crime and drug dealing cartels. After one 17-month undercover operation, South Texas law enforcement agencies had evidence for charges ranging from racketeering, gambling, weapons, drugs, theft, and stolen property as well as 187 abused animals valued at up to $3000 each in the illegal market (Leahy & Khanna, 2008). Still, the newness and infrequency of animal-oriented investigations means that officers are often inexperienced and untrained in cases such as dogfighting. In a recent New Mexico case, two brothers accused of operating dogfights had charges dropped and their dogs, many of whom were injured or ill, returned to them when a court ruled that there were errors in the search warrant. In an interesting move, the Gadsden Independent School District the former employer of one of the men went to court to claim "five of the dogs in lieu of a debt of $20,000 in legal bills incurred after the former teacher's contract was not renewed" (*Las Cruces Sun-News*, 2009).

THE PROSECUTION OF CRIMES AGAINST ANIMALS

Most jurisdictions only have a limited number of laws and codes dealing with the treatment of animals. In Las Cruces, New Mexico, cases of animal hoarding appear to have snowballed with media coverage of one case seemingly leading to another and another much like the social problems literature suggests. Four cases unfolded in a span of less than two months. In May, 2007 an electrical fire at a house led to the deaths and discovery of 73 cats under the care of one woman. She was soon found with another 21 cats in her downtown office. She pleaded no contest to 73 counts of failure to adequately provide proper care and maintenance and one count of violating a kennel license. A few days later, 129 cats were removed from another Las Cruces area home and all were euthanized due to poor health (feline leukemia and AIDS). The next day, 34 live and 16 dead cats were found in yet another Las Cruces home. It is unclear whether charges will be brought against these owners but charges were quickly filed against a fourth person after county Sheriff's deputies removed 125 animals from his property. In this case, the newspaper indicates that "a call from a neighbor" led to the investigation. The man's confrontations with authorities entering his property appeared to lead to a more aggressive response. In addition, his position as a public-school speech pathologist seemed to generate more controversy and concern about the status of his mental health. Soon, the newspaper reported that a Las Cruces man faced animal cruelty charges when it was discovered that his horse was suffering from malnutrition and a broken leg. The newspaper even printed short clips about cases in other jurisdictions including an elderly woman bitten by the more than 100 pet rats she kept in Los Angeles. Thus, the appearance of a social problem seems to have led to pressure on law enforcement authorities to deal with the cases as more and more are highlighted in the press. Newspaper editorials and blogs in Las Cruces raged back and forth between the issues of privacy, the encroachment of regulation, definitions of cruelty and standards of animal care.

Traditions of rural living, along with exaggerated feelings of personal freedom and privacy may lead some hoarders to reduced expectations of social contract and government intervention. Inhabiting unincorporated areas or those outside the city limits may lull owners into the perception of life without restrictions. The law, too, has consistently reinforced notions of home as private castle, which may allow some people, perhaps more so those with personal and mental-health problems to misjudge the public's tolerance for lifestyles that deviate significantly from the norm.

For Las Cruces, the exponential growth of the area in a very short time has generated a number of controversial issues reflecting the sharp divide between a traditional Hispanic farmland and a contemporary retirement mecca. Part college town, part military retirement area, the city is viewed by many as suffering from being distinguished by top national magazines as one of the best places to live. In a relatively short period of time the population almost doubled, introducing a rapidly-changing value set into the community. Ironically, the care and treatment of animals has figured prominently into the culture conflict as new residents arrive and crowd into previously-open spaces that used to separate homesteads with privacy. Economic hard times also drive concerns over property values leading to calls for code enforcement and animal control over anything viewed as a potential detriment to the area.

Animal Cruelty and Human Violence

A recent newspaper article about senseless animal shootings bemoans the fact that the few protection laws that do exist seem to cover pets and not livestock. Ironically, the cattlemen's lobby groups which are now looking for protection of their assets are the same ones who for years successfully avoided incorporation of their livestock under cruelty measures lest their treatment and slaughter be somehow evaluated in a context of animal rights. The article captures the essence of social problem construction: "While there are no statistics on such crimes, newspapers detail scores of cases" (Glionna, 2007). The author goes on to say

> Two Texas college students were indicted in 2006 for slashing a horse's neck before stabbing it in the heart with a broken golf club handle...three joy-riding men killed a pony named 'Ted E. Bear' that belonged to a 4-year old boy...two Tennessee teenagers shot and killed 24 cows, many of them pregnant.

The article fuels potential panic with its claim that

> Studies suggest that youths who engage in animal cruelty often commit violent criminal behavior as adults. Among those who preyed on animals before people were infamous mass murderers Jeffrey Dahmer, Ted Bundy and Albert DeSalvo, the "Boston Strangler."

It is precisely these links to psychopathology and the idea that the animal abuser of today is the serial killer of tomorrow that pushes legislators to adopt more serious interventions in cases of detected delinquency.

One of the reasons that criminologists are wary of the animal-abuse/serial-killer link is that the cases we know of are determined retrospectively, in that we analyze a person after the fact. The finding of a history of animal abuse in a number of the very small subset of serial killers may seem significant but that implication diminishes once the overall prevalence of animal abuse in the general population is gauged. In a research study where participants answered an ad offering pay for participation, Lea (2007) was able to determine that 22% of male respondents admitted to some involvement with animal cruelty. After studying the more than 550 youth in this survey, she concluded that while there is no direct support for the idea that abusive behavior towards animals is linked to human-directed violence, the relationship is nonetheless complicated. It appears that young people may engage in animal abuse as a form of stimulation, excitement and risk-taking behavior and in some cases to alleviate frustration. However, she also found that these behaviors seemed to be associated with other forms of less serious forms of delinquency, most of which appeared to be non-violent. In her study, Lea found that a number of youth experimenting or going along with others in animal-abuse activities altered their behaviors once they realized the harm or suffering caused and reported guilt over the incident. However, "some admitted abusers, of course, never experienced such an incident and thus simply seemed to outgrow abusive behavior without incident, perhaps finding little social support for such acts as they took on more adult roles" (Lea, 2007, p. 120).

Still, research findings on the animal-abuse/later-violence relationship are mixed. Many of the studies that do find correlations are small sample studies using participant interviews. Comparing 45 violent and non-violent offenders in prison, Merz-Perez, Heide and Silverman (2001) found that childhood violence against animals was related to future violence against people. Examining attitudes about the treatment of animals in college students, Henry (2004) found that those who had either observed or had actually taken part in animal cruelty scored higher on indicators of delinquency on a self-report scale.

A number of studies have looked at animal abuse as another facet of domestic violence. A companion pet can viewed as an attractive target of violence as it may be emotionally tied to the well-being of the human victim. In one study of women at a battered woman's shelter, over 70 percent of those interviewed reported that a pet had been killed, harmed or threatened with harm—most were actually harmed. And, more than one-half of the women reported that one of their children had hurt or killed a pet (Ascione, 1998). Repeating this study, this time with a control group of women who had not suffered domestic violence, Ascione and his associates (2007) found that not only were women in shelters 11 times more likely to have had pets injured or killed but that they reported being distraught and emotionally devastated by the harm, which may have been the intent of the abuser. In fact, in the first case of battered-women's syndrome used as a defense to murder in Salt Lake City, Utah, Peggy Sue Brown testified to such abusive conduct by her husband. After repeatedly beating, raping and locking her up, as well as torturing members of her family, Bradley Brown "hung a pet rabbit in the garage and summoned his wife. When she came with the baby on her shoulder, her husband began skinning the animal alive. Then he held the boy next to the screaming rabbit. 'See how easy it would be?' Bradley said." Mrs. Brown was acquitted (Ascione, 1998, p. 130).

In some instances, battered women have indicated that concern for a pet may have even delayed their decision to seek safety in a shelter. Again, children were often exposed to pet violence and also reported distress over the incidents. In a more recent study in Australia, female victims of domestic violence were asked about pet abuse and were compared to women in non-violent domestic settings. Those with a history of family violence were more likely to report that the partner abused a pet, threatened to abuse a pet, or other family members in the home engaged in pet abuse. Mothers referred from domestic violence services also reported that children were more likely to have witnessed and engaged in pet abuse than in homes without domestic violence (Volant, et. al., 2008).

Research seems to indicate that pets may serve as an outlet for youth who are frustrated and acting out over violence in the home or are mimicking or learning violent reactions to stress. In a study using a community control-group, Currie (2006, p. 425) found "children exposed to domestic violence were significantly more likely to have been cruel to animals than children not exposed to violence." She also found that it was older youth who engaged in the cruelty if they came from domestic violence settings as compared to kids who were cruel to animals but had not been exposed to family violence. A closer look at this relationship was found in a study by Clifton Flynn (1999) who determined that boys who were subjected to corporal punishment from their fathers up through the teenage years were more likely to commit animal abuse. This association appeared to hold even after controlling for child abuse, parental domestic violence and the father's education level. This is one of the few studies that specifically addressed gender distinctions in its outcomes.

Legal Responses to Animal Victims

Pressure from animal rights activists and their effective use of the media has certainly enhanced the likelihood of prosecution of animal hoarders and abusers. This would not be possible, however, were we not in a time where public sentiment favors such a course of action. Experts appear on a host of animal-related issues including an Anti-Cruelty Initiatives subcommittee of the SPCA and many law schools, including South Texas College of Law, now offer permanent courses in animal law (Bryant, 2007). Harris County, Texas, employs a special assistant district attorney for prosecuting animal abuse cases.

According to Allen (2005), in the past decade, most states have upgraded their animal-cruelty statutes from mostly misdemeanors to at least some felony offenses, a move the author credits to the effective lobbying of the Humane Society. States with larger Humane Society memberships were more likely to have statutes that are more punitive, as was the case for states that bordered other states with more punitive statutes. Allen also found that states with higher numbers of hunters were less likely to enact the more-punitive sanctions and states with more democratic leadership or more political party competition were also more likely to have added the felony punishments for animal cruelty. Today, Arizona law sets the largest possible fine at a maximum of $150,000, while those convicted in Louisiana and Alabama face sentences of up to 10 years of incarceration.

While animal-abuse statutes may be more specific and offenses easier to detect and prosecute, it's often much more expensive and time-consuming to investigate instances of animal hoarding. Part of the expense involves the cost of providing care to the animals during the potentially lengthy investigation period, an expense born by public and private animal shelters and animal control facilities. Overnight, an animal hoarding case can increase the population of a shelter to the point that it is forced to refuse taking in other animals until the case is resolved, which can easily take weeks and months. Animals that have been hoarded may have contagious diseases or need medical care. In most cases, these animals cannot be released until the animal cruelty case is resolved. The animals live in a sort of legal limbo during this time period. According to the Hoarding of Animals Research Consortium (HARC) , approximately one-third of the states have laws that allow a defendant in an animal cruelty or neglect case to post a security bond to pay for the costs of caring for the animals while the case is being adjudicated. This way, defendants can keep legal ownership of the animals and the private or public shelter facility does not bear the expense of caring for the seized animal.

In many instances, the individuals investigating hoarding cases (police, judges, prosecutors, and defense attorneys) fail to recognize the seriousness of the hoarder's conduct. The media has portrayed some hoarders as eccentric lovers of animals who are well-meaning but "things just went wrong" or they "tried to help too many animals." And, in the past, prosecutors and judges did not appear to be willing to seek or impose strict sentences, even for hoarders who are recidivists. All of this changes, however, when the social context of a problem makes it politically-expedient for the criminal justice system to change its priorities on certain types of cases. As a recent case in Houston demonstrates, both civil and criminal codes are being fine-tuned to respond more quickly than ever before. In October of 2009, more than 1,000 animals were seized from a man who was selling them at local flea markets. Although most were birds, iguanas, hamsters and rats, there were other larger pets, most cramped into small cages. Up to 200 of the animals were dead or died shortly after they were confiscated. Reports indicated that "ducks and geese were drinking from puddles that had dead chickens in them, and one trailer was filled with caged animals kept in the dark with no food, water or heat...some of the mice had cannibalized each other" (O'Hare, 2009). In an unusual ruling, a civil remedy was reached with the owner agreeing to turn over the home and property, valued at approximately $150,000 to the county to pay for the rescue and care of the animals which is estimated at over $213,000. Criminal charges may still follow.

Berry, Patronek, and Lockwood (2005) report that it is difficult to study animal hoarding cases because there is no national law-enforcement data base that lists people who have been prosecuted and convicted of hoarding animals and no standard for reporting the cases. As a consequence, there is little or no data available about the long-term outcomes of animal-hoarding cases where charges have been filed. Added to that is the significant diversity among state statutes and local ordinances that authorities use to prosecute hoarders. In their study of 56 animal-hoarding cases from 26 different states in which charges had been filed and follow-up information was available, Berry et al. found that in 41 cases the primary defendant was charged with at least one misdemeanor count of animal cruelty and in five of those cases, he or she was also charged with at least one felony count of animal cruelty. Many defendants were also charged with violating local ordinances such as failure to maintain sanitary conditions, violation of a pet limitation ordinance, failure to provide rabies vaccinations, failure to license animals, and other charges including criminal nuisance and business and zoning violations. Although these charges can be brought as one count for each animal, typically the charges were reduced because of redundancy. In only in one-fourth of the cases did the court order the defendant to undergo pretrial psychological assessment or a mental-health evaluation. Of the 42 cases in which there was a guilty verdict or plea-bargain, 40.5% of the defendants were given a sentence of jail time, with almost one-half of those sentences for less than six months. Almost one-half of those 42 were fined and 25% ordered to pay restitution. Only eight of the defendants were ordered into post-trial mental health counseling. In three cases, the defendants were prohibited from ever owning or possessing animals in the future. Others were prohibited from owning or possessing animals during probation or given limits on the number of animals they could own or possess. The authors of this study concluded that officials often had a difficult time striking a balance between helping the hoarder and protecting the animals. Officials were pressured in some situations to seek plea bargains or forego filing charges in order to prevent the animals languishing in shelters for a long time pending resolution of a case. They also reported that in several cases there was little communication and a lack of shared information between the different county and state agencies involved in the case. Interestingly, the researchers found that in nine cases, the defendants claimed they were involved in animal rescue organizations. The researchers in this case were not able to collect follow-up data to determine if the convicted animal hoarders actually served their sentences, where the hoarder was currently located, or whether follow-up visits were actually conducted in those cases where they were ordered.

Illinois is currently the only state with a specific statute addressing animal hoarding (Avery 2005; Berry, Patronek, & Lockwood, 2005). Signed into law in 2001, it defines the term "companion animal hoarder," and imposes specific penalties against hoarders that can even result in felony convictions. Animal hoarders are defined as:

> [A] person who i) possesses a large number of companion animals; ii) fails to or is unable to provide what he or she is required to provide under Section 3 of this Act; iii) keeps the companion animals in a severely overcrowded environment; and iv) displays an inability to recognize or understand the nature of or has a reckless disregard for the conditions under which the companion animals are living and the deleterious impact they have on the companion animals' and owner's health and well-being.

The Illinois law increases the penalties for animal abuse from a misdemeanor to a Class 4 felony, and increases the penalties for subsequent offenses. Judges can also order psychiatric examination and treatment for offenders, at the convicted offenders' expense. Animal hoarders are required to pay a bond for the care of animals seized in abuse cases and to provide assistance to shelters charged with the animals' care. If the bond is not posted within five days of the animals' seizure, their ownership is transferred to the agency providing shelter and they can be offered for adoption. The law also allows veterinarians, animal welfare investigators, or law enforcement to take animals into protective custody without a court order if they believe the animals have been abused or their lives are in danger.

Animal hoarding is prosecuted in other states under anti-cruelty to animals' statutes (Berry, Patronek, & Lockwood, 2005). Those statutes require people who own companion animals to provide for their care and impose criminal penalties for failure to do so; however, they sometimes leave room for interpretation. How much food, water, and shelter can be considered adequate in a particular situation? Some cities avoid the ambiguity of the state laws by relying on a mix of local ordinances dealing with pet limitations, animal licensing, dangerous animals, rabies vaccination, health and safety codes (including child and elderly adult welfare laws), wildlife statutes, and even agriculture or market codes (see Huss, 2005 for a discussion of the constitutionality of some of those ordinances) Some states allow prosecutors and animal protection agencies to seek counseling and community service for animal hoarders, seizure or forfeiture of the animals, and restitution from the offender to reimburse the agency that cared for the animals pending resolution of the case.

Most state courts have upheld their states' animal cruelty statutes against challenges that they violate the U.S. or state Constitutions under *void for vagueness* which would be found if they are not written clearly enough to give adequate notice as to what conduct is allowed or forbidden. In *Wilkerson v. State* (1981), the offender was convicted of torturing a raccoon. He contended that the Florida law's definition of animal was vague and overbroad. The Florida Supreme Court held the term "animal" and "every living dumb creature"—the definition of an animal—are not unconstitutionally vague and upheld Wilkerson's conviction. The court concluded that the state legislature intended raccoons to be included in that definition. In *State v. Hirsh* (1924), the Missouri Court of Appeals upheld Hirsch's misdemeanor conviction for unlawfully failing to supply his horses with sufficient water, food, shelter, and protection. The local sheriff found two horses and 17 Shetland ponies confined on his property without sufficient food. The sheriff found no food on the property and bare ground in the pastures. Two horses had starved to death and had been buried on the property. Hirsch argued that the evidence was insufficient to convict him of intentionally failing to provide necessary food and water or that he was indifferent to their care. The court concluded that malice and intent could be imputed from the facts of the case and malice could be inferred by showing that Hirsch confined the animals without food. The state legislature, decided the court, provided that it was not necessary to show the act was done maliciously but a malicious act could be inferred if it was done wrongfully, intentionally, and willfully. When a wrongful act is committed under the facts of a case like Hirsch's, the court concluded it could infer the acts were intentional.

The defendant was charged with willfully and intentionally confining 27 cows on his farm without food in *Missouri v. Brookshire* (1962). Brookshire argued that he lacked criminal intent because he had a physical injury that made it difficult for him to get food for the cows. The court concluded that Brookshire confined the cattle on his farm in the winter without food, knowing they would require 500 or so bales of hay and that several days without food could result in their starving to death. These facts were sufficient, held the court, for the jury to find malice and criminal intent as required by the statute.

The Florida District Court of Appeals upheld the constitutionality of a statute that prohibited depriving an animal of sufficient food, water, air, and exercise in *Florida v. Mary Elizabeth Wilson* (1985). Wilson was convicted of confining 77 poodles in cages in the back of her van without food, water and air. The court found that the statute's language conveyed sufficient definite warnings of the illegal conduct. The statute's language was definite enough about the need to provide a sufficient amount of food of good quality and water, and similarly definite in its proscription against keeping animals in enclosures without sufficient exercise and a change of air. Persons of common intelligence would understand the law's requirements.

In *People v. Speegle* (1997), a California appellate court noted that it would be impossible for an animal-cruelty statute to describe every possible way that offenders could be cruel to animals. In that case, animal control officers removed 200 dogs, three horses, and one cat from unsanitary and filthy conditions that included no food or water, and corpses of dogs and puppies in Speegle's freezer. Vets who examined the dogs stated they were anemic, malnourished and underweight, suffering from bug infestations and parasites. The horse was unable to walk without severe pain because his hooves had not been trimmed. Speegle was convicted of eight counts of animal cruelty—subjecting her animals to unnecessary suffering as prohibited by state law. Speegle challenged her conviction and alleged the statute was unconstitutionally vague because the language was too general and left individuals to guess as to what the law required. What is meant by necessary sustenance, proper food and drink, or subjecting an animal to needless suffering? The court held, however, that the meaning of the statute could be reasonably ascertained and that a statute does not have to furnish detailed plans or specifications of the prohibited acts. Statutes can use ordinary language that has a common usage. Terms such as "necessary," "needless," and "proper" give people notice of what a reasonable standard of care for animals is.

Images of Animal Abuse and Freedom of Speech

If commonsense definitions of animal cruelty are constitutional, what do courts say about the creation of images of such abuse? In 2009 the U. S. Supreme Court agreed to examine a case (*U. S. v. Stevens*) that pits animal-cruelty groups against free-speech advocates who argue that even disgusting and inhumane footage of animal torture and abuse should be protected under the Fifth Amendment (making the First Amendment applicable to the states)(Savage, 2009). In striking down Stevens' conviction for animal cruelty in a case where the defendant sold videos of dogfights and the use of pitbulls in hunting down and killing other wild animals, the court could not find a compelling state interest that would outweigh the First Amendment rights at stake. The legal reasoning was that while the law clearly penalized those conducting such actions, it is less likely that it would be constitutional to punish a person not directly involved in any of those activities, meaning the holder or promoter of the films. According to Savage, "Some media lawyers worry the law could be used against movies, TV shows or books that show bullfighting, hunting with bows and arrows or documentaries exposing conditions in a slaughterhouse." Although Federal law had made it a crime to market "crush" or torture videos, it had specifically aimed the law away from hunting, fishing and the regulated slaughter of animals for food (Savage, 2009, p. A20). Still, a U. S. Appeals court has recently overturned that law on freedom of speech grounds, leading critics to claim a resurgence of such clips, animal "snuff" films and underground footage of kittens being set on fire, on the internet.

Alternatives to Formal Legal Interventions

One of the arguments against the development of new criminal laws and offenses is the existence of adequate measures in civil codes to address these problems. As Berry, Patronek and Lockwood (2005) explain, most jurisdictions have an array of anti-cruelty laws that would cover the circumstances in hoarding cases. They use pet limitation, animal licensing, dangerous animal, rabies vaccination requirements, as well as health, zoning, fire, safety, and wildlife statutes along with agriculture and market codes.

HARC encourages communities to establish an interdisciplinary task force to address hoarding situations with a multi-pronged and coordinated approach. Such a task force would include representatives from public health agencies, social service agencies, local housing and building code enforcement agencies, and animal protection public and private organizations. Local housing and health codes often include minimal standards of cleanliness and safety that can be enforced to deal with some animal hoarding. Health departments can be called in to investigate complaints dealing with such things as inadequate ventilation, non-functioning bathroom and kitchen facilities, lack of garbage disposal, and rodent infestations—the kinds of conditions that authorities frequently discover during animal abuse and cruelty investigations.

Determining appropriate sanctions for offenders would also go a long way in reducing potential victimization and prevention of recidivism. In the Harris County, Texas, case of the killing of the popular deer, Mr. Buck, the defendant received 18 months in jail. As a consequence of the felony conviction he will also likely lose his license as an insurance adjuster (Rogers, 2010). In one Las Cruces, NM, case Marilyn Davis was given one year of probation and 500 hours of community service working in animal shelters, which certainly would be challenged by mental health professionals. Her pathology is the inability to separate normal service and caring from hoarding; thus, psychologically, this may not be an appropriate or healthy sanction. Isn't it a bit like putting a child molester to work in a day-care center or an alcoholic to work in a bar?

ANIMAL VICTIMS IN PERSPECTIVE

In many societies today there are values and attitudes supporting the idea that some animals, as well as people, may be more vulnerable to victimization and thus need additional protections and services. Pro-testers commonly boycott industries selling furs or processing meats, and commit crimes by breaking into and liberating zoo exhibits and laboratory experiments. Most lawful actions are tolerated and accommodated to some degree by our appreciation of free expression and diversity. Still, we must each attempt to prioritize in some logical schema which victims we will devote our limited resources to. Deciding where to place animals and whether to distinguish between pets, lifestock and wildlife is part of developing a meaningful continuum of victims. A survey sponsored by the American Veterinary Medical Association in 2002 found that 47 percent of those questioned viewed their pets as members of the family (Donn, 2007). It is not surprising, then, that they would see care and justice issues in that light and campaign for stronger laws and harsher sentences for those abusing animals. And, perhaps, they would also argue for more lenient sentences for those who violate the law in their efforts to protect the lives of animals.

References

Note: All references to HARC's recommendations and findings are from the HARC website.

Allen, M. D. (2005). Laying down the law? Interest group influence on state adoption of animal cruelty felony laws. *The Policy Studies Journal, 33*, 443–457.

Ascione, F. R. (1998). Battered women's reports of their partners' and their children's cruelty to animals. *Journal of Emotional Abuse, 1*, 119–131.

Ascione, F. R., Weber, C., Thompson, T., Heath, J., & Maruyama, M. (2007). Battered pets and domestic violence: Animal abuse reported by women experiencing intimate violence and by nonabused women. *Violence Against Women, 13*, 354–373.

Avery, L. (2005). From helping to hoarding to hurting: When the acts of "good samaritans" become felony animal cruelty. *Valparaiso University Law Review, 39*, 815–858.

Bentham, J. (1948). *An introduction to the principles of morals and legislation.* New York: Kegan Paul (Orginal work published 1789).

Berkowitz, L. (2010, February 24). Booming industry. *Houston Chronicle*. E4.

Berry, C., Patronek, G., & Lockwood, R. (2005). Long-term outcomes in animal hoarding cases. *Animal Law, 11*, 167–194.

Bryant, S. (2007, October 20). More U.S. law schools going to the dogs. *Houston Chronicle*, B1, 6.

Costin, L. B. (1991) Unraveling the Mary Ellen legend: Origins of the "cruelty" movement. *Social Service Review, 65,* 203–223.

Currie, C. (2006). Animal cruelty by children exposed to domestic violence. *Child Abuse & Neglect, 30,* 425–435.

Donn, J. (2007, March 18). Medical bills soaring for American pets. *Los Angeles Times,* A14.

Flynn, C. P. (1999). Exploring the link between corporal punishment and children's cruelty to animals. *Journal of Marriage and Family, 61,* 971–981.

Gilbert, J. (2010, January 24). Awareness campaign targets chained dogs. *Las Cruces Sun News.*

Glionna, J. M. (2007, August 24). State laws failing to guard the flock. *Houston Chronicle,* A18.

Henry, B. C. (2004). The relationship between animal cruelty, delinquency, and attitudes toward the treatment of animals. *Society & Animals, 12,* 185–207.

Henry, G. (2007, July 20). Michael Vick's off-field troubles suspend release of Nike product. *Las Cruces Sun News,* 3B.

Huffstutter, P. J. (2007, July 15). Who gets custody of Fido? *Los Angeles Times,* A13.

Huss, R. (2005). No pets allowed: Housing issues and companion animals. *Animal Law, 11,* 69–129.

Kamil, N. (2006). Of animal history and human cruelty in the New England tradition. *Reviews of American History, 34,* 1–11.

Kirk, B. (2007, June 30). Possible hoarding charges pending. *Las Cruces Sun News,* A1, 9.

Las Cruces Sun-News (2009, December 23). El Paso twins get four pit bulls back, barred from taking five more by court order.

Lea, S. R. (2007). *Delinquency and animal cruelty: Myths and realities about social pathology.* New York: LFB Scholarly Publishing.

Leahy, J., & Khanna, R. (2008, November 16). Search continues for suspects in Harris dogfight ring. *Houston Chronicle.*

Medina, J., & Kirk, B. (2007, June 29). 'Deplorable' man has 30 dogs, dozens of cats. *Las Cruces Sun News,* A1, 7.

Merz-Perez, L., Heide, K., & Silverman, I. (2001). Childhood cruelty to animals and subsequent violence against humans. *International Journal of Offender Therapy and Comparative Criminology, 45,* 556–573.

O'Hare, P. (2009, October 1). Man forfeits home, 1,000 animals. *Houston Chronicle*, B1.

Rogers, B. (2010, February 5). Killer of 'Mr. Buck' gets 18 months in jail. *Houston Chronicle*, B5.

Savage, D. G. (2009, September 27). Should images of animal cruelty be protected speech? *Houston Chronicle*, A20.

Singer, P. (1999). *Practical ethics, 2nd Ed.* Cambridge, UK: Cambridge University Press.

Snyder, K. S. (2009). No cracks in the wall: The standing barrier and the need for restructuring animal protection laws. *Cleveland State Law Review, 57,* 137–166.

Volant, A., Johnson, J., Gullone, E., & Coleman, G. (2008). The relationship between domestic violence and animal abuse. *Journal of Interpersonal Violence, 23,*1277–1295.

Law Cases

Florida v. Mary Elizabeth Wilson, 464 So.2d 667 (Fla. Dist. Ct. App. 1985)

Missouri v. Brookshire, 335 S.W.2d 333 (Mo. Ct. App. 1962)

People v. Speegle, 53 Cal. App. 4th 1405 (Cal. 1997)

State v. Hirsch, 260 S.W. 557 (Mo. Ct. App. 1924)

Wilkerson v. State, 401 So. 1110 (Fla. 1981)

U. S. v. Stevens (05-2497)

Discussion Questions

1. When would you define an animal as a victim?
2. How do you think animal victims compare to human victims in our society and why?
3. Discuss the various laws and legal options that we have developed to protect animals and prosecute animal abusers in terms of their actual and potential impact. What are the strengths and weaknesses of these measures?

Books You May Want to Read

Beirne, P. (2009). *Confronting animal abuse: Law, criminology and human-animal relationships.* Lanham, MD: Rowan Littlefield.
Eisnitz, G. (2006). *Slaughterhouse: The shocking story of greed, neglect, and inhumane treatment inside the U.S. meat industry.* Amherst, NY: Prometheus Books.
Strouse, K. (2009). *Badd newz: The untold story of the Michael Vick dog fighting case.* North Charleston, SC: BookSurge.

Movies You May Want To See

Monster (2003) Charlize Theron
Boys Don't Cry (1999) Hillary Swank

Web Links

www.animallaw.info
http://www.aspcapro.org/
http://www.pet-abuse.com/

CHAPTER 11

The Victim in News Media, Film, and Literature

INTRODUCTION

The way the media interprets crime is often an emotional presentation that some critics might say amounts to exploitation. Unless you have had a direct experience that allows you to counteract or offset the media's version of crime effects, you are likely to see their images of victimization as reality. Strong emotional depictions are an essential part of crime news. First, stories need to show that victims are "just like you and me" which compels viewers to see themselves as the possible victim of such a crime. The event is also described in enough detail to allow you to feel some small part of exactly what the victim endured (McShane & Williams, 1992) . And, unlike newscasts of the past that strove to be strictly factual, reporters today use adjectives like "horrendous," "devastating," and "brutal" to describe a victimization that has taken place. This "colorized" version ascribes emotions, feelings, and subjective sentiments to events. It is likely that most citizens do not even realize these values and images are being imposed on the event "stories."

In the process of "sharing" the victimizing event, or vicarious victimization, the viewer identifies with the victims and becomes bonded with them. Blogs and feedback comments on internet news pages attest to this phenomenon. The story usually implies that the victim has been forever changed by the events and will, somehow, never be the same again, potentially leaving us, as consumers of that information, with a type of haunting fear that we could be next. And, because research indicates the percentage of news focusing on crime has increased over the years (Callanan, 2005), it is likely that our perceptions of the amount of crime that is taking place has been disproportionately inflated.

The media coverage of the 1993 murder of Polly Klass, according to journalist Peter Sussman (1997, p. 13), was one such example of this process, which he argues is not only unbalanced, but non-journalistic.

California journalists chose to tell—to overtell—the story of Polly Klass with the erroneous implication that it was somehow a representative crime. Coverage that was factual on its face became a serious form of media distortion because the emphasis itself was misplaced.

Cases, like those of Klass, a middle-class, white pre-teen, represent perhaps some of the most statistically rare crime events, namely an older child abducted from her bedroom at night by a stranger while a parent was home. Trends in data indicate that most murdered children are under the age of one and that most older children are killed with firearms and by an adult family member. In addition, murder victims 12 years of age or older are more likely to be Black (Harms & Snyder, 2004).

Our American obsession with crime television ballooned with the advent of cable and around-the-clock reality programming. As Callanan explains, the blending of news and entertainment as "infotainment" has perhaps culminated in the appearance of unique channels dedicated solely to the coverage of crime, courts and victim stories. In addition, anywhere from 75 to 95 percent of Americans and Canadians surveyed report that mass media is their major source of crime information (Callanan, 2005, p. 55). And, even though many viewers recognize that media is distorted, inaccurate or biased, they still continue to rely on it as their only source of information about crime.

Of course the goal of any media outlet is to attract and retain viewership in order to drive up the price and the desirability of advertising space. The simplest way to do that often seems to be appealing to the public as potential victims. It is therefore more effective and efficient to use stories where the theme is clear cut: good versus evil and images of offenders as physically-threatening strangers who are unlike us.

FEAR OF CRIME

Research has consistently supported the relationship between exposure to media and fear of crime (Chiricos, Padgett & Gertz, 2000; Eschholz, Chiricos & Gertz, 2003; Guo, Zhu & Chen, 2001). Studies have found that some types of media exposure, such as local news about crime or crime dramas, are influential in increasing individual levels of fear of crime. Even back in 1947, the FBI's infamous director, J. Edgar Hoover, used a magazine article to stir up the country and most likely get additional crime fighting funds. In an article in American Magazine he told the country that our women and children would never be safe until rapists were cleared from the streets. Using fear tactics, the title itself, "How Safe is Your Daughter?," implied that females everywhere were at risk.

More recent research has indicated that there are certain people, such as white females, for whom the media is an even stronger influence on their fear of crime (Dowler, 2003). While Williams and McShane (2003) found that significant others were a more important source of one's degree of worry about crime, there are indications that the information our significant others get is directly from television and other forms of media. And, there is plenty of criticism of media's abuse of crime victims and their circumstances. As Sussman (1997, p. 13) argues, in many cases, "...the story titillates rather than educates. It panders to and reinforces widespread public fears instead of informing with a valid sense of context."

Fear of crime has also been associated with the perception of one's environment as dangerous and disorderly (Quarles, 2003). Features of a neighborhood such as incivilities and aesthetics are also thought to be associated with potential victimization and thus higher levels of fear of crime among residents (Snell, 2001). Official or informal designations of places as high-crime areas or hot spots become part of the reputation that makes an area undesirable.

Social scientists also refer to fear of crime as a secondary or indirect victimization. In this scenario, the effects of crime appear to restrict our activities and diminish the quality of our lifestyle as we take precautions to avoid places, times, or events that might increase our risk of becoming a victim. This has social costs as we refrain from going to clubs, movies, or other cultural events that might enhance our community both economically and socially. In a sense, we are all victimized as a group when more diverse interactions are reduced or cut off entirely.

For many victims, fear of crime also means fear of repeat or subsequent victimizations. Those who have been abused, harassed or stalked often attempt to relocate to avoid being the target of subsequent crimes. Currently, 28 states have enacted an Address Confidentiality Program (ACP), which allows a victim to use a legally-recognized separate and substitute address that is provided for them (Syrnick & Applegarth, 2009). In most cases the program is administered by an Office of Victim Advocacy (Pennsylvania), Victims Services Office (New Hampshire, North Carolina), the Office of the Attorney General (Florida, Indiana, Texas), or the Secretary of State (California, Oklahoma, Washington), all of which make sure that applicants meet the criteria for this protection feature. These addresses can be used to fulfill the "residence" requirements of court and government records, such as drivers' licenses, library cards, public utility billings, traffic tickets, motor vehicle registrations, employment security, workers' compensation, school records, and court petitions. The state also assumes the responsibility of safeguarding the actual addresses of program participants. The intent of these programs is to limit the ways that victims might be tracked, particularly through the use of open records mandates which effect most government records and public documents.

VICTIMS AND THE MEDIA

In our society, First Amendment concerns about protecting speech often mean that some groups will be offended by graphic and violent images and language in the media, including expressions in art, music, film, television or video games. And, from time-to-time, cases develop where defendants attempt to blame these media entertainment sources for their criminal conduct. The implication is that their criminal conduct was somehow caused by the media and that the offender was himself or herself a victim of that media.

The research findings have been very mixed about the possible relationship between violent media, video games, and music, and subsequent violent behavior by its consumers. In one notorious case, Ronald Ray Howard argued that his constant exposure to the "cop killer" lyrics of rapper Tupac Shakur was the force behind his gunning down a law enforcement officer outside of Houston,Texas in 1993 (Philips, 1993). His defense depicted Howard as a robotic automaton, helpless to ignore the messages playing over and over in his head and blaring from his car stereo. Not believing this defense, the jury convicted Howard and he was given the death penalty and executed in 2005. Despite the apparent futility of the argument, the same defense was entered by two teens in Wisconsin who took part in the sniper slaying of an officer in 1994. The defendants in that case, Curtis Lee Walker and Denziss Jackson, seventeen at the time of the murder, were both sentenced to life in prison and will not be eligible for parole until 2045 (Philips, 1994). Ironically, Shakur himself was gunned down and killed a short time later in Las Vegas, Nevada, at the age of 25.

News Media

While the results of research on the effects of these various forms of media on behavior are inconclusive and methodologically problematic, many still believe that some restrictions on media are best for society. In the mid-1980s, Tipper Gore, wife of then-senator Al Gore, worked to form the Parents' Music Resource Center (PMRC) that pushed for a more uniform system of warning labels to identify certain types of graphic content in music sold to youngsters. The PMRC published a list of its "Filthy Fifteen"—the songs they believed should be banned for explicit language about sex and violence or the glorification of drugs and alcohol. Tipper Gore testified before Congress about possible government restrictions; her testimony was then countered by the music industry and advocates for freedom in music expression. The latter group emerged mostly victorious on the issue, as it continues to be interpreted as one of suppression and artistic censorship; although, today, most music with explicit lyrics does contain a warning label or sticker. The concession to provide a parental guidance/explicit lyrics warning was the music industry's way of neutralizing an issue that had been politically volatile. The measure mirrored the use of similar ratings in film and did not seem to have any significant impact on sales.

Victimologists and those involved in victim support also appear to have a general consensus that media, particularly news media, need to be more sensitive to victims as live crime stories are covered. While some states have restrictions on releasing the names of juveniles or sex crime victims, identities are easy to discern when parents, employers or neighbors are photographed or interviewed. Karmen (2001) suggests that journalists should develop a code of ethics pertaining specifically to victims. This code would involve explaining to victims their "media rights" before interviewing them about their experiences.

The news media is also criticized for focusing on current or unfolding explanations of events and then failing to go back and explain later developments that might implicate a victim, exonerate an offender, or clarify the context of a crime. The same can be said for coverage of new legislation or policies. For example, while there was substantial media space devoted to the passage of Megan's Laws in all 50 states, there has been virtually no discussion in the same media about the lack of evidence that the law has had any desired effect. In fact, a study in the law's originating state, New Jersey, found that the legislation had no significant impact on the length of time sex offenders spent released in the community prior to a rearrest. The researchers also found the law did not lower the rate of sexual reoffending, nor did it reduce the number of victims involved in sexual offenses. And, although sentences received by sex offenders following passage of the law nearly doubled, time served in prison or jail was relatively unchanged. Further, the costs of implementing the bill increased steadily and ended 2007 at roughly $3.9-million in expenditures for the New Jersey communities studied. Although the authors of the report (Zgoba, Witt, Dalessandro & Veysey, 2008) conclude that the costs may not be justified given the lack of positive results, it is unlikely that anyone would speak out against the measures, given the widespread notoriety of the family of the victim for whom the measures are named.

The media can also become involved in stories that would then cause readers or viewers to suspect their neutral reporting of that issue. For example, Spivak (2011) explains that *Ms. Magazine* funded a research study on rape that was part of coverage they were doing on the topic. As his description conveys, politicians contribute to media interest and all parties seem to have a vested interest in the various aspects of victim studies.

The issue of rape victimization prevalence being tied to survey definitions was most notably demonstrated in the controversy surrounding the so-called *Ms.* Study.... The popular name of the study came from *Ms.* magazine, which had reported on an earlier survey...leading to sponsorship of the latter study...by the magazine's Campus Project on Sexual Assault (Warshaw 1988/1994). The authors of the study asserted that one-quarter of their sample reported having been the victim of rape or attempted rape since they were fourteen years old (Koss et al., 1987). The results of the survey, popularized in Robin Warshaw's book *I Never Called It Rape*, became a sensation in the late 1980s and early 1990s. The "one-in-four" figure was regularly invoked by activists at "Take-Back-the-Night" rallies, and even cited by Senator Joseph Biden in support of the Violence Against Women Act (Schoenberg and Roe, 1993). The study was also cited in Naomi Wolf's (1991/2002) *The Beauty Myth* and defended in a Newsweek op-ed by Susan Faludi (1993, p. 61), who stated that "the one-in-four figure does not include women who felt sweet-talked into sex"...numerous other studies bear these figures out (Spivak, 2011, p. 12).

In the short space of the paragraph above, politicians, activists, magazines, books and a number of researchers and research projects are intricately tied to the outcome of a survey. Examining the potential vested interests of each of the actors described above, we can see why cultural criminologists consider information to be "filtered" through the lens of different ideologies before it reaches the consumer public.

Media and Gendered Violence

Womens' advocates have long argued that the media often supplies crime images and interpretations that contribute to dated stereotypical portrayals of female victims of violence. Rap music lyrics, the adult film industry and even some forms of art have been criticized for glorifying abuse of females and perpetuating domestic violence. In some cases, feminists point out, issues of race and social class will supplant gender as in the O. J. Simpson murder trial. Simpson's notoriety and use of wealth to employ an expensive legal defense, along with the attention paid to his treatment by race, seemed to overshadow the domestic violence context of the case (Foley, 2010). Although he had a history of domestic violence, and even a conviction for domestic battering (Taslitz, 1998), the fact that his wife seemed to have benefited from the glamorous days of his career, despite the abuse, seemed to impugn her character rather than his. Some may even argue that the bi-racial aspect of their marriage may have altered society's interpretation of Nicole Simpson as a victim of domestic violence (Carbado, 1997).

Malloy and Miller (2009) contend that in order to be depicted as a "pure victim" a woman must be the "good girl" who conforms to ideal wife and mother roles. Those who are viewed as promiscuous or engaging in more masculine achievement pursuits will be seen as more blameworthy in their victimization. In fact, Cowan and O'Brien (1990) found that the sexuality of female characters in films was associated with their eventual murder. As they explain:

> In slasher films the message appears to be that sexual women get killed and only the pure women survive. This message that the good woman is asexual and the bad (and therefore dead) woman is sexual may be almost as pernicious as the message conveyed in pornography that violence can be fun for women (pp. 194–195).

The case of the "Central Park Jogger" is an excellent example of a real-life victim who garnered national and international support along the lines suggested by feminist theorists.

The Central Park Jogger
Every so often the case of a particular victim will captivate the media and elevate the incident to a prominence that is difficult to explain. In 1989, during a period where gangs of "wilding" youth were on unprecedented crime sprees in the area, a young woman was attacked and raped while jogging in the early evening. She was discovered in a ditch hours later thrashing about from a severe brain injury she had suffered in the beating. The anonymous woman lapsed into a coma and was kept on life support with little hope of survival (although she did).

Having suffered multiple stab wounds, she had lost almost 80 percent of her blood and one eye was dislodged from the orbital socket as a result of the beating itself. As Meili (2003, p. 20) reports, the crime shocked and outraged the city which was reflected in the media coverage.

It is the lead story on local and national television for many days, and the newspaper coverage is even more extensive. Beyond the papers in the immediate area, the story is picked up within days by the *Boston Globe, San Francisco Chronicle, Los Angeles Times, Northern Virginia Daily, USA Today, Seattle Times, Detroit News, Pittsburgh Post Gazette, Houston Chronicle, Dallas Times Herald* and *Milwaukee Journal,* among others. The *International Herald Tribune* runs a long story on the Jogger, and the case is covered both in the *Evening Standard* of London and *La Presse Etrangere* in Lebanon. A special hospital spokesperson is assigned to brief the media first hourly, then daily. As soon as they can, weekly and monthly magazines feature the Jogger and/or her alleged assailants. All three major women's magazines...have comprehensive coverage. In December, the Jogger is chosen as one of *Glamour's* Women of the Year and *People* magazine names her one of the Year's Most Interesting People.

The victim herself, later reflected on the notoriety that followed that fateful night that changed her life so dramatically (Meili, 2003). Shying from the public, it was fourteen years before she would openly admit her identity. Still, she is genuinely grateful for the outpouring of support she received from all over the world.

In the intervening years, there have unfortunately been innumerable beatings and countless rapes (during the week I was attacked, twenty-eight other rapes were reported across the city), yet my case is remembered.... Perhaps it is because this assault revealed the basest depravity human beings are capable of—the attack was believed to have been committed by a group of teenagers between the ages of fourteen and sixteen, out only to have some "fun" and people shuddered to realize such cruelty exists in our exalted species. Perhaps it is also the randomness of the attack—the sense that "there but for the grace of God go I." And perhaps it is because people wanted to affirm that there is a better, higher part in the vast majority of us and could display that nobility in their desire to comfort me(Meili, 2003, p.7).

While some may argue that the attractive, young, white, investment banker made a stereotypical storybook heroine, there is no doubt that her miraculous physical recovery was a "feel good" story that brought hope and encouragement to millions around the country and around the world. One man who followed the story was compelled to write to her after he opened the newspaper and saw the headline "She's Jogging Again." He said, "One didn't need a scorecard to know who 'she' is. I did a double-take, felt goose bumps swelling all over, and entered into a state of blissful euphoria" (Meili, 2003, p. 115).

For Trisha Meili the experience meant dealing with the way victims are perceived and labeled in society. It was difficult for her to learn of media accounts that predicted her "brain damaged" limitations and pitied her "forlorn" and "pathetic" appearance. When she finally testified in court, one paper headlined "Jogger: She Was a Walking Crime Scene." Understandably, much of her battle to recover was fueled by the determination to challenge the images that had been created through the media.

McMartin Pre-School Case

One element of victimization events that draw media attention is child victims. In a quintessential example of what was a virtual media frenzy, the sensational trial of the operators of the McMartin Preschool, who were accused of the bizarre and ritualistic abuse of almost 300 children in their care, dominated American newspapers throughout the 1980s. Seven workers at the Manhattan Beach, California, facility were charged. Five had their cases dismissed and only two went forward in trials, both of which ended in hung juries. Many called it the trial of the century, and up until the O.J. Simpson case or the Rodney King incident, it perhaps was. Almost 300 child victims were interviewed and gave varying accounts of satanic, ritualistic abuse that included the torture of animals, hot-air balloons, secret tunnels, nuns and churches which all unfolded in over 62,000 pages of transcripts (Butler, 2001). At the time, it was the longest and most expensive criminal case ever prosecuted in this country. Critics argued that leading questions by interviewers contaminated the witness pool and no real physical evidence was validated. There was finger pointing, counter-lawsuits, several books, and an HBO movie following the trials, all of which threatened to obscure the real lessons learned from the events. Indeed, those lessons did not really receive any media attention.

First, we learned that while attempts to prosecute the alleged perpetrators of what would have been traumatic abuse are intrinsically noble, they also raised criticisms of the political nature of justice system responses. The case was from a prosperous Los Angeles suburb and involved a trusted family with a good reputation and many influential parents. The ability to bring about pressure to try what prosecutors considered an unpopular case, especially at a time when the legal precedent in this area was uncharted wilderness, demonstrates the power of local politics. If reports come from this elite community, though, it stands to reason that they are in other places as well. So, many asked, "where are the cases from other neighborhoods, from less fashionable and even unlicensed facilities? At that time, a three-year study of child sexual abuse in day care found that there were over 2,500 child victims in over 500 facilities reported during the years 1983–85 (Finkelhor & Williams, 1988) . Why then, did the McMartin case rise to such prominence? Some argue that it may have been the bizarre nature of the alleged rituals and terrorist threats reported by the children. Some argue that it was the large number of reported victims or the substantial period of time over which the abuse was believed to have occurred. Still others would say that reports of such events at such an unlikely place play upon our worst fears and focus us on the details.

Undoubtedly, there have been many positive effects from the media attention paid to potential sex abuse in day care. Many policies were implemented, ranging from architectural design standards to pre-employment checks of staff to insure that the environment is healthy and safe. Education programs targeted awareness and prevention for children and parents were taught how to detect, respond to and report suspected problems. Parents have been encouraged to choose facilities that allow them access at all times and to make random, spontaneous visits to these sites once their children are enrolled. Staff are better screened and more training is given on appropriate adult-child interaction. More supervision is given to employees and staffing has increased during the higher-risk times such as naptime, and high-risk areas such as bathrooms. Facilities are being designed with fewer visual barriers and closed doors, fewer closets, and more open spaces and windows.

What disappoints many experts about the media attention given to day-care cases is the way that the problem of child sexual abuse is distorted. In truth, given the chances of victimization, a child is at greater risk at home than in a day-care center. In calculating the rate of abuse in day care, data seem to suggest that approximately five children per 10,000 enrolled in day care are sexually-abused, while almost nine out of 10,000 children of the same age are victimized in the home (Finkelhor & Williams, 1988) . Another problem with the focus on day-care abuse cases is that it creates unnecessary fears and anxiety in parents. This fear undermines the faith that is needed for the inevitable child-care support necessary for working parents. Employment statistics tell us that roughly forty percent of mothers with children under age three are employed outside the home. The need for safe day care is an important aspect of our contemporary lifestyle.

LITERATURE AND FILM

Today, there may be more of a blending of roles between literature and other forms of media than ever before. Many different formats are used to attempt to "tell a story" and effect changes in people's attitudes and perceptions about issues beyond the simple reporting of facts. Sculpture, paintings, documentaries, poetry and songs, all address the issues of victims and their need to be supported. There is literature about victims of crime, offenders who began as victims, victims who began as offenders, and families, much like our own, drawn into the drama of surviving and healing from the effects of crime.

It can be argued that the history of this country and our culture includes the history of victims. Their stories chronicle important events, as well as political and economic controversies, that can often best be understood through the experiences of the individual. For example, a number of books have been written about victims of crimes who were related to the civil-rights movement in the late 1960s. The assassination of a well-known leader in the NAACP, Medgar Evers, has been chronicled in works that feature his life story and civil-rights work, as well as the trial of his assassin. Parallel to that are works like the film *Murder in Mississippi* that focus on the slayings of lesser known civil-rights workers who were also targeted for violence.

It is not surprising that stories of vigilante victims, those who become empowered to seek out revenge against their attackers, are popular entertainment. This theme in movies such as *The Burning Bed* and *The Brave One* seem to give us courage and inspiration but the role is, in reality, illegal and unlikely. On the other hand, commentary on victims who are abandoned and powerless is equally compelling.

In *Thirty-Eight Witnesses: The Kitty Genovese Case,* Rosenthal recounts events of 1963 when a young woman was attacked for over an hour on the streets of New York below a large apartment building. No one called the police. To many, this crime epitomized a time and place that desperately needed to be addressed with greater human engagement and social accountability. Communities across the country looked for ways to build citizenship and responsiveness. Many jurisdictions passed Good Samaritan laws that released individuals from liability when they stopped and rendered aid to persons in distress. Still, you might argue that, today, a victim like Kitty Genovese would not be ignored. Witnesses would pick up cell phones with auto-911 features, some would record the scene on their camera phones and area surveillance cameras would provide footage of the crime. Documentaries tell us that much has changed over the last fifty years in responses to crime victims; however, one of the slowest areas for change has been in correctional institutions.

The Prisoner as Victim in Literature

Prison data indicate that violence in institutions is common with both offenders and officers/staff the target of assaults. In order of frequency we see prisoners assaulting prisoners, prisoners assaulting officers/staff, and officers/staff assaulting prisoners. Perhaps the most compelling accounts of prison violence are sexual assaults. While statistics indicate that close to 5% of prison inmates reported being sexually victimized in 2009 (Houston Chronicle, 2010), among some populations, such as juveniles, and in some facilities, such as the Estelle unit in Huntsville, Texas, the rate may be as high as 16%. In fact, half of the U. S. prisons with the highest rates of sexual violence are found in Texas. More disturbing than the numbers, however, are the stories of those who have suffered silently in the wake of such abuse.

Often, reports of sexual victimization are published from inmate narratives from inside the prisons, from information that is relayed to writers outside prison, and from inmates immediately following their release. In "A world apart: Women, prison and life behind bars," Cristina Rathbone, a researcher, interviewed a woman after her release about sexual victimization at a Massachusetts facility. While working on a cemetery detail, Marsha was sexually abused by a city employee who threatened his victims by emphasizing his contacts in the State Police Department. The abuser was later investigated but cleared of any wrongdoing and the women who were victimized were punished for having cigarettes which the perpetrator had supplied to them. As the author relates, the official interpretations of the charges were that the man had sex with the women but that it had been consensual. This "double victimization" describing both the offense and the treatment in the system is a common theme in prison literature. The stigma of being a convicted offender often means that you are not worthy of being a victim or your accusations are not believed. Rathbone (2005, p. 61) explains Marsha's dilemma:

> "I was afraid" she told me. "Bob, I knew, had friends who were cops. He made that very clear to me when he told me that nobody would ever believe me, because if I told people, who were they going to believe, an inmate or a cop's friend?.... "What did the police tell you?" I asked. "Nothing. I think they understood why I was afraid. And the state cop told me if I was afraid, then I should write a statement that I didn't want to press charges at that time."

It is difficult to imagine a viable criminal justice system where any victim who is fearful of her attacker would be encouraged to avoid pressing charges.

Another format that allows us to gain insight into the experiences of the victim is through a published work released later in life, long after the events have occurred. In *Fish: A memoir of a boy in a man's prison*, T. J. Parsell tells the story of his incarceration as a juvenile. The cyclical nature of predatory sexual behavior, moving from victim of assault to offender would seem to be a clear indication of the importance of addressing youth violence in institutions. Parsell (2006, p. 225) describes going to the hospital after one rape caused serious injuries to his rectum.

> The doctor at MTU sent me over to the infirmary at Riverside.... I thought about asking the hospital staff if they would keep me there. I had filed several grievances, requesting a transfer back to Riverside, but the response was always the same: "Without a disciplinary reason or compelling need for protection, your request is denied." If I were to complain of being raped, I would have to tell them who it was that raped me.

Knowing that snitches received far worse consequences than the abuse he was currently experiencing, Parsell concentrated on finding protective relationships and avoiding potential attack scenarios. Unfortunately, his story is fairly typical of the young offender, yet this literature seems to have little impact on the field. The accounts more commonly serve as an example of the struggle for survival and the rite of passage from "fish" or new convict to a member of a powerful prison force to be reckoned with.

In, *I cried, you didn't listen: A survivor's expose of the California Youth Authority,* Dwight Abbot explains how as a fourteen-year-old he was incarcerated, not for any juvenile offense, but because then in the late 1950s a child without parental supervision was subject to state custody. In fact, it was not uncommon to have children who were sexually abused by a family member removed from the home and placed into a state juvenile center "for their own protection." While a ward of the state, Abbot was preyed upon by older, tougher delinquents until he finally developed the skills to victimize others. To prove he was not a "sissy" he first physically, and then later sexually, assaulted a younger, weaker inmate. He explains (2006, p. 72),

I smelled his fear, and a door inside my brain opened. Knowledge poured forth and overcame me in waves. We fought to hide our fear, to maintain our positions as predators rather than as victims. In reality, we were all victims.

Self-Exploration or Self-Promotion

Many therapists will argue that the process of healing requires facing the memories and the feelings of past victimization and evaluating one's responses and developing productive mechanisms for dealing with them. Pop-rock icon, Brian Wilson of the Beach Boys, authored a book, *Wouldn't it be Nice* (1991), detailing the abuse he suffered at the hands of his father and the toll that trauma played in his adult life. Readers are left to wonder if his music talent was aided or hampered by the emotional pain he could not seem to resolve.

Bibliotherapy, or reading about incidents that may trigger cathartic progress in counseling, may be followed with encouragement to write about one's experiences to aid in self-discovery. While most writing takes the form of personal journals, poetry and letters, occasionally, some of these narratives become popular literature, either in memoirs or self-help books. Some of these more popular works are even adapted for film.

In the documentary *What I Want My Words To Do To You*, playwright Eve Ensler conducts a writing workshop with about a dozen female prisoners. She directs them to write about their victims and the role those victims play in their sentences. Despite what many may believe about criminal remorse, the inmates bring vivid images to life about the haunting scepter of those they have hurt, not only those murdered, but the pain experienced by those left behind, including members of their own families.

More so than literature, the cinema is closely equated with what would be equated to our society's popular culture. Images developed through films are now a critical part of the study of criminology and victimology. Nicole Rafter, author of *Shots in the mirror: Crime films and society* (2nd Ed., 2006) argues that studying the discourse of the internet, film, television, rap music, and newspapers gives us unique insights (which she refers to as "popular criminology") that are as valid as traditional empirical studies of crime (Rafter, 2007) .   The   stories of victims of infamous crimes, such as the Columbine High School shootings, or famous people and their victimization such as John Lennon or Gianni Versace, may produce better-selling books but everyday crimes that happen to ordinary people have also generated popular narrative works. The ability of victims to overcome adversity and to share inspirational messages through literature and film has been the essence of the popularity of this genre. Dave Pelzer's chronicle of an abusive childhood suffered at the hands of his mentally-ill mother has resulted in seven best-selling books and a career in motivational speaking. Still, critics attack some writers and their recollections as this posting by David Plotz (2000) demonstrates

> Dave Pelzer, the most famous author you've never heard of, has three books on the *New York Times* nonfiction paperback best-seller list this week. Pelzer, whose most insistent piece of advice is "don't dwell on the past," dwells on it very profitably. At 39, he has already written a trilogy of memoirs. *A Child Called "It": One Child's Courage To Survive* chronicles how his mother tortured him from age 4 to 12. It has sold 1.6 million copies and spent two and a half years on the best-seller lists. Its sequel, *The Lost Boy: A Foster Child's Search for the Love of a Family* rehashes the maternal abuse and documents his wild teen-age years. It has sold a million and had 18 months as a best seller.... He has turned child abuse into entertainment. Pelzer likes to be known as the guy who "makes child abuse fun." ...Pelzer's books come programmed for big sales. They straddle all the trendy genres: confessional memoir, childhood trauma, triumph-over-adversity, and self-help. Pelzer also owes his success to tireless marketing.

While some victims may find personal insight and relief in the publicizing of their experiences, others use the medium to address shortcomings in the way we treat victims today. Many of these accounts bitterly criticize the criminal justice system and its treatment of victims and provide insight into the ways that we could better address their needs through more meaningful programs, policies and services.

BEST USES OF MEDIA

To date, victimology has not paid much attention to the role of the media in creating images that may not promote the best interests of victims. Jenkins and Katkin (1988) argue that, in many cases, the media engages in and promotes sensationalistic aspects of crimes instead of fulfilling a watchdog role where consumers are guided through a more fact-based analysis of events that transpire. They caution that media seem to even create more victims by broadcasting unsubstantiated information that may be prejudicial in future legal proceedings. Even with disclaimers, first impressions seem to drive public opinion and once it is no longer a breaking news story, there is seldom any motivation to go back and correct inaccuracies. Getting information out seems more important than getting *accurate* information out.

After the infamous trial of O. J. Simpson for the murder of his wife, Nicole, and a friend, Ron Goldman, Goldman's family produced a book that told their story, *His name is Ron: Our search for justice* (1997). Members of the Goldman family spoke about their reactions to the murder of Ron, and the subsequent trials and how the constant media focus affected their grieving process. What emerges from their book is a contemporary view of how media uses victims and victims use media in a somewhat symbiotic relationship.

The literature written by and about victims can serve as our window into their world, yet books and Hollywood films are perhaps outdated formats. With cell-phone cameras and access to streaming online video, it can be argued that more footage and accounts of victimization are transmitted through YouTube than any other media genre. Fights, attacks on police, assaults by police and sex crimes seem to be on our computer screen around the clock. The challenge for the criminal justice system today is to provide meaningful and creative ways to educate the public about victimization and crime prevention. While it will be impossible to eliminate the distortions and biases of media images, we can at least work toward a more realistic justice.

References

Abbott, D. (2006). *I cried, you didn't listen: A survivor's expose of the California Youth Authority*. Oakland, CA: AK Press.

Butler, E. (2001). *Anatomy of the McMartin child molestation case*. Lanham, MD: University Press of America.

Callanan, V. (2005). *Feeding the fear of crime*. New York: LFB Scholarly Publishing.

Carbado, D. (1997). The construction of O. J. Simpson as a racial victim. *Harvard Criminal Law, 32,* 49.

Chiricos, T., Padgett, K., & Gertz, M. (2000). Fear, tv news, and the reality of crime. *Criminology, 38,* 755–785.

Cowan, G., & O'Brien, M. (1990). Gender and survival v. death in slasher films: A content analysis. *Sex Roles, 23,* 187–196.

Dowler, K. (2003). Media consumption and public attitudes toward crime and justice: The relationship between fear of crime, punitive attitudes and perceived police effectiveness. *Journal of Criminal Justice and Popular Culture, 10*(2), 109–126.

Eschholz, S., Chiricos, T., & Gertz, M. (2003). Television and fear of crime: Program types, audience traits and the mediating effect of perceived neighborhood racial composition. *Social Problems, 50,* 3, 395–415.

Finkelhor, D., & Williams, L. (1988). *Nursery crimes: Sexual abuse in day care*. Thousand Oaks, CA: Sage.

Foley, A. J. (2010). Book review: Women, violence and the media. *Violence Against Women, 16,* 715–721.

Goldman Family (1997). *His name is Ron*. New York: Avon.

Guo, Z., Zhu, J., & Chen, H. (2001). Mediated reality bites: Comparing direct and indirect experience as sources of perceptions across two communities in China. *International Journal of Public Opinion Research, 13,* 398–418.

Harms, P., & Snyder, H. N. (September, 2004). Trends in the murder of juveniles, 1980–2000. *Juvenile Justice Bulletin*. Washington, DC: Office of Juvenile Justice and Delinquency Prevention.

Hoover, J. E. (1947). How safe is your daughter?. *American Magazine, 144*(32–33), 102–104.

Houston Chronicle (2010, April 9). Stopping prison rape (editorial). *Houston Chronicle,* B10.

Jenkins, P., & Katkin, D. (1988). Protecting victims of child sexual abuse: A case for caution. *The Prison Journal, 68*, 25–35.

Karmen, A. (2001). *Crime victims, 4th Ed.* Belmont, CA: Wadsworth.

McShane, M., & Williams, F. P. (1992). Radical victimology: A critique of the concept of victim in traditional victimology. *Crime & Delinquency, 38*, 258–271.

Meili, T. (2003). *I am the Central Park jogger.* New York: Scribner.

Meloy, M., & Miller, S. (2009). Words that wound: Print media's presentation of gendered violence. In D. Humphries (Ed.). *Women, violence and the media: Readings in feminist criminology* (pp. 29–56). Boston: Northeastern University Press.

Parsell, T. J. (2006). *Fish: A memoir of a boy in a man's prison.* New York: Avalon.

Philips, C. (1994, October 17). Gangsta rap: Did lyrics inspire killing of police? *Los Angeles Times.*

Philips, C. (1993, July 15). Rap Defense Doesn't Stop Death Penalty. *Los Angeles Times.*

Plotz, D. (2000, September 29). David Pelzer, the child abuse entrepreneur. Retrieved from http://slate.msn.com/ id/90532/.

Quarles, T. (2007). Predicting recidivism in a cohort of juvenile probationers: A risk assessment instrument. Unpublished Dissertation, Prairie View, Texas: Prairie View A & M University.

Rafter, N. (2007). Crime, film and criminology. *Theoretical Criminology, 11*, 403–420.

Rathbone, C. (2005). *A world apart: Women, prison and life behind bars.* New York: Random House.

Snell, C. (2001). *Neighborhood structure, crime, and fear of crime.* New York: LFB Scholarly Publishing.

Spivak, A. (2011). *Sexual violence: Beyond the feminist-evolutionary debate.* El Paso, TX: LFB Scholarly Publishing.

Sussman, P. (1997). Crimes of silence: The politics of regulating prisoners and the press. *Social Pathology, 3*, 8–15.

Syrnick, J., & Applegarth, V. (2009, January). *Relocation Project.* Boston: Greater Boston Legal Services and the Safety Net Project, National Network to End Domestic Violence.

Taslitz, A. E. (1998). An African-American sense of fact: The O. J. trial and black judges on justice. *The Boston University Public Interest Law Journal, 7*, 219–249.

Williams, F. P., & McShane, M. (2003, November). Correlates of learning in worry about crime. Paper presented at the annual meeting of the American Society of Criminology, Denver.

Wilson, B. (1991). *Wouldn't it be nice: My own story.* New York: Harper Collins.

Zgoba, K., Witt, P., Dalessandro, M., & Veysey, B. (December 2008). *Megan's law: Assessing the practical and monetary efficacy.* Report 225370. Washington, DC: U. S. Department of Justice.

Baunach, P. (1979). *The families of inmate mothers: Perceptions of separation from their children.* Paper presented at the National Institute of Mental Health's Conference on Incarcerated Parents and their Children. Bethesda, MD.

Discussion Questions:

1. How do you think the media selects certain types of victims and certain victims' cases to focus on? In what ways are consumers or the public in general responsible for these selections?
2. What protections should victims have from the media? What choices should they be able to make in terms of media access to their cases?
3. Why do you think that victims' stories are popular forms of literature? What types of stories about victims would you be most likely to read and why?

Books You May Want To Read:

Meili, T. (2003). *I am the Central Park Jogger: A story of hope and possibility.* New York: Scribner.

Pelzer, D. (1995). *A child called it.* Deerfield Beach, FL: HCI.

Spencer, L. (2007). *Shattered dreams: My life as a polygamist's wife.* New York: Center Street.

Movies You May Want To See:

Innocent Voices (2004)
Indictment: The McMartin Trial

Web Links:

http://dnaquiz.ncvc.org/quiz.html
http://salem.lib.virginia.edu/Commemoration.html

CHAPTER 12

Rethinking the Victim-Offender Relationship

INTRODUCTION

Today's complex and multicultural society provides us with many opportunities for interactions with strangers. Trust, Marc Riedel (1993) tells us, is the basis for orderly and predictable exchanges with strangers and is the key to living without fear. Victimization violates our sense of well-being and may cause us to restrict our lifestyle and limit exposure to less predictable circumstances. Logically, however, victimization at the hands of family, friends or acquaintances should be more dramatic and difficult to recover from, as would abuses by members of trusted occupations such as priests, doctors, scoutmasters and teachers. The dynamics of victim-offender relationships are often contaminated by subjective and ongoing interpretations of motives and reactions.

Some crimes, like consumer fraud, are more likely to be perpetrated by strangers, while others such as rape or homicide are more likely to involve victims and offenders who know each other. In fact, only 14 percent of homicides involve a perpetrator who is a stranger (Fox & Zawitz, 2010). And, homicides where the offender and victim are family members or acquaintances are much more likely to result in charges not being filed, or grand juries failing to return an indictment (Reidel, 1993). According to a research study by Koss (1988) only two percent of women who were raped by an acquaintance even reported the victimization. The relationships between victims and offenders and the official as well as the informal outcomes of the crimes they share contribute much to theory building in victimology.

Many of the theories we have discussed so far are specific in the types of victim/offender relationships they address.

THEORY AND RESEARCH ON VICTIM-OFFENDER RELATIONSHIPS

Criminology's rational theories, particularly lifestyle theory and routine activities theory, tell us that victims and offenders often come together to occupy the same time and place. Geo-spatial studies plot and graphically display the areas that are likely to produce higher concentrations of victim targets and motivated offenders. Research often demonstrates that the demographics of offenders and victims closely resemble each other and that they often shift back and forth between the two roles. Reducing exposure to crime-prone individuals, at higher-risk times and places is the basic strategy for preventing victimization.

Gender, a factor that shapes lifestyle, is also predictive of victimization risk. While marriage seems to decrease the risk of violent crime for males, it increases the risk for females (Maston, 2010). Studying homicide victims of youthful offenders over a 30-year period in Chicago, Laurikkala (2009) found that almost 90 percent of both victims and offenders were male. This finding is most recently attributed to the gang-related nature of many of the homicides. As we will see in this chapter, there are also many ways that victims can be created through the actions and activities of the criminal justice system thus complicating traditional conceptions of the victim-offender relationship.

LAW ENFORCEMENT OFFICER-OFFENDER VICTIMIZATION

The Creation of Victims in the Criminal Justice System

While the police beating of Rodney King in a traffic stop was an infamous case that led to intensive legal analysis of patrol operations and sweeping administrative changes, there are a number of other cases that have served over the years as the policy building-blocks of the justice system. A country's reputation, including its accomplishments in democracy and citizenship, is often measured by the level and consistency of its justice. Organizations like Amnesty International, the NAACP, LULAC and the American Civil Liberties Union monitor the justice system to minimize the risk of harm for persons who come in contact with law enforcement.

The ultimate harm for anyone processed into the criminal justice system is perhaps a false conviction. In November of 2008, an article in *Texas Monthly* profiled 37 men in Texas who were eventually exonerated for crimes for which they had served a collective 525 years. Although they were eventually released, few were able to get their lives back on track. Each had to overcome not only the stigma of prison time but also the toll the years had taken on personal lives. Texas has, according to the article, the greatest number of prisoners cleared by the Innocence Project, a legal-assistance program that has been instrumental in the release of over 222 wrongly-convicted persons nationwide. One of the difficulties for the organization is that each state handles the process of reviewing cases and releasing exonerated defendants differently. In Texas, for example, each year spent in prison under a false conviction is payable at $50,000 as long as the recipient forfeits their right to later sue (Hall, 2008).

Victims of Police

There are a variety of ways that people might conceive of themselves as being victimized by police. Conflict theory would argue that, overall, police power is controlled by wealthy policy-makers and that abuse of power would be disproportionately inflicted on the poor, those with less influence and access to resources. Police corruption is a phenomenon that would victimize all of society as would systematic violations of civil liberties. Many believe that procedures adopted during the drug war have had a disparate impact on innocent citizens, particularly minorities, and half of Americans believe racial profiling is widespread (Carlson, 2004). According to Amnesty International (2004), there are currently 32 million victims of racial profiling and another 87 million will be at risk over their lifetimes.

Police have at their disposal a number of weapons and instruments of control, including some newer forms of restraint and submission. From batons and TASERs to canine units and pepper sprays, those who come in contact with police may suffer some type of injury. In a 2004 report, the Los Angeles County Sheriff's Department was criticized for the frequency with which police dogs bit minority citizens. Because the percentage of those bitten by police dogs who were minority has never fallen below 80%, the report asked the department to do some "soul searching" to decide if the deployment of the animals was a *de facto* form of racial profiling (Usher, 2004).

In many jurisdictions, the TASER, a brand name for a conductive energy device (CED), has replaced the use of chemical sprays for incapacitating suspects. The manufacturers of the TASER, adopted by over 12,000 law enforcement agencies by 2008, claim greater officer safety and an effectiveness rating of about 86–88% in deployments (Hougland, Mesloh, & Henych, 2005; Spriggs, 2009). Because of the nature of the instrument, persons at risk for injury and death via the use of a CED include those who are:

- are handcuffed or restrained when the weapon is deployed
- are mentally-ill or on drugs
- have heart disease or a pacemaker
- pregnant or elderly

In addition, the CED must be used in a recommended manner with strict constraints on the use of multiple shots and the maximum energy cycle length and it is not to be used with minors or the physically handicapped. Deviations from the accepted standards may result in higher levels of harm resulting from its use. Perhaps the greatest concern however, is the danger people face from the improper use of deadly force.

Police Use of Deadly Force

When Pam and Steve Hobart called the police to help them get their 19-year-old, mentally-ill son into treatment, the last thing they expected was that the officer would shoot and kill the distraught young man. In a lawsuit filed against the city of Stafford, Texas, the parents argued that the officer's abuse of deadly force was directly linked to the fact that he had received no training in handling the mentally ill. Although Aaron Hobart had no weapon, the officer reported that he "feared for his life" when he fired twice, which the parent's claim was excessive given the possible range of alternatives the officer might have used (Flood, 2009).

Theoretically, police shootings go hand-in-hand with citizen shootings of police in an environment of risk, fear and expectations about what the other person in a possible confrontation will do. In recent years, Harris County Texas has seen a steady increase in the number of cases involving an officer's use of deadly force and a record number of resulting fatalities. In 2007 there were 12, in 2008 there were 16, and in 2009 the total was 20. In this same time period, felony and misdemeanor assaults against law enforcement officers in the area has increased 32 percent (Pinkerton 2010. Depending on who you talk to, there are a number of explanations for the rise in officer-involved shootings. These include (Pinkerton, 2009; 2010):

1. a depressed economy
2. permissive law enforcement supervision
3. the failure of the prosecutors' office to aggressively respond to these cases
4. a lack of social services that address the needs of the drug-addicted and mentally-ill
5. changes in the law that allow more carrying and concealed carrying of weapons while at the same time making it more difficult to file charges for unlawful carrying
6. residual tensions over the influx of offenders and weapons from Hurricane Katrina some years ago

The police shooting of unarmed citizens is perhaps one of the most controversial homicides played out in our society today. After-the-fact analysis, and *post-hoc* debate are used to advance the sides of debates on all types of issues from how the streets are more violent and unpredictable to how training or supervision may be lax. Still, juries are usually reluctant to find that officers intentionally violated the rights of a citizen encountered under stressful circumstances. In the case of New York City police officers firing forty-one rounds into an unarmed 23-

year-old immigrant, Amadou Diallo, all four officers charged were acquitted. Subsequently, family members settled a wrongful-death lawsuit against the department for three million dollars (Albertson, 2009). Likewise officers accused in the video-taped beating of Rodney King were also acquitted, which resulted in days of intense rioting throughout Los Angeles and a settlement of 3.8 million dollars.

It seems as if there is a degree of victimization recognized in cases of citizen/police conflict, but only to the degree that damages may be compensated; criminal liability is less likely to be established. Exceptions may be those cases that rise to a level that shocks and appalls society with types of force prohibited under any circumstances. One such example was the case of Haitian immigrant Abner Louima who was brutally attacked by officers inside a police station, one of whom jammed a plunger into his rectum and his mouth. In that case, Officer Justin Volpe's criminal conviction carried a sentence of thirty years (Albertson, 2009).

The types of people likely to become involved in police use of force vary considerably as does their risk of injury or death in that encounter. Characteristics of the responding officers, as well as the type of weapons or suppression devices available, affect the outcomes of these confrontations. The mentally-ill or persons with certain types of medical conditions or disabilities may be at greater risk of injury or death from physical struggles or from the application of physical or chemical restraints.

The accumulation of data on both attacks on police and police use of force has helped to shape the way officers are taught to assess their risk and respond. For example, research indicates that officers engaging an armed suspect who is as close as 32 feet may have less than two seconds to react. This two seconds is the estimated time it takes a suspect to proceed 32 feet. In *Estate of Larsen v. Murr (2008)*, the court agreed that the use of a "21-foot rule" in applying deadly force represented a defensible standard. The 21-foot rule evolved from evidence that an average suspect can cross a distance of 21 feet in 1.5 seconds. Law enforcement officers may be more prepared to use deadly force as they assess unfolding events and weigh the fact that a suspect's actions are often faster than their own reactions (Mesloh, Henych & Wolf, 2008).

LAW ENFORCEMENT OFFICERS AS VICTIMS

Most people are familiar with California's swift implementation of a "Three Strikes" law after the murder of young Polly Klaas, who was abducted from her bedroom in the middle of the night. Much less is known about the effect of "three strikes" and other habitual-felon statutes on the risk of law enforcement officers being killed in the line of duty. When California Highway Patrol Officer Don Burt was gunned down at close range during a traffic stop, the killer was facing his third strike after convictions for forgery, escape, weapons violations, burglary, and assault with a deadly weapon. After Officer Burt conducted a routine search and discovered evidence of organized crime activity in the trunk of the car, the killer shot him seven times and then fled.

In two recent Houston, Texas, cases, one officer was shot in the back of the head by an illegal immigrant who was arrested and sitting in the back of his patrol car. Another was slain pursuing a parolee through a high-crime area. Although both offenders had lengthy criminal histories, only one was given the death penalty. Differences in the details of the offenses, characteristics or actions of the victims and offenders, and the composition of the juries may have been responsible for the different outcomes for the two capital murder cases, even though both had a similar aggravating circumstance of murdering a peace officer.

Attacks on law enforcement officers are considered one of the more serious crimes in our society. The Federal Bureau of Investigation tracks injuries and deaths in law enforcement professions and reports them annually. In 2007, 57 officers were killed in 51 different incidents. Those who lost their lives tended to be male, averaged 37 years of age with 10 years of experience on the job, and assigned to vehicle patrol. The most common circumstances of the murders were that officers were affecting an arrest, engaged in a traffic pursuit or stop, or victims of an ambush (FBI, 2008). Most of those killed were with another officer at the time and most were slain by handguns, about half of which occurred at close range. Although most were wearing protective armor, the fatal wounds were to the head or neck. The known assailants were younger than the officers, all were male, and most had prior criminal records (FBI, 2008).

CORRECTIONS SYSTEMS: OFFENDERS AND VICTIMS

It is often interesting to ask people to compare the victimization risk of police officers and correctional officers and to hear the variety of opinions on this subject. Many see the outside world as more dangerous and unpredictable while others see a prison as a high-risk environment filled with murderers and rapists with no incentive to behave. Realistically, it is hard to accurately compare the professions, as the two field's definitions of assault may differ as well as the rules and procedures governing encounters with their respective "publics." Correctional officers, for the most part, work without weapons, although they have a number of control mechanisms at their disposal.

Probation and parole officer positions are characterized by features of both policing and corrections. In an early study of victimization within that field, Parsonage and Bushey (1987) found that roughly 50% of Pennsylvania parole and probation officers carrying active caseloads had been victim of some type of assault or threatened assault. Further studies seemed to indicate that rural areas, more experienced officers, and those who carried weapons were more likely to be involved in confrontations with clients (Renzema, 1987). This last characteristic, arming community-corrections personnel, has been controversial. Many jurisdictions have elected to do so over the years, while others decided to team police with probation/parole officers to more effectively pursue warrants and arrests.

Of all criminal justice areas, prisons have historically been considered a closed and largely "hidden" world. The general public was not privy to the many ways disagreements played out between members of what Goffman (1961) called the "total institution." Today, through research and literature, we know quite a bit more about the risks of victimization within prisons, jails, and juvenile institutions. We are aware of the long-term effects of depression and post-traumatic stress that can accompany injuries suffered by any type of law enforcement officer. Few of the officer hostages from the Attica riot and none of the officers brutalized in the Santa Fe riot ever returned to work inside a prison. Some theorists acknowledge that criminals' involvement in a "subculture of violence" increases the risk of assaults and others recognize that the structure and operations of incarceration facilities makes it difficult to avoid confrontations and conflict.

Prisoner Assaults on Prisoners

Prisoner assaults on other prisoners is the most common form of prison violence. Much of prison violence is gang-related and often racially motivated. Rates of inmate-on-inmate assault appear to be higher in more crowded facilities and more likely to involve younger, more aggressive inmates (Lahm, 2008). The recent decline in the number of inmates who become victims of homicide in prison could be credited to better classification, increased security measures for detecting lethal weapons and improved medical responses to injuries.

The prison world is one where an elaborate hierarchy of status governs inmate relations and activities. Certain criminal histories like rape and sexual assault of a child are considered despicable even within the offender world and thus these prisoners are deemed worthy of further abuse. Persons who are viewed as having cooperated with authorities are also singled out for attacks. Most offenders can easily calculate whether another prisoner's sentence is below the norm and thus, an indicator of someone who "ratted out", or testified against a co-defendant. Those considered snitches inside the institution, or who fail to pay on bets or debts are also likely to be singled out for violent retribution. Although some seek protective-custody status that insures they will have only limited exposure to other inmates, it is more expensive to operate this type of housing. For that reason, the process for obtaining protective-custody classification is often administratively difficult. As a result, potential victims are discouraged from pursuing it.

In a highly-publicized case, a lifer previously convicted of murder, armed robbery and assault strangled fellow inmate, John Geoghan, an ex-priest serving a six-year term for indecent assault of a child. Although the Diocese settled 86 individual cases tied to this cleric, most victims interviewed felt that staying behind bars rather than being killed was the most appropriate punishment. Lawyers and therapists seemed to agree that outcomes like this bring little closure or peace to the survivors. Although many prisoners foster resentment and threaten abuse against child molesters, this particular inmate, Joseph Druce, had a history of violence while incarcerated and had often expressed not only racist ideology but hatred of homosexuals (Nestruck, 2003).

In 1994, infamous serial-killer Jeffrey Dahmer, serving 17 life sentences was beaten to death in prison by another inmate. The prosecutor acknowledged that Dahmer's sensational crimes, murdering young boys, having sex with the corpses, cutting up and eating pieces of his victims, meant that he was always a "marked man" while incarcerated (Dallas Morning News, 1994). Although Dahmer spent his first year in protective custody, he was moved to the general population and given a regular job assignment. While this usually means a more normal and active lifestyle for prisoners, there were soon warning signs that Dahmer was in danger. In July of 1994, four months before the fatal attack, another inmate attempted to cut his throat with a homemade plastic knife while in a church service. Family members of Dahmer's victims admitted that they often received phone calls from persons claiming to be inmates at the Wisconsin prison where Dahmer died. The callers vowed to provide justice for the families, to take care of the situation (Dallas Morning News, 1994).

Prisoner Victims of Correctional Staff

In the 1995 case, *Women Prisoners v. the District of Columbia Department of Corrections (DCDC)*, federal judges found ample evidence of a pattern of sexual abuse of female prisoners. This abuse included "forceful sexual activity, unsolicited sexual touching, exposure of body parts or genitals and sexual comments." The justices found that the extensive sexual harassment allowed there created a "sexualized environment" where "boundaries and expectations of behavior are not clear." One facility administrator even commented that "You just get this sense that [sexual misconduct] has always happened and it is always going to happen." This is not something that a court would appreciate hearing.

The court in this case was alarmed not only by the many instances of sexual assault but also by the administration's failure to address them. The court heard evidence like the following:

> ...a correctional officer at the Jail, sexually assaulted Jane Doe Q while she was a patient in the infirmary.... The officer fondled her breasts and vagina, tried to force her to perform oral sex and then raped her...a correctional officer at CTF forced Jane Doe RR to perform oral sex on him while Jane Doe RR attempted to empty trash as part of a work detail....

The individual officers who assaulted Jane Doe Q and Jane Doe RR warned the women not to report the attacks...a correctional officer at CTF grabbed Jane Doe W's buttocks and vagina while he escorted her from the medical unit where she had received prenatal care.... A CTF foreman tried to rub up against Jane Doe Z, and steward hands and different officers fondled women prisoners' breasts, legs, arms and buttocks.... Another CTF officer attempted on several occasions to fondle Jane Doe K's breasts, vagina and buttocks in the television room.... A teacher in the print shop would frequently try to pull Jane Doe OOO to him and kiss her.... An officer in the garment shop attempted to paw and kiss women prisoners.... One officer in particular discovered that Jane Doe V was going to take a shower and said, "Well, you go ahead and do that and I'll be in there to stick my rod up in you".... Male prisoners and correctional officers at the Annex also direct sexually explicit comments toward women prisoners.... Officers at the Jail verbally harass women by making derogatory references about women prisoners' breasts and buttocks.

In cases like the one above, the defense may attempt to argue that an inmate, unlike those described in the *Women Prisoners* above, has agreed to engage in sexual conduct with an officer. However, the courts have explicitly established that this can never be the case. The reasoning behind this position reflects the legal status of the prisoner as a ward of the state. Despite what offenses prisoners may have committed, and regardless of what may transpire between officers and inmates either in conversations or agreements, the legal precedent is indisputably clear that the relationship between an officer and an inmate is a custodial one. The officer is representing the state and its interest in maintaining control, not abusing its authority. There is, then, no recognition of "implied consent" to any sexual relations. As long as a prisoner is incarcerated against his or her will, participation in such an activity must be construed to be exploitative. The liability, civil and criminal, for such actions will rest upon the officer and his organization.

In *People v. Lovercamp* the court went so far as to recognize the potential need to escape from a facility if the targeted victim faces threat of imminent attack, sexual assault or serious harm. Still, the guidelines for successfully using this rape-duress defense to the charge of escape are rather narrow and very specific. The prisoner must meet the following criteria:

1. must face a specific threat of death, forcible sexual assault or substantial bodily injury in the immediate future,
2. must have no time to complain to authorities and no prior history of frivolous complaints,
3. must have no time or opportunity to resort to the courts,
4. must commit no violence against prison personnel during the escape, and
5. must report immediately to prison authorities upon escaping.

Preventing the victimization of those in the care of the state has been a priority not only for the courts but for legislators as well. *The Prison Rape Elimination Act of 2003* has provided not only for tracking and reporting incidents that occur nationwide but for research on this issue. As discussed in Chapter Two, confidential survey techniques have made it possible to gain a clearer picture of the sexual abuse problems in institutions. Already studies from this data have helped develop models to identify the context of predatory sexual behaviors and to predict victimization. For example, training has been suggested to help officers develop stronger boundaries that may reduce the potential for the sexual exploitation of inmates (Warren, Jackson, Loper & Burnette, 2009).

While sexual assault is probably the most common form of prisoner victimizations, there are many other forms including unwarranted disciplinary action, assault and even medical malpractice. Deliberate indifference to an inmate's serious needs has been found in several cases, such as when a prisoner was denied proper shoes that would have addressed his circulation problem thus avoiding the amputation of his leg (McShane, 2008).

Correctional Officers as Victims

During the 1990s, all forms of prison violence appeared to be at record levels. Although statistics indicate that inmates are almost twice as likely to assault other inmates than they are staff (McShane, 2008), the rate of assaults against correctional officers was also unprecedentedly high. In 1995, there were over 14,000 assaults on staff members working in prisons, which represented a 32% increase from five years earlier (Stephan, 1997). The subsequent 2000 prison census reported 18,000 inmate assaults on staff (Stephan & Karberg, 2003). The number of staff injured in juvenile facilities was also high (6,900 in one year) (Parent, et al., 1993). There are many possible explanations for the increased violence. Overcrowding fueled by longer sentences for drug and gang offenders, along with the reliance on a number of older facilities whose designs created safety gaps, were partly to blame. Employment practices that minimized training and the proliferation of a number of privately-managed institutions have also been cited as factors related to inmate-on-staff violence. Further, a lack of timely automated-systems information made it difficult to classify potentially violent inmates appropriately.

A 1998 study by Warchol indicated that the rate of 218 nonfatal workplace assaults per 1,000 correctional officers made it the second highest in occupations, right after policing (306 per 1,000). A California Department of Corrections (2000) report a few years later indicated that there were over 3,200 assaults on officers by inmates in 1999 alone and almost half of these involved the use of weapons created by inmates. Overall, assaults against correctional staff in that state increased more than 300% in the ten-year period from 1990 to 1999, at the beginning of which there were 1,002 assaults against officers, with only 201 involving weapons. The report drew attention to the fact that an average of nine correctional peace officers and staff were suffering assaults each day in California facilities—which was a significant increase over the previous average of five per day.

Research on staff assaults seemed to indicate that facilities with higher staff-to-inmate ratios had higher assault rates (Lahm, 2009). This is most likely attributed to the fact that such units have a higher security-level inmate population, one that is predictably more assaultive. However, the newer "supermax" facilities, designated specifically for this population, appeared to have lower rates of assault on staff (Sundt, Castellano & Briggs, 2008), a fact that can probably be attributed to the contemporary design and operation involving less physical contact with their higher-risk inmate population.

Today, correctional officers are far less likely to be killed on the job than in the past (Lahm, 2008). While lethal attacks on officers appear to have decreased, managers are still well-aware that the risk of assault on correctional officers is related to employee stress, job satisfaction, and turnover. To address this, state and federal corrections officials have instituted a number of measures designed to improve staff safety. Today, modern podular designs, direct supervision techniques (Wener, 2006), architecture that utilizes technology and remote surveillance, as well as better training with updated equipment for managing aggressive inmates all seemed to have increased the amount of control an officer can exercise across prison space. In addition, more sophisticated analysis that examines prison violence by time and place has assisted administrators in better staffing and equipping of "hot spots" and higher-risk shifts. For example, a 1991 study by Steinke focused on situational factors believed to be related to prison violence. It was determined that violence against staff was more likely in dining, recreation, and bathroom areas where inmates were involved in less-structured activity and where they were more likely to encounter officers one-on-one. With this information, authorities can work toward reducing officer risk. By 2004, the California Department of Corrections and Rehabilitation had reduced the number of assaults on staff (from 3,200 to 2,869) despite a growing inmate population and reducing by almost half the number of cases involving an inmate weapon (California Department of Corrections and Rehabilitation, 2005). While the nature of prisons and prisoners will always hold the potential for conflict and violence, the more it can be predicted and addressed, the safer the environment will be for all.

VICTIMS IN SCHOOLS

School violence takes many forms, from students bullying each other to attacks on teachers by students and even by parents. While these problems may have always existed in schools, the expanse of media coverage and the range of legal responses to them have changed significantly in the last few decades. Over the last two decades we have seen considerable change in the way violence and crime have been defined and addressed in public schools. The creation of school police, the use of metal detectors, and a range of zero tolerance policies have been adopted in order to reduce victimization in schools and improve the safety of the learning environment (Mueller & Lawrence, 2007).

Teachers as Victims

According to Duhart (2001), teaching is one of the five professions at highest risk of potential victimization. The literature cites a number of expenses involved in addressing the aftermath of assaults on teachers including workers'-compensation claims, work-days lost, and medical reimbursements related to assaults on teachers and assistants. Liability insurance, legal fees and new security equipment, as well as its repair and maintenance, are all part of the rising expenses of dealing with violence in the schools (Kalenda, 2010).

The educational climate of any school is related to perceptions of safety. Research indicates that this may be influenced by the amount of training teachers have in dealing with aggressive students (Alvarez, 2007). Although support from administrators is a key factor in addressing teacher fears and stressors, legislation and state policies may make it difficult to control classroom confrontations in the most effective ways. For example, Kalenda (2010) explains that laws imposing zero tolerance for guns or weapons in school do not necessarily apply to students with disabilities. Instead, these laws seem to be superseded by *Individuals with Disabilities Education Act* amendments that limit the amount of time disabled students, who represent a disproportionate percentage of those manifesting classroom problems, can be sent to alternative schools.

In 1993 one-in-nine teachers reported being the victim of violence; six years later that rate had risen to one-in-six (Louis Harris & Associates, 1999). Elementary- and secondary-level teachers were equally likely to be victimized and 90 percent of the perpetrators in those incidents were students. Still, the most common form of violence against teachers appears to be verbal threats and verbal attacks with well over 60 percent of teachers in one study reporting these (Petersen,

Pietrzak & speaker, 1998). Teachers in public schools are also more at risk of victimization from violent behavior and threats (Kalenda, 2010).

Hazing

Incidents of hazing as profiled in the media are often extreme cases: young men sodomized with broom sticks, players being doused with urine and vomit, brutal assaults with paddles, and teens dying from alcohol poisoning. And yet, estimates are that about 1.5 million high-school students are hazed each year (Weir, 2003) as are about 55 percent of college students who are involved in clubs and athletics (Allan & Madden, 2008). Critics argue that pledges and young recruits to these organizations are vulnerable as they look up to and admire the older members of these clubs. Subculture theory tells us that teams, fraternities and gangs hold values and attitudes separating them from the rest of society. Initiations into these groups are a traditional rite that forges bonds of belonging, which may account for their disproportionate representation in hazing statistics.

In the first part of fall semester 2008, five deaths of fraternity pledges were registered, four from alcohol poisoning. Five percent of university students involved in fraternities practice hazing and more than a quarter-million collegiate athletes were involved in some form of hazing. One survey found that 20 percent of all student athletes were victims of serious and even criminal abuse in the form of hazing (Nuwer, 2005), half of which involved being forced to drink some form of alcoholic beverage or participating in drinking contests (Hoover & Pollard, 2000). Data also indicate that males are exposed to more hazing than females and participants in college sports such as swimming, lacrosse, soccer, football, and ice hockey reported higher rates of hazing.

In an NCAA-assisted study, researchers at Alfred University found that, of those surveyed, 68 percent of male and 63 percent of female athletes, acknowledged participating in criminal, dangerous or alcohol-related incidents of hazing. In another study of hazing conducted at Alfred University, almost half of the high-school students surveyed indicated that they were hazed as part of joining a group, including church-related organizations. One-third of those students admitted performing some type of illegal act as part of initiation. Many said that there was no point in reporting such events to an adult and most of them considered the activity exciting or fun (Hoover & Pollard, 2000).

In Katy, Texas, members of the high-school cheerleading squad alleged that they were just having fun when they blindfolded and bound junior varsity cheerleaders and pushed them into a swimming pool (Eriksen, Rogers & Turner, 2008). The seven oldest offenders were charged as adults and indicted by a grand jury for the class B misdemeanor of hazing. Also facing charges in juvenile court were the five younger members of the varsity squad. Luckily, all of the victims survived.

Nearby in Prairie View, Texas, a young college student was less fortunate. Donnie Wade collapsed and died after being forced into intense physical exercise by a fraternity that has since been given a three-year suspension by the university. Although a post-mortem examination subsequently determined that Wade suffered from a medical condition that contributed to his death, the fraternity's engagement in hazing practices, their failure to seek medical aid for the collapsed pledge, and their intent to cover up their involvement and impede the investigation were all factors in the sanctions. The victim's parents have sued the fraternity, Phi Beta Sigma, for wrongful death, arguing that the systemic practices including a bread-and-water diet, paddling, and strenuous exercise without hydration created unreasonable risk (Horswell, 2010).

Almost all states now have anti-hazing laws and most campuses have developed "zero-tolerance" policies on hazing. Nuwer (2005) also suggests that annual surveys be undertaken to monitor hazing and students be given anonymous means to report such activity. He also supports educational programs to promote awareness, as well as firing athletic coaches or personnel who do not take affirmative action against hazing incidents that are uncovered.

UNCHAINING THE VICTIM AND OFFENDER

Throughout this book we have tried to look at traditional as well as nontraditional images of victims. Those who work in the criminal justice system will find it helpful to understand the degree of emotional processing that is involved in social determinations of one victim being worthy and another less worthy. Decisions about the authenticity or validity of certain victims have implications for how we allocate our criminal justice resources as well as the types of laws and policies we focus on passing.

It is also important that we craft a clear and consistent role for the victim in our justice system. That role should be balanced and fair to all parties if we are concerned with carrying out a meaningful justice process. Should the degree of emotional outrage and articulate response of one victim versus another determine the severity of a convicted offender's sentence? If so, does that mean we have no need of sentencing guidelines and uniform sentencing practices?

When a young girl was killed in a drunken-driving accident, the parents sued the offender for several million dollars. Instead of awarding the sum in full, the judge ordered the defendant to send the couple a check for $5 every week for the rest of his life. Believing that the amount of money was not the issue for the parents or the court, the judge felt that somehow this might be a more continuous and painful reminder for the probationer. Justice was viewed as the weekly task accompanying the recognition that some type of debt was owed. That debt, the judge reasoned, would be more impressive as a sentence similar to the never-ending suffering that the family has endured. And while this resolution may seem an appropriate one for the offender, it may not meet the needs of the family who may choose to find closure in some other type of activity or process. This highlights the importance of not assigning uniform outcomes to cases involving victims.

Judges must be careful in creative sentencing schemes and not let popular feedback and media interest override the basic sensibilities of punishments. If the creation of a victim-impact statement is to have any meaning at all, it would be the recognition that all victims do not view the criminal justice system in the same way. Whether standardized or customized punishments are appropriate will vary from case to case. The media also bears the responsibility of sifting carefully through issues so that the potential harm of resurrecting some issues is weighed against the most likely benefits of some stories. As the mother of one murder victim explained regarding publicity over an offender's alleged murderabilia enterprise (which arose long after she had finally come to some type of closure regarding the crime): "I had reached the point after he was convicted and sentenced to life without parole that I could look, you know, remember Elena without seeing his face. All that has come back now" (Schooler, 2007). In fact, this particular victim had no interest in receiving any of the proceeds of such arrangement despite the efforts of activists to develop such provisions.

While both criminology and victimology use research and theory to study problems of crime in America and to make recommendations about policy and programs, reliance on generalizations across populations or anecdotal experiences is very limiting. And, too often we equate victim satisfaction and meeting the needs of the victim with meting out punishment to the offender. We tend to see greater punishment of the offender as more justice for the victim. Unchaining the victim from the offender and viewing victims as unique individuals, separate from the offenses and the offenders, is perhaps the first step to a more meaningful interpretation of justice.

References

Albertson, L. M (2009). *The influence of jurors' race on perceptions of complex scientific evidence.* Unpublished doctoral dissertation, University of Delaware, Newark, DE.

Allan, E., & Madden, M. (2008, March 11). *Hazing in view: College students at risk.* Orono, ME: University of Maine.

Alvarez, H. (2007). The impact of teacher preparation on responses to student aggression in the classroom. *Teaching and Teacher Education, 23,* 1113–1126.

Amnesty International. (2004). *Threat and humiliation: Racial profiling, domestic security, and human rights in the United States.* New York: Amnesty International

California Department of Corrections and Rehabiliation, (2005) *Inmate incidents in institutions.* Sacramento, CA: CDCR.

California Department of Corrections. (2000) *Inmate incidents in institutions.* Sacramento, CA: CDC.

Carlson, D. K. (2004, July 20). *Racial profiling seen as pervasive, unjust.* Retrieved from http://www.gallup.com.

Dallas Morning News. (1994, November 29). Jeffrey Dahmer slain in prison; Inmate is questioned in attack. *Dallas Morning News,* A1.

Duhart D.T. (2001): *Violence in the workplace, 1993–99.* National Crime Victimization Survey. Washington, DC: Bureau of Justice Statistics.

Eriksen, H., Rogers, B., & Turner, A. (2008, November 20). Morton Ranch cheerleaders indicted in hazing. *Houston Chronicle.*

Estate of Larsen v. Murr, 511 F. 3d 1255, 2008

Federal Bureau of Investigation (October, 2008). *Law enforcement officers killed and assaulted, 2007.* Washington, DC: U. S. Department of Justice.

Flood, M. (2009, October, 16). Plea to spare other parents. *Houston Chronicle,* B1, 2.

Fox, J., & Zawitz, M. (2010). Homicide trends in the U. S. Washington, DC: Bureau of Justice Statistics. Retrieved from http://bjs.ojp.usdoj.gov/content/homicide/homtrnd.cfm

Goffman, E. (1961). *Asylums.* Garden City, NJ: Doubleday.

Hall, M. (2008, November). The exonerated. *Texas Monthly, 36*(11), 148–165.

Horswell, C. (2010, April 20). Prairie View disbands frat after pledge's hazing death. *Houston Chronicle,* A1.

Hoover, N. C., & Pollard, N. (2000, August). *High school hazing: Initiation rites in American high schools.* Final Report. Alfred, NY: Alfred University.

Hougland, S., Mesloh, C., & Henych, M. (2005). Use of force, civil litigation and the taser: One agency's experience. Retrieved from http://www.ncjrs.gov/App/AbstractDB/AbstractDBDetails.aspx?Id =209260

Kalenda, T. (2010). *The victimization of teachers: A routine activities analysis.* Unpublished masters thesis. Houston, TX: University of Houston-Downtown.

Koss, M.P., Dinero, T., Seibel, C., & Cox, S. (1988). Stranger and acquaintance rape. *Psychology of Women Quarterly, 12,* 1–24.

Lahm, K. (2009). Inmate assaults on prison staff: A multilevel examination of an overlooked form of prison violence. *The Prison Journal, 89*(2), 131–150.

Lahm, K. (2008). Inmate-on-inmate assault: A multilevel examination of prison violence. *Criminal Justice and Behavior, 35,* 120–137.

Laurikkala, M. (2009). *Different time, same place, same story? A social disorganization perspective for examining juvenile homicides.* Unpublished dissertation. Orlando, FL: University of Central Florida.

Louis Harris & Associates (1999). *The Metropolitan Life survey of the American teacher, 1999. Violence in America's public schools— five years later.* New York. Louis Harris & Associates.

Maston, C. T. (2010, March 2). *Crime victimization in the U. S.— 2007.* Washington, DC: Bureau of Justice Statistics.

McShane, M. (2008). *Prisons in America.* New York: LFB Scholarly Publishing.

Mesloh, C., Henych, M., & Wolf, R. (September 2008). *Less lethal weapon effectiveness, use of force, and suspect and officer injuries: A five-year analysis.* Report 224081. Washington, DC: U.S. Department of Justice,

Mueller, D., & Lawrence, R. (2007). Cops in the classroom: Assessing the appropriateness of search and seizure case law in schools. In M. McShane & F. P. Williams (Eds.), *Youth violence and delinquency: Monsters and myths* (Chapter 10, pp. 149–167). Westport, CT: Praeger.

Nuwer, H. (2005, October 4). Rights v. rites on hazing. *The Globe and Mail* (Canada), A19.

Parent, D., Leiter, V., Kennedy, S., Levins, L.,Wentworth, D., & Wilcox, S. (1993). *Conditions of confinement in juvenile detention and correctional facilities: Crowding pervasive in juvenile facilities.* Washington, DC: Bureau of Justice Statistics, U.S. Department of Justice.

Parsonage, W. H., & Bushey, W. C. (1987). The victimization of probation and parole workers in the line of duty: An exploratory study. *Criminal Justice Policy Review, 2,* 372–391.

People v. Lovercamp, 43 Cal App 3d 823, 118 Cal. Rptr 110 (1974).

Petersen, G. J., Pietrzak, D., & Speaker, K. M. (1998). The enemy within: A national study on school violence and prevention. *Urban Education, 33,* 331–359.

Pinkerton, J. (2010, Jan 23). Shootings by area lawmen already at six. *Houston Chronicle,* B1.

Pinkerton, J. (2009, September 28). Police shootings of citizens jump; why is not clear. *Houston Chronicle,* A1.

Renzema, M. (1987). *Report on an exploratory survey.* Kutztown, PA: Kutztown University.

Riedel, M. (1993). *Stranger violence: A theoretical inquiry.* New York: Garland.

Schooler, L. (2007, July 30). Texas law would prevent sale of "murderabilia." *National Public Radio.* Retrieved from www.npr. org/templates/story.

Skinner v. Uphoff, 234 F. Supp 2d 1208 (2002).

Spriggs, M. J. (2009). "Don't tase me bro!" An argument for clear and effective taser regulation. *Ohio State Law Journal, 70,* 487–518.

Steinke, P. (1991). Using situational factors to predict types of prison violence. *Journal of Offender Rehabilitation, 17,* 119–32.

Stephan, J. J. (1997). *Census of state and federal correctional facilities, 1995.* Washington, DC: Bureau of Justice Statistics.

Stephan, J. J., & Karberg, J. C. (2003). *Census of state and federal correctional facilities, 2000.* Washington, DC: Bureau of Justice Statistics.

Sundt, J. Castellano, T. C., & Briggs, C. (2008). The sociopolitical context of prison violence and its control: A case study of supermax and its effect in Illinois. *The Prison Journal, 88*(1), 94–122.

Usher, N. (2004, August 14). Canine detail a pocket of concern. *Los Angeles Times,* B1.

Warchol, G. *(1998). Workplace violence, 1992–96.* Washington, DC: Bureau of Justice Statistics.

Warren, J., Jackson, S., Loper, A. B., & Burnette, M. (2009, December). *Risk markers for sexaul predation and victimization in prison.* Washington, DC: National Institute of Justice.

Weir, T. (2003, December 9). Hazing issue rears ugly head across USA. *USA Today,* 1C.

Wener, R. (2006). Effectiveness of the direct supervision system of correctional design and management. *Criminal Justice and Behavior, 33*(3), 392–410.

Women Prisoners v. the District of Columbia, 899 F. Supp 659 (1995).

Discussion Questions

1. What do you think could be done to reduce the number of injuries and deaths that result from offender/police interactions or from correctional officer/inmate interactions?
2. What factors seem to influence whether someone is determined to be a victim or an offender in an incident when the two have a pre-existing relationship?
3. Why do sports, and fraternities seem to engage in more hazing practices than other social and recreational groups? What can be done to address the culture of hazing or is hazing going to occur no matter what sanctions are developed?

Books You May Want to Read

Carcaterra, L. (1993). *A safe place*. NY: Villard Books.
Gaines, E. (1992). *A gathering of old men*. New York: Vintage.
Nuwer, H. (1999). *Wrongs of passage: Fraternities, sororities, hazing, and binge drinking*. Bloomington, IN: Indiana University Press.

Movies You May Want to See

Bury My Heart at Wounded Knee
A Gathering of Old Men
Changeling (Angelina Jolie)

Web Links

http://bjs.ojp.usdoj.gov/content/homicide/homtrnd.cfm
http://www.insidehazing.com/
http://www.stophazing.org
http://www.hazingstudy.org/publications/hazing_in_view_web.pdf

Index

A

Abu Ghraib, 51
Address Confidentiality
  Program, 224
AIDS/HIV, 204
Amber Alert, 76, 122
American Civil Liberties
  Union (ACLU), 245
Amnesty International, 245,
  246, 261
Animal rights, 203, 206, 209
Arson, 26, 70, 185, 186, 187
Auschwitz (concentration
  camp), 182

B

Battered persons syndrome,
  104
Battered woman syndrome, 17,
  101, 102, 104
Bentham, Jeremy, 57, 201
Bias crime, 19 (see hate crime)
Bibliotherapy, 236
Booth v. Maryland, 92
Bullying, 69, 139, 140-142,
  148, 256
Burglary, 8, 27, 96, 106, 249

C

Campus crime, 31, 45, 76, 80,
  81, 84
Campus Project on Sexual
  Assault, 227
Catholic Church, 120, 144,
  147, 149
Child abuse, 46, 82, 119, 143,
  153, 159, 162, 163, 164,
  166, 167, 168, 208, 237
Child neglect, 119, 165
Child Protection Act of 1990,
  72, 91
Child protective services, 82,
  118, 119, 143, 164, 167
Child sexual abuse, 47, 72,
  103, 120, 121, 144, 166,
  166, 167, 231, 232
Child sexual abuse
  accommodation syndrome,
  103, 104
Civil lawsuit, 112
Civil rights, 26, 41, 71, 186
Clery Act, 76, 80
Cloward, Richard, 53
Cockfighting, 199, 203
Cohen, Albert, 53
Cohen, Lawrence, 58

Missouri v. Brookshire, 213
Monetary damages, 87
Mothers Against Drunk
Driving (MADD), 84, 91,
114
Ms Magazine, 226, 227
Murderabilia, 79, 80, 260

N

National Center for Victims of
Crime, 91
National Center on Elder
Abuse (NCEA), 137
National Crime Information
Center (NCIC), 94, 95, 143
National Crime Survey (NCS),
27, 29, 38, 164
National Crime Victimization
Survey (NCVS), 27, 29, 37,
116
National Incidence Studies of
Missing, Abducted,
Runaway, and Thrownaway
Children (NISMART), 165
National Incident-Based
Reporting System (NIBRS),
30, 45
National Institute of Justice,
117, 165

O

Oklahoma City (bombing),
177

P

Panel design, 27
Parental liability, 53, 99

Parents' Music Resource
Center, 225
Parents of Murdered Children
(POMC), 84, 108, 122
Patriarchy, 17, 51, 52, 55, 161
Patriot Act, 82, 89
Payne v. Tennessee, 92
Pedophile, 166, 191
Pelzer, Dave, 237
Pennsylvania v. Rutherford, 66
People v. Lovercamp, 254
People v. Prince, 93
People v. Speegle, 214
People v. Zamudio, 93
Physical abuse, 47, 102, 138,
139, 164, 165, 166
Plea bargain, 211
post-traumatic stress disorder
(PTSD), 12, 17, 104, 134,
250
Prevalence (rate), 35
Prison Rape Elimination Act,
31, 254
Prison violence, 233, 251, 255,
256
Psychological abuse, 156

R

Racial profiling, 245, 246
Rafter, Nicole, 236
Rape, 2, 9, 11, 16, 23, 29, 31,
32, 33, 35, 36, 37, 38, 39,
46, 52, 56, 71, 76, 181, 226,
227, 229, 235, 243, 251,
254
Rehabilitation, 66, 87, 89-91,
116, 124, 134, 211, 213,
256

Restitution, 66, 87, 89-91, 116,
117, 124, 211, 213
Restorative justice, 117
Restraining order, 71, 94, 97,
125, 160, 202
Retribution, 3, 107, 251
Revenge, 107, 141, 233
Robbery, 5, 29, 37, 106, 191,
251
Routine Activities theory, 35,
58, 59, 244

S

Sapp, Allen, 10
Schafer, Stephen, 7, 8, 45
School violence, 256
Sexual abuse, 23, 46, 49, 72,
84, 88, 102, 103, 120, 134,
139, 166, 254
Sexual Allegation in Divorce
(SAID), 167
Sexual assault, 23, 29, 31, 33,
34, 39, 53, 88, 90, 106, 123,
125, 168, 181, 233, 251,
252, 254
Sexual harassment, 52, 252
Shakur, Tupac, 225
Shelters, 23, 90, 113, 120, 124,
136, 146, 161, 207, 208,
209, 210, 211, 212, 213,
216
Shepard, Matthew, 77
Simon and Schuster v.
Members of the New York
State Crime Victims Board,
78
Simpson, O.J., 14, 65, 79, 187,
227, 230, 238
Social control (theory), 55

Society for the Prevention of
Cruelty to Animals (SPCA),
162, 202
Society for the Prevention of
Cruelty to Children (SPCC),
163, 202
Sodomy, 166
Son of Sam laws, 75
South Carolina v. Gathers, 92
Spousal abuse, 154
Spousal assault, 14, 153
Spousal rape (see Marital
rape), 52
Stalking, 11, 29, 47, 65, 74
State v. Brewer, 130
State v. Hirsh, 213
State v. Kelly, 102
State v. Oliver, 153
State v. Smith, 52
Steffensmeier, D., 160
Stockholm syndrome, 17, 105,
106, 107
Subculture of Violence, 54, 55,
250
Subculture theory, 54, 258
Substance abuse, 61, 131, 134,
154
Suicide, 8, 99, 113, 140, 141
Supremacist (racial), 10, 70, 77
Supreme Court, U.S., 66, 71,
78, 92, 215
Sussman, Peter, 222, 223
Sykes, Charles, 17
Sykes, Gresham, 56

T

Tarasoff v. The Regents of the
University of California, 98
Telescoping, 27